LC

D0992349

PAUL AND QUMRAN

PAUL AND QUMRAN

Studies in New Testament Exegesis

Edited by

Jerome Murphy-O'Connor, O.P.

Pierre Benoit, O.P.
Joseph A. Fitzmyer, S.J.
Joachim Gnilka
Mathias Delcor
Jerome Murphy-O'Connor, O.P.
Karl Georg Kuhn
Joseph Coppens
Franz Mussner
Walter Grundmann

GEOFFREY CHAPMAN
LONDON DUBLIN MELBOURNE 1968

Geoffrey Chapman Ltd
18 High Street, Wimbledon, London SW 19

Geoffrey Chapman (Ireland) Ltd
5-7 Main Street, Blackrock, County Dublin

Geoffrey Chapman Pty Ltd
44 Latrobe Street, Melbourne, Vic 3000, Australia

© compilation 1968, Geoffrey Chapman Ltd
First published 1968

This book is set in 11 on 13 point Baskerville
Printed in Great Britain by
Clarke, Doble & Brendon Ltd, Cattedown, Plymouth

CONTENTS

v

ABBREVIATIONS

AER	*American Ecclesiastical Review*
BJ	*Bible de Jérusalem* (Eng. trans. *The Jerusalem Bible*)
BZ	*Biblische Zeitschrift*
CBQ	*Catholic Biblical Quarterly*
CSEL	*Corpus Scriptorum Ecclesiasticorum Latinorum*
DBS	*Dictionnaire de la Bible: Supplément*
ETL	*Ephemerides Theologicae Lovanienses*
EvQuart	*Evangelical Quarterly*
EvTh	*Evangelische Theologie*
IEJ	*Israel Exploration Journal*
JBL	*Journal of Biblical Literature*
JSS	*Journal of Semitic Studies*
NRT	*Nouvelle revue théologique*
NT	*Novum Testamentum*
NTD	*Neues Testament Deutsch*
NTS	*New Testament Studies*
PG	*Patrologia Graeca*
PL	*Patrologia Latina*
RAC	*Reallexikon für Antike und Christentum*
RB	*Revue biblique*
RdeQ	*Revue de Qumran*
RGG³	*Religion in Geschichte und Gegenwart*, 3rd. edition
RHPR	*Revue d'histoire et de philosophie religieuses*
RSR	*Recherches de science religieuse*
ST	*Studia Theologica*
TLZ	*Theologische Literaturzeitung*
TrierTZ	*Trierer Theologische Zeitschrift*
TRu	*Theologische Rundschau*
TWNT	*Theologisches Wörterbuch zum Neuen Testament*
TZ	*Theologische Zeitschrift*
VD	*Verbum Domini*
VT	*Vetus Testamentum*
ZAW	*Zeitschrift für die alttestamentliche Wissenschaft*
ZNW	*Zeitschrift für die neutestamentliche Wissenschaft*
ZTK	*Zeitschrift für Theologie und Kirche*

QUMRAN MANUSCRIPTS

CD	*Damascus Document*
1QS	*The Rule of the Community*
1QSa	*The Rule Annex*
1QSb	*The Book of Blessings*
1QH	*The Hymns* ('Hodayoth')
1QpHab	*The Commentary on Habakkuk*
4QpPs 37	*The Commentary on Ps 37*
1QM	*The War Rule*

FOREWORD

The contribution that the Dead Sea Scrolls can make to a more profound and accurate understanding of the New Testament and the milieu in which it took shape has become increasingly more evident in recent years—at least to those who are in a position to keep an eye on the tremendous scholarly output devoted to this area. Unfortunately not all who are interested in the progress of this research have access to the periodicals in which the most original and constructive work appears, and in some quarters this has given rise to accusations of a conspiracy of silence on the part of Christian scholars. It is said that they are afraid to publish the results of their investigations because they threaten the uniqueness of the Christian faith. This is certainly untrue, but it is undeniable that a communication gap has developed due to inability to handle foreign languages and lack of library facilities. My sole object in compiling this book was to bridge this gap by rendering more accessible some of the more significant articles devoted to study of the contacts between the Pauline writings and the Essene documents.

The term 'Pauline writings' is used deliberately because I have included material bearing on Ephesians and the Pastoral Epistles. This is not because I accept the full Pauline authenticity of these writings, but because I feel that the debate is still open and that the consideration of comparative material from Qumran may aid in the formation of a consensus. The Epistle to the Hebrews has been excluded, despite the many contacts it has with Qumran, because it falls into a completely different category. I limited myself to this area both for the sake of homogeneity, and because, if the articles presented here are added to those which have already appeared in *The Scrolls and the New Testament* (edited by Krister Stendahl, New York, 1957), practically all the note-

worthy contributions that have been made in this domain are
now available in English.

While the ultimate responsibility for any defects in the translations lies with me, the actual work was done by the following
to whom I must express my deepest gratitude for their coopera-
tion : Sister M. Keverne, O.P., Heather Hanna, Anthony Manly,
O.P., Henry Wandsborough, O.S.B., John Stephenson, and
Derek McCullough.

My awareness of the importance of the Qumran material for
the study of the New Testament is due in great measure to
Professor Karl Georg Kuhn, and I would like to take this
opportunity to thank him for the kindness and generosity he
showed me during the two semesters I attended his seminars on
the Essene documents at the University of Heidelberg. The
'Qumranarbeitsgemeinschaft' which he founded has made many
significant contributions to the elucidation of the Scrolls, and it
was a privilege to participate in the stimulating discussions in
which absolutely nothing was taken for granted.

This book I dedicate to K. Ashe whose friendship, encourage-
ment, and support mean so much to me, and without which it
may never have seen the light.

JEROME MURPHY-O'CONNOR, O.P.

Ecole Biblique, Jerusalem

1
QUMRAN AND THE NEW TESTAMENT*

Pierre Benoit, O.P.

THESE reflections were first proposed at the closing session of the Meeting of the *Studiorum Novi Testamenti Societas* held at Aarhus in 1960 and they do not claim to be a detailed study of the relations between the writings of Qumran and the New Testament, which would be an immense undertaking, nor even a report on the present state of research, which would entail comprehensive analyses and bibliographies. They are no more than an attempt to disengage a few guiding principles from the evidence now available. Many comparative studies of the doctrines or literary forms of both movements have already been published. Some of the conclusions drawn emphasize strongly the analogies between the two, while others, manifesting a definite mistrust, reject them. Some emphasize the similarities and conclude to a close relationship, others insist on the differences and contrast the two movements. In this situation there would appear to be a definite advantage to be gained from a number of reflections on method. I would put forward three.

I

The first would be a *warning against an imprudent tendency to accept as immediate contacts arising from direct influence what in fact may be no more than independent manifestations of a common trend of the time.*

* Published in *NTS* 7 (1960-61), pp. 276-96.

1

We must accept as beyond dispute that many passages in the recently discovered writings of Qumran and the New Testament exhibit contacts that are very close, even striking. While this may be the result of an immediate dependence (in which case the New Testament must be the borrower), it may also be an example in the two communities of a way of thinking and speaking common throughout Palestine at the beginning of the Christian era. This does not mean that we are faced with a dilemma; both explanations have their value, and a decision between them has to be made in each particular case. But here it is necessary to be prudent, and not accept too hastily the first to the detriment of the second.

To see all Judaism at the time of the New Testament in the writings of Qumran would be an optical illusion. Not long ago we experienced such an illusion, when we accepted, if not in theory, at least in practice, the rabbinical writings as typical of Judaism at the time of Christ. Everything else, especially the 'Apocrypha', enigmas without definite historical connections, were more or less ignored. The privilege of providing a true picture of Judaism, which could be set beside early Christianity, was accorded to the mishnaic and midrashic writings. But in fact, these writings were composed only from the second century onwards. They had their origin not alone in a particular movement, Pharisaism, but in one of its branches, the school of Hillel, and—still more distinctive—they present Judaism in the narrow, integrist and hardened form, imposed upon it by the hard struggle for survival after the catastrophe of A.D. 70. It was obvious that such writings could not accurately reflect Judaism as it was earlier; yet, lacking anything better, people were satisfied with it.

Now a wonderful piece of good fortune has given us the library of a sect (which, with your permission, we shall term Essenian), which existed before the ruin of the Temple. It is an extraordinary find, whose value is inestimable, yet which tempts us to yield to another illusion: to think that this time we possess all of first century Judaism, and that any connections with it in the New Testament are necessarily with the Essenes. Such an illusion would be no less a distortion than the former. For it would attribute to one particular movement many ideas which in fact belonged to others much larger and from which both Essenism and Christianity borrowed.

We feel that Judaism during the last few centuries before its ruin in 70, was both a living and varied movement. On one hand, messianic expectation and apocalyptic calculations, stimulated by set-backs in politics, strengthened belief in the imminence of a crisis, which would lead to deliverance. Disappointed by the failure of some abortive actions and by the defeat of a number of false messiahs, dreams were dreamt and plans elaborated, which varied according to the different spirit of each sect. On the other hand the influences of the Gentile world had been brought closer by historical events—the Babylonian and Iranian world, into which the Exile had led, the Greco-Roman world created by Alexander, which had become the Jewish 'Diaspora'—and were active now even within Palestine itself, enriching the doctrines and the hopes of the different groups. Palestine was a fertile breeding-ground of hopes and esoteric doctrines, of which the Essenism of Qumran is an example of infinite value, though it cannot claim to be the only one. The same causes must have given rise to the same effects in other places as well. Its fortunate recovery is no reason to deny the existence of other likely examples, now unfortunately lost to us, which in similar ways would have served the same causes and used the same sources.

If not the Sadducees, doubtless less fecund than others because of their conservatism, the Pharisees at least must also have been familiar with these more or less adventurous speculations, which were effaced by the Hillelite orthodoxy of Jamnia. Moreover, Josephus's catalogue of these important movements cannot be thought of as including all the fluid variety of tendencies and the writings to which they gave rise. At that time there were many eschatological and apocalyptic enthusiasts, and there is no reason to assemble them all within the walls of Qumran. It has already been correctly noted that some of the writings in the library of Qumran were not written by members of the sect; some, like the writings of Enoch, could have arisen in distinct centres. Thus, it is possible that more than one doctrine, which we know only through Qumran, had its origin elsewhere, and that Qumran is only the channel by which it reaches us.

Of course, there is no question of denying the originality of the doctrines and writings of the Essenes, or their original way of handling the material common to the Jewish world of their day. Yet the following important distinction remains both licit and necessary, viz. between the doctrines which are truly characteristic of the sect at Qumran and those which came from much wider movements and were shared by other groups. If our present state of knowledge makes the application of this distinction difficult in practice, it is none the less valid, and should prevent us from too easily applying the term 'Essene' to things which do not warrant this identification.

As an example, we may take the dualism which sets Good against Evil like two kingdoms in conflict. It is licit to see here a reflection of Iranian speculations; it may even be held that the beginnings of it are already found in the Old Testament. At the same time, it is very likely that this view of the world, which was also favoured by certain schools of Greek philosophy, was at that time quite widespread in the syncretist circles of Judaism, and by no means a monopoly of the Essenes. The same must be said of the doctrines related to this dualism, e.g. angelology, and the effect of this conflict in the very being of man. Such doctrines are found in germ in the bible, and they developed under Iranian influence, though not without being somewhat purified by monotheism. Other groups in Palestine at this period were also influenced, for example, Pharisaism. With regard to such traditional themes as the advent of the messianic age, the necessary trials of a Servant, the eschatological purification by the Spirit, with far greater reason it can be correctly claimed that these also were developed in places other than Qumran, even though they remain unknown to us today. Finally, the attention given to 'the mysteries' of the divine plan, certainly a theme of later origin, is too characteristic of the apocalyptic speculation to be confined to one group alone. In these and other similar fields the contacts of the New Testament with Qumran do not imply more than that both made use of common sources. And very often that common source is none other than the Old Testament.

But the case may be different when these contacts concern distinctive features of these themes which are more characteristic of Essenism. It is quite certain that these features exist, and it is extremely important that they be recognized. Their identification is not easy, as we have already sain, since we lack sufficient information to furnish an independent check of the Qumran material. At least, our knowledge of the origins and the history of this purist and reactionary priesthood may suggest certain traits which are proper to it. Some of these may be their retention of the old calendar, already abandoned by official Judaism, or their hope for two Messiahs, where the traditional Davidic Messiah is placed in juxtaposition with a priest-Messiah of the line of Aaron, and even overshadowed by him, or again their claim to be building a spiritual temple in the desert, whose prayer and sanctity are preferable to the defiled worship of the Temple at Jerusalem.

It is on these and suchlike points that a comparison with the New Testament will be most fruitful and similarities here may well signify direct contact.

We must not omit to add the sphere of literary forms, for here especially a milieu leaves its own mark, and produces a community tradition. Common doctrines, received into the community, are expressed in a unique way. In this matter, especially, similarities can hardly be explained except by direct influence.

Now, there is no doubt that the New Testament, besides certain general analogies which prove little, also evidences certain affinities in distinctive points of doctrine or formulation with the Qumran writings which imply a definite relationship. It must suffice here to evoke one passage, 2 Cor 6 : 14-7 : 1, which is Qumranian in both thought and style; a meteor fallen from the heaven of Qumran into Paul's epistle. Other examples will be noted later.

The first methodological observation which we have just

suggested would restrict research on the relationship between
Qumran and the New Testament to a narrower field than that
normally assigned to it. But although it is restricted, it is still
there. Essenism had some direct influence on Christianity, less
than some have suggested, but none the less real. It remains to
discover, *when* : whether at the beginning or later on; and *how* :
whether in essential matters or only in secondary, through passive
reception or a transforming reaction? The two following observations on method are intended to be of assistance in answering
these new questions.

II

*In the measure that direct influence of Qumran on the New
Testament appears to be established, it does not necessarily
follow that this influence was exercised at the very beginning, so
that Christianity would derive from Essenism as from its
source. This influence could rather have been exercised at a later
stage, and would have assisted the new movement only to express
and organize itself, but would in no sense have created it.* It is
suggested here that the second alternative is more often the truth.
The contacts with Qumran came less through John the Baptist
and Jesus, than through Paul, John, and even the faithful of
the second generation.

Chronologically, the first contact could have arisen in the
person of John the Baptist. The content of his preaching and
the proximity of his sphere of activity to the Dead Sea all suggest
that some form of connection existed between the Precursor and
the community at Qumran. Yet, it is questionable whether these
facts justify exaggerating this relationship, for example, by
making him an Essene, who first of all belonged to the sect, and
then left it to accomplish his own mission. This is not impossible;
but the evidence does not support it. Not only is John the Baptist
clearly distinguished from the Essenes by certain features, but
even those traits which are common may be nothing more than
parallels without immediate contact.

Expectation of the Messianic age was far too widespread at
that time to say that John must have received it from Qumran.

And the manifestation of the Messiah in the desert was then very common (cf. Mt 24 : 26; Acts 21 : 38; Josephus, *B.J.*, II, § 259-61; VII, § 438), so that it is not necessary to say that the choice of the place and the application of the prophecy of Isaiah 40 : 3 by both John the Baptist (Jn 1 : 23; cf. Mk 1 : 3ff.) and Qumran (1QS 8 : 13-14; 9 : 19-20) demands direct dependence. The hermit Banos also lived in the desert, wore special dress, lived on a sparse diet, and emphasized ablutions (Josephus, *Vita*, § 11), all of which make him like John the Baptist, yet no one claims him as an Essene.

It is true that John the Baptist sought to win converts and preached a baptism of penance, whose counterpart and origin some have tried to find at Qumran. But this really seems to be forcing the analogy. Frequent ablutions with a ritual value were at that time quite common in Judaism. Those practised at Qumran are a typical, but not unique, example. Their purpose was to maintain or re-establish the state of ritual purity demanded by a holy life, and in particular by participation in the common meal. While related to moral conversion, it was not its cause (1QS 5 : 13-14), but only added to it levitical purity of body. What Josephus incorrectly writes about John the Baptist (Josephus, *Ant. Jud.*, XVIII, § 117), is true in fact of the Essenes. No one has yet proved that they practised a baptism of initiation which had a moral value. Washing in lustral water that purified the flesh (1QS 3 : 8-9), but which was of no value before the conversion of the heart (1QS 3 : 3-6), and which appears only after the moral purification by the Spirit (1QS 3 : 6-8), was nothing other than the daily ablutions of ritual purity, whether those probably performed by the postulant (Josephus, *B.J.*, II, § 137—he was given a loin-cloth), or those of the proficients in 'purer' waters (Josephus, *ibid*, § 138), to which the candidate was admitted after one year's noviciate (1QS 6 : 16-17). The different stages are by themselves sufficient proof that it is a question of ritual, not moral, purity. And the purer ablution, to which the novice accedes, is only the first step of a series, which he then repeats every day; far from being an unrepeatable action, it is like the common meal which the newly professed will be allowed to share after the second year (1QS 6 : 20-21) and will continue to do for the rest of his life. By contrast the baptism of John, performed but once (there is no justification for saying that it was followed by further ablutions) and expressing interior conversion of heart, exhibits the qualities of a rite of initiation and of moral purity. Whatever be the nature of proselyte-baptism, whose existence before John the Baptist still lies in doubt, the baptism performed by the Precursor retains its clear distinctiveness in relation to Qumran.

The eschatological purification by the Holy Spirit constitutes another parallel between John the Baptist (Mk 1 : 8 and parallels; Jn 1 : 33) and Qumran (1QS 4 : 21), but is, however, adequately explained by the Old Testament (Ezek 11 : 19; 36 : 25-27; 39 : 29; cf. Is 32 : 15; 44 : 3; Jn 3 : 1-2). The coming of the Holy Spirit on the Messiah (Mk 1 : 10 and par.; Jn 1 : 32ff.), although already adumbrated in Is 11 : 2; 42 : 1, would be a more striking parallel, if it appeared in Qumran; but this theme is not contained in 1QS 4 : 20ff., where 'the man' is more naturally understood in a collective sense, that is to say, the group, whom God will purify from among 'the sons of man', because he has chosen *them* for an eternal covenant (line 22).

No longer need we have recourse to Qumran, nor to Iranian influence by way of Qumran, to explain eschatological retribution by fire, for 1QH 3 : 28ff. speaks of it using expressions drawn from the Old Testament (Ezek 21 : 3; Is 34 : 9; Amos 7 : 4), where the image is frequently encountered (Is 9 : 17-18; 10 : 16; 66 : 24; Jer 21 : 14; Dn 7 : 9-10; Zeph 1 : 18; Ps 21 : 10; 83 : 15). In point of fact, the precise image of 'the river of fire' is doubtful in 1QH 3 : 28ff. and absent from the gospels.

The phrase 'brood of vipers' (Mt 3 : 7; Lk 3 : 7), which recurs elsewhere in the gospels (Mt 12 : 34; 23 : 33), evokes another biblical image (cf. Deut 32 : 33; Is 59 : 5; Jn 20 : 14-16) which inspired 1QH 5 : 10 and 27, and does not imply a direct dependence of John the Baptist on the menacing poetry of 1QH 3 : 12-18.

We are not trying to minimize the possible contacts between the Precursor and Qumran, the most important one being their common concern to prepare the converted hearts for the eschatological intervention of God expected imminently. But this concern, and the actions and words used to express it, do not seem to imply, on either part, anything more than influences received from the same surroundings.

Even supposing that John the Baptist did depend on the Essenes, Christianity would owe them nothing on that score. It is only apropos of Jesus that the question becomes crucial. Yet here the dependence is still less likely.

Jesus could not have been ignorant of the Essene movement, with its centre at Qumran and its disciples throughout Palestine. So his silence about them is all the more remarkable. References to them in the gospels are few and uncertain. The eunuchs by choice (Mt 19 : 12) are probably the Essenes, as the religious ideal of celibacy is not attested anywhere else in Palestine at that period. Among them also the command to 'hate one's enemy' may be found (Mt 5 : 43; 1QS 1 : 4 and 10 : 9, 21-22), while it has no traces in the Old Testament. The prohibition of having oneself called *kathēgētēs* 'teacher' (Mt 23 : 10) could also be an illusion to the *Moreh ṣedeq*. Finally, it has been noted that the procedures for excommunication set forth in Mt 18 : 15-18 are somewhat similar to those in 1QS 5 : 25-6 : 1. However, these connections are rather tenuous, and it is remarkable that they are all supplied by the gospel of Matthew alone. While it is certain that this gospel preserves some very ancient material, especially in the case of the logia, it also seems that it sometimes expresses the preoccupations of a later Judaeo-Christian milieu, of which the above-mentioned passages may be examples.

Leaving aside such specific but debatable contacts, may we not find in the thought of Jesus certain key-concepts about his own person and mission, which would have been originally inspired by analogous ideas at Qumran? What has so far been written on this point has not been very convincing, either relative to the similarities—which, however, are adequately explained by the Old Testament and Judaism in general—or to the differences—which indicate a totally different spirit.

There is no need to reconsider the dualistic opposition between the two kingdoms of God and Satan; it is not proper to Qumran, with the possible exception of some of its vocabulary. For this reason it is striking that Jesus speaks of Beelzebul, and not of Beliar, as the sect does (the very Qumranian passage of 2 Cor 6 : 15 is the only place in the New Testament where this distinctive name occurs). As for the Light-Darkness terminology, which is more characteristic of Qumran, we may note that it is not used by the Jesus of the Synoptics, but by the Johannine Christ.

Of supreme importance is Jesus's own awareness of himself and his mission. Despite some of the critical doubts, I hold that Christ regarded himself as one sent by God, with whom he enjoyed, as a Son with his Father, relations of extraordinary closeness, that he proclaimed himself as the Messiah or, better, as the Son of Man of Daniel, at least in hope, i.e. he expected to attain that state completely after his triumph over death, since he first had to lay down his life to expiate the sins of men, like the Servant of Yahweh.

In spite of what some have proposed, no such person is to be found in the Qumran writings. The title 'Son of Man' never occurs in them. Instead two Messiahs were expected, of Aaron and Israel. These two are not so much two definitive real persons as the representatives of the two traditional authorities in Judaism (cf. 1QSb 3 : 2 and 4—the posterity of the eschatological High Priest): the new Israel will regain for ever both her sacerdotal and regal dynasties, when the theocracy is restored after the triumph of the Light over Darkness. In fact, these two messiahs did not have an important place in the preoccupations of the sect. They appear mostly in the eschatological community, where they preside over the banquet (1QSa 2 : 11-22) and where they perform their traditional duties, one that of sacrifice and worship (1QSb 1 : 21-5 : 19?) and the other that of government and justice (1QSb 5 : 20-29). Their role in the eschatological conflict is very obscure. Even if we identify them with 'the chief priest', head chaplain of the forces, (cf. 1QM 2 : 1ff.) and with 'the prince of the whole congregation' (1QM 5 : 1), they only participate with the other members in the common victory, which is won by all the sons of light, their angelic partners, and, above all, the All-Holy God, the King of Glory, Mighty in War (1QM 12 : 7-9) who is present in the midst of his people, and conducts the battle.

There is nothing here of a unique Messiah, who personally plays an essential part in the realization of salvation. More important, there is no mention of a suffering Servant, who is to acquire this salvation by expiating the sins of man. While granting that the theme of the Servant is exploited at Qumran, here again we must be careful to avoid making hasty comparisons. First of all, the expiation mentioned in 1QS 5 : 6; 8 : 6 is of a liturgical nature; as in the ancient worship of the Temple, this expiation will be assured henceforth by the Community of the Covenant, which has become the eschatological sanctuary. The holy lives of the sons of light, perfectly conformed to the Law, will expiate sin more efficaciously than material sacrifices (or with the help of such sacrifice, if one accepts the *mem* of 9 : 4 as a *mem* of origin and not comparison), that is to say, it will cleanse the Holy Land defiled by impiety. There is no question of an expiation in favour of, and in place of, sinners; for they will receive their 'retribution' (8 : 7). Neither is there any special mention of the Servant. This theme is not the inspiration of 1QS 4 : 20ff., which deals with the eschatological purification, not of one Man, who is the Servant-Messiah, but rather of man in general, that is to say, the elect whom God has called with his angels to eternal life.

The figure of the Servant of Yahweh appears more clearly in the Hodayoth, where he is identified with the author of these hymns, who is, no doubt, the Teacher of Righteousness, and then through him with the whole community, which he founded and which shares his fortune. But even here, the identification rests on the inevitable trials of the eschatological crisis rather than a special role of vicarious and redemptive suffering, effective for others through substitution. The author, broken by his sufferings, weighed down by his sins, persecuted by his enemies, and yet sustained by God, who has revealed his mysteries to him and will

give him ultimate victory, so that he will be able to enlighten
his own disciples and lead them on the way of salvation: these
are the themes which constantly recur in the hymns, and are
expressed with all the imagery of the bible—the erupting storm,
the strong city besieged on all sides, the trials of a woman in
child-birth. (In 1QS 3: 7ff. as in 5: 30ff. it is the author who
brings forth the community, while being its foster-father, 7: 20ff.
No reference to the Mother of the Messiah.) The Isaian theme
of 'the Servant', who was misunderstood, disregarded, and
distorted, yet always remaining in God's safe keeping, appears
in these comparisons without its one specific characteristic:
vicarious suffering, which bears the sins of others, makes expiation
for sinners, in a word, the surrender of a life in ransom, and
the shedding of blood for many (Mk 10: 45; 14: 24 and
par.).

The Teacher of Righteousness is the one person at Qumran
who doubtless reminds us most of Jesus. But, however striking
his religious personality may be, it only serves to highlight the
unique and transcendent person of Jesus. Leaving aside the
questions of an incarnation, a crucifixion and a resurrection (the
writings of Qumran offer no support for the attribution of these
to the Teacher of Righteousness), he is not even a saviour whose
coming in itself will inaugurate the eschatological age. Since he
is a man of weakness and sin, as he continually repeats, he stands
in need of pardon and purification. The only title, though one
of eminence, that he can claim is that of Prophet, or more
accurately, of inspired Exegete, who has received an illumination
from heaven to understand the mysteries of revelation, and to
instruct his disciples in the ways of God, especially during the
last days. (Cf., among other passages 1QpHab 2: 2-10; 7: 4-14;
1QH *passim*). As 'a true Teacher' he enables others to attain
salvation through this instruction, which leads them to observe
the law perfectly, and prepares them for 'the mystery to come',
which is, of course, the eschatological crisis. There is nothing in
this which transcends the categories of the prophetic movement
in Israel. There is also nothing approaching the messianic
consciousness of Jesus, who inaugurates the eschatological king-

dom of God in his own person, and establishes it by his own suffering and triumph over death.

If Jesus appears to be ignorant of the Essenes and is not influenced by their doctrines, his practical behaviour distinguishes him still more from them. Instead of forming a separatist group, he consciously and freely associates himself with official Judaism, even though he censures its faults. He frequents the Temple, and teaches obedience to the doctors and Pharisees as the official leaders who occupy the chair of Moses (Mt 23 : 2-3). Jesus has no part with those schismatics who, far away in the wilderness, despise the Temple and claim to be alone in perfect obedience to Moses.

The evening meal, which Jesus celebrated before his death, resembles the common meal at Qumran no more than it does those of the many religious associations of Judaism, where the blessing of bread and wine was the normal practice. What makes it so radically different from them is its paschal character, whence its meaning of 'passing over' from the captivity of sin to the liberty of salvation. Its celebration on Tuesday evening remains a debatable hypothesis, which is not supported by the gospels, and which, should it be proved, would only connect it with 'an ancient priestly calendar', possibly still in use at the time, and not only at Qumran.

But what places Jesus poles apart from the sectarians is his liberty with regard to the Law and his love of sinners. At Qumran an absolute and even integrist return to the Law was extolled and its members were careful to keep away from the unclean, the sinners, the sons of darkness, who did not belong to God's chosen company. By his liberal interpretation of the Law, seeking its spirit while dispensing with the letter, and by his love of sinners, which brought him into contact with some of the most notorious, Jesus could only have scandalized the Essenes, even more than the Pharisees. To say that Jesus was not one of the Essenes is an understatement.

Essenism, then, did not provide primitive Christianity with its basic inspiration, neither through the Precursor John the

Baptist nor, still less, through its founder Jesus. Yet, a certain influence, reflected in the New Testament, seems undeniable. But, could it not be that this influence is a later development, occuring after the death of Jesus, in the primitive community, and then, in subsequent generations? This kind of influence, real but secondary, is easily explained, whether through converted Essenes, who brought their doctrines and practices into the life of the community, or by a deliberate policy of the new-born Church with regard to an important religious movement in Judaism. It is not only possible, but very likely, that some zealous and sincere Essenes gradually accepted and joined the infant Church; some exegetes have suggested that the priests of Acts 6 : 7 or those to whom the epistle to the Hebrews was sent were such Essenes. It is possible that the Judaeo-Christian movement, Ebionism, could have its origin here. From a different point of view, leaving aside the question of such converts, it is easy to understand why Christianity in its early stage was influenced in its own development by this older sect with its strong organization and its system of doctrine, either by directly borrowing from it or by having to react against it.

In fact, it is in the two spheres of community organization and theological speculation that the influence of Essenism is visible, and not in the realm of basic inspiration. To avoid exaggerations, however, it should be noted that, even at this later stage, this influence is subject to limitations, both of time and degree.

The influence of the Essenes is more obvious in the field of the Church's organization and liturgical life at a relatively late period than in its early years.

For example, liturgists consider that the times of prayer, vigils, and quarter-tense came to the Church from Qumran. The historical connection of Christian monasticism with the common life of the Essenes, which seems so probable to us now, will no doubt be established by scientific studies in the future. It is stated in the Syrian *Didascalia* of the third century that the Christian *episkopos* is nearest to the *mebaqqer* of the Essenes. We have already referred to the procedures of excommunication set out in

Mt 18 : 15-18, which would seem to have been inspired by those of Qumran; at the same time we noted that this passage of the first gospel could well represent a later stage of the gospel tradition.

On the other hand, when we go back to the primitive community at Jerusalem, the traces of Essenism are far less evident. Some have claimed to discover them, but, in my opinion, only by forcing the evidence. Whatever one's first impressions, the common life practised by the first Christians was quite different from that which existed at Qumran. Theirs was obligatory, total, and enforced by penalties; at Jerusalem it was left to the choice of the individual and developed out of the practice of social assistance, which existed in all the Jewish communities. Barnabas' gift to the apostles of the price of his property was an act of generosity, which merited special mention (Acts 4 : 36-37), while Ananias and Sapphira were punished for lying to the Holy Spirit (Acts 5 : 3, 4c, 9), and not for keeping back money, which no one obliged them to place in the common treasury (Acts 5 : 4a). It is true that there are statements of the principle, such as those in Acts 4 : 32, 34ff., but firstly they are phrases in brief summaries, which generalize on the basis of particular cases; and, secondly, they belong to a later redactional stage (Acts 2 : 44-45, inserted into the summary 2 : 42-43, 46-47).

The proposed connection of the 'Hellenists' of Acts 6ff., with the Essenes of Qumran is most improbable. Whatever be the precise meaning of this rare and puzzling term, which may have been invented by Luke or his sources, it certainly designates those Jews who had more or less accepted Greek language, customs and way of life together with the liberal and cosmopolitan outlook that accompanied it. At the opposite end of the scale are the Essenes, who advocated a total return to the Law of Moses, accepted a self-imposed ghetto, materially and spiritually, and whose separation from the Temple at Jerusalem was motivated by personal and transitory reasons.

Nor does the organization of the Essenes appear to have influenced the Church's hierarchy in its early years. There is no need to discuss the twelve apostles, whose choice by Jesus himself is sufficiently explained by the number of the twelve tribes which made up the chosen people (cf. Mt 19 : 28; Lk 22 : 30); nor of the three, Peter, James and John, who, in fact, have nothing in common with the three *priests* who pertained to the council of the community *in addition to* the twelve (1QS 8 : 1). The 'presbyters', who form with the apostles the top level in the church at Jerusalem (Acts 11: 30: 15: 4 etc.), were quite common in most of the Jewish communities in Palestine and the Diaspora. The mention of the *zeqenim* taking their place in the community in 1QS 6 : 8; 1QM 13 : 1, does not imply any special contact. Bishops and deacons only make their appearance in areas of Paul's mission (Phil 1 : 1; Acts 20 : 28; 1 Tim 3 : 1ff., Tit 1 : 7), under the influence of Hellenism, where such offices were known. If the Christian bishop was modelled on the *mebaqqer* of the Essenes, he should have first made his appearance in the Palestinian community, and his office held by only one person at a time. However, this is not the case : James rules the church at Jerusalem as 'the brother of the Lord' and not as 'bishop'. For a long period in the Pauline churches we find only colleges of bishops, and it is not until the close of the first century that the single bishop emerges, at Antioch according to our most ancient sources (Ignatius). It is possible that the Essenes, or rather Essenizing Judaeo-Christianity, contributed to this development, which only confirms our thesis : that the influence of Essenism on Christianity took place in its later development rather than during its early years.

Doctrine is another important sphere where the influence of the writings of Qumran on the New Testament is perceptible. But once again this did not take place on the level of the primitive inspiration received from Jesus, but on that of the subsequent theological systems of a Paul or a John.

For this, Paul and John must have been familiar with the writings of Qumran, or others like them, and, whether approving or opposing them, made use of them to formulate and express the Christian message. Outside of Palestine, Asia Minor, especially the region of Ephesus, was an area which would have favoured such contacts. As J. B. Lightfoot suspected, and recent discoveries have confirmed, the error combated by the epistle to the Colossians appears to be tainted with Essenism. A return to the Mosaic Law by circumcision, rigid observance concerning diet and the calendar, speculations about the angelic powers; all this is part and parcel of the doctrines of Qumran. Paul himself can hardly have been unaware of the writings of the sect when writing Col 1 : 12-13. Literary influence of Qumran is still more striking in Ephesians, which was written at the same time and addressed to the churches of the same region. This is evident not only in the themes of passages such as Eph 5 : 6-13; 6 : 10-17; but, more significantly, in the stylistic mannerisms, such as have been noted by Prof. K. G. Kuhn.[1] The only explanation for all this is that either Paul or a disciple, who was entrusted under his direction with the final redaction of the epistle, had a first-hand knowledge of the writings of Qumran.

Tradition assigns the same region as the place of composition of the Johannine writings, and this may explain why they, especially 1 John, are so strongly coloured by the writings of Qumran. Since the discoveries at Qumran, we can see that it is no longer necessary to invoke Greek Gnosticism as the original milieu of the Fourth Gospel, since now we have one, which is more ancient and closer, in Palestine itself. This point is relevant and should be remembered. Yet, it does not follow that the origin and development of this gospel should be confined to the Holy Land, for its history is a long and complicated one. Whatever its older portions, which, for other reasons also must be connected with an eye-witness of Jesus and the Holy Land, it is permissible to maintain that the later portions attained their final form in some other place. So the tradition that the gospel was completed at Ephesus may be confirmed by the existence of these islands of an Essenizing Judaism or Judaeo-Christianity.

How did these come to Ephesus? On this matter we can only fall back on conjecture. Maybe the Alexandrian Apollo and the Johannites of Ephesus (Acts 18: 24-5; 19: 2-3) and their incomplete Christianity, which stopped at the baptism of John, can supply the links of the chain which joins the Essenism or

[1] See below, pp. 116ff.

Judaeo-Christianity of Ephesus to that of Palestine, via the Therapeutae of Alexandria.

At the same time, we should not make the province of Asia the only place where Paul could have come into contact with the thought of Qumran. The epistles to the Thessalonians which are interior to his story at Ephesus, manifest important analogies; passages such as 1 Thess 6 : 1-11 on the eschatological crises and the conflict between light and darkness, and 2 Thes 2 : 6ff. whose affinities with 1Q 27 : 1 are striking, are good examples. We know little about the diffusion of Essenism in the Diaspora, and Palestine remains for us the principal region, where a John or a Paul could have made use of it. Although the actual historical contacts, the when and where of the possible influence on Paul or John, escape us today, it is clear that it took place on a secondary level of their thought, and was not its source. This point is supremely important, and it calls for a reconsideration of the borrowed elements: were they central or only minor themes? Were they accepted without change, or were they modified in the process?

III

A question may be asked: are we not conceding that Christianity owes much to the Essenes in admitting that their doctrines have left their mark on Christian theology, even if only in the secondary period? There is an opinion which minimizes the creative role of Jesus and makes Paul and John the true authors of Christian thought: in this perspective, if we admit that Paul and John used Essenian ideas, are we not saying that these ideas have penetrated the entire system of Christian theology?

This view is contradicted by two important considerations. Firstly, *the themes which are borrowed are secondary and do not form the essence of the Christian message.* Secondly, when they are used, *they are profoundly transformed, precisely because they are put in the service of a new and original reality.* Jean Guitton's distinction between 'spirit' and 'mentality' has an application here. The forms of thought and expression of the Essenes, which Paul and John found in use among their con-

verts or opponents, arose from a 'mentality', which was widespread in the areas where they worked, but the message which
they proclaimed, while accommodated to their hearers, arose
from a totally diverse 'spirit', which mastered this mentality to
the point of completely transforming it.

For Paul as for John, the heart of the Christian faith is the
death of Jesus, the Son of God made man, who made expiation
for the sins of men by his blood, and his resurrection, which saves
man and enables him to become a friend of God. This is the
central 'kerygma', rooted in history, which both proclaim in their
own way, one emphasizing that in Jesus the creative Word came
to destroy the old order and recreate a new humanity, the other
seeing in Jesus the revealing Word, who dispels the darkness of
sin and enlightens man with the true knowledge of the God of
glory. But neither the fundamental historical event nor their
presentation of it came to them from Qumran. One seeks in
vain there, provided that one does not supply what one seeks,
for the belief in a delegate of God, who was crucified and rose
from the dead; even the notion of a Messiah, Son of Man or
Servant, who is to realize salvation in his own person is absent
from these writings. Those, then, who deny that Jesus was the
first so to reveal his own person and mission must look elsewhere
for the source used by Paul and John to develop their theological
creations, either in the Old Testament or some other Jewish
movement.

Even more particular doctrines, which are at the same time
part of the essential message of Christianity, as, for example, the
Logos of John, or the heavenly Man of Paul, are not explained
by Qumran. Once again, the similarities are most evident in the
secondary elements of the presentation, where they are given a
new meaning by a different application. We shall take three
examples to show this, all of which are found especially in Paul :
the conflict between light and darkness, the revelation of the
mystery, and justification by grace alone.

The theme of opposition between *light and darkness* occurs
quite often in Paul's writings, from his earliest (1 Thess 5 : 1-10),

through 2 Cor (4 : 6; 6 : 14; 11 : 14) and Rom (2 : 19; 13 : 11-13) to his last letters (Col 1, 12-13 : Eph 5 : 6-14). Admittedly, a passage like Rom 2 : 19 implies nothing more than a general use of a theme found in the prophetic and sapiential books, and which is sufficiently explained by the Old Testament (cf. Is 42 : 6-7; 51 : 4; Wis 18 : 4). The same may be said for Phil 2 : 15. However, most of the other passages appear in contexts of eschatological crisis and conflict (1 Thess 5: 1-8; Rom 13: 12-13), of dualistic opposition between two hostile camps (2 Cor 6 : 14), and even of angelic intervention (2 Cor 4 : 3-4; 11 : 14). This aspect makes the parallel passages in Qumran very close, especially when such distinctive phrases are used as 'sons of light' and 'sons of darkness', which even at Qumran are only found in 1QS and 1QH, and are perhaps proper to the Teacher of Righteousness.

This common imagery only serves to highlight a radical difference about the coming of the eschatological age. At Qumran the hour of the conflict is yet to come and remains undetermined : for Paul, the decisive event has already taken place, and the final outcome of history is never in doubt. While the actual day remains unknown (1 Thess 5 : 2), it is near (Rom 13 : 12), because Christ has already conquered and distributed the armour of light (Rom 13 : 12, 14; 1 Thess 5 : 8-10; cf. 2 Cor 4 : 4, 6) so that the faithful even now are the sons of light (1 Thess 5 : 5; Eph 5 : 8). No doubt the sectarians of Qumran are also sons of light, but the reasons for this are different, and they exemplify the differences between the two systems.

The members of Qumran are sons of light as it were by definition, made to belong to one side, which has always existed, by a divine predetermination (1QS 4 : 24-25; 1QM 13 : 9-12). It appears that at the very beginning of time, God established the two armies of light and darkness with their two rival leaders (1QS 3 : 25). The covenant of Moses and its renewal from time to time through the prophets strengthen the forces of light (e.g. CD 5 : 17ff.; 6 : 1), but they do not change a primordial situation which existed before them and will continue until the day when God will decree the final conflict. Qumran always remains in the Old Law. It believes the great event to be very near, but it has not arrived. Since Moses, there has been no change, unless we except the Master of the sect, who as the last of the prophets, endeavours to find in a total return to the Mosaic covenant the final preparation, which will ensure victory (1QS 1: 1-11; 8: 15-16, etc.). Paul's position is quite different: the battle has already been fought and victory won by a single individual, Christ. The fighting that still remains will be done by the rear-guard, who follow their leader who has achieved the main victory. More than this, the impression is given that the people of light did not exist before Christ came, but, on the contrary, was brought into existence by him. Before Christ, it was night (Rom 13: 12) and the kingdom of darkness, from which he has rescued his elect and brought them into the kingdom of light (Col 1, 13; cf. 2 Cor 4: 4-6). In principle, of course, Paul never denied that the Old Testament and the Law of Moses brought some degree of light (cf. 2 Cor 3: 7-13), but when he contemplates the whole history of salvation, it seems more accurate to him to describe all the ancient economies of belief, Jewish as well as pagan, as darkness, ruled by 'the elements of the world', and to reserve the name of 'light' for the new economy brought by Christ.

The same thing, and with more truth, may be said of St John. For him Christ *is* the Light, who has come into the world to overcome the darkness that rules there. Those who receive Christ in faith receive the light from him. In this way, the determinism, which the doctrines of Qumran seem to force on him, especially in 1 Jn, is disposed of. 'To be born of light' no longer means for St John that one is made a member of the eternal people of light by an irresistible decree of God, but rather that a person enters the kingdom of light, established by Christ, through a free choice of faith and love.

The second theme which calls for our attention is the *mystery* of the divine plan, from old a hidden secret, and now at last revealed. In fact, this theme has its roots in traditional Jewish sapiential, and especially apocalyptic, literature, where it is expressed with a distinctive vocabulary, and these common sources are quite sufficient to explain even the literary similarities. At the same time the importance it has in the writings of Qumran (especially in 1QS and 1QH, but also in CD, 1QpHab., etc.) and of Paul (especially Col 1 : 26-27; 2 : 2-3; Eph 1 : 9-10; 3 : 3-12; before them in 1 Cor 2 : 7-10; 15 : 51; Rom 11 : 25; 16 : 25-26) implies the possibility of direct contact and suggests that a comparison would at least be rewarding.

At the outset we must recognize the profound differences regarding the time and manner of the revelation of the mystery, as well as its content. There is no equivalent at Qumran to the eschatological 'now' of St Paul. The revelation given to the Teacher of Righteousness and his disciples seems to be no more than the final part of a very ancient revelation, which has lasted through the centuries (1QS 9 : 13), beginning even before the patriarchs (CD 2 : 17-3 : 4), but given especially through Moses and the prophets (1QS 1 : 3; 8 : 15; CD 2 : 12). Among those who have received this revelation are the 'sons of Sadoq' (CD 5 : 4-5). At the end of this line stands the Teacher of Righteousness (1QpHab 2 : 2-10; 7 : 4-14) as the successor of the prophets. His revelation is the most recent, yet it belongs to the same order; for its main purpose is to effect the restoration of the ancient laws, which had been lost and rejected by the crimes of Israel (1QS 1 : 8-9; CD 3 : 12-18). Even those words, which he receives from the mouth of God about the last days, are no more than an authorized interpretation of the prophets (1QpHab 2 : 2-10; 7 : 4). His charism works through religious contemplation of scripture. He is a contemplatively inspired exegete of divine revelation. In the Hodayoth he does not mention the source of his illumination, about which he continually speaks; but, to judge from his great familiarity with sacred scripture (shown by his numerous more or less explicit quotations), we may assume that it arises from his meditation on the holy books. It is important to note that the term *raz* 'mystery' almost always appears in the plural in the Qumran writings, denoting all the wonderful works of the divine plan from the beginning. The singular, when not used in a generic sense (1QH 12 : 13), signifies either the

mystery of the abasement in which God has placed the Community of the Covenant with their leader for a short time (1QS
5 : 25; 8 : 6, 11; 9 : 23), or 'the mystery to come' (IQS 11 : 3;
1Q26, 1 : 1, 4; 1Q27, 1 : 1, 3, 4). This latter, while remaining
very obscure, must concern eschatological destinies, and in
particular those of the elect, who are at the centre of the thought
of the Teacher of Righteousness : God's call of sinners to salvation by pure grace, and their elevation to the lot of the angels
(1QS 11 : 5-9; 1QH 8 : 26-31; 11 : 9-19). Such vision, expressed
with unusual intensity, without doubt manifests an authentic
religious experience. Yet, we may suggest that they are 'revelations' only in a wide sense, having their source in the profound
intuitions of a mystical personality, and based on continual
meditation on the ancient revelation.

How different it is with Paul. Of course, we must grant that
he was no less a mystic and contemplative than the Teacher of
Righteousness. Because of this, his way of speaking often recalls
the Teacher of Righteousness, as for example when he applies
the 'mystery' to the glorious destiny of the elect (Col 1 : 27;
Eph 1 : 17-18; cf. 1 Cor 2 : 7-10), or when he uses it to describe
the unexpected ways of the divine plan (Rom 11 : 25), or a
detail of the eschatological scenario (1 Cor 15 : 51), and finally,
when he speaks of the related themes of 'wisdom', 'knowledge',
'understanding', either in God or in those whom he has illumined.
There is no denying the resemblance of the vocabulary. A passage
like 2 Thess 2 : 6-8 suggests even the possibility of direct borrowing from some Qumran text (cf. 1Q27 1 : 1). However, behind
these resemblances of 'mentality' lie very clear differences of
'spirit'.

The Mystery for Paul is a secret, never revealed to anyone,
hidden from past generations (1 Cor 2 : 9; Col 1 : 26; Eph 3 : 5),
even from the heavenly powers (1 Cor 2 : 8; Eph 3 : 10), and
only 'now' revealed to the 'saints' who are the Christians and,
in particular, the 'apostles and prophets' of Christ (Col 1 : 26;
Eph 3 : 5). The writings of the prophets, now that they have
been made clear by the event, have a place in the preaching of
the faith (Rom 16 : 26), yet by themselves they were not able to

reveal it (cf. 1 Pet 1 : 10-12). Paul's knowledge of the mystery is not the result of meditation; it is due to a direct 'revelation' of Christ (Gal 1 : 16; Eph 3 : 5, 8), who 'took hold' of Paul (Phil 3 : 12) to send him to preach the Good News to the Gentiles. This mystery is not given to recall men back to a strict observance of the divine laws, nor is it only the consoling assurance that the sins of the children of light have been gratuitously forgiven; it brings a message, absolutely unheard of, unexpected and without parallel, of salvation achieved through the cross of Christ (1 Cor 2 : 7-8), offered to Gentile as well as Jew (Col 1 : 27; Eph 3 : 6, 8, 12; cf. Rom 11 : 25ff.), and which will finally result in the union of the whole universe in Christ (Eph 1 : 9-10). The idea of salvation available to all through faith with no need of the Law of Moses (Rom 1 : 17 and *passim*), would have been inconceivable to the Teacher of Righteousness, and was accepted by Paul only because of the overwhelming vision on the road to Damascus. These two mystics, one a reformer, the other an apostle, can use the same language, common to their epoch, but it clothes totally different realities. We have already seen this verified in the case of the Light-Darkness theme. The former still lives in the world of the Old Law and his revelations never go beyond the prophets, while Paul stands at the dawn of the new age, the herald of a mystery only lately revealed, whose splendour will win the faith of the world.

Justification by grace alone is a theme which, while characteristic of Paul, is found already in Qumran, and would thus seem to have its origin there. This is our last test case, and its solution, in fact, will be the same as the previous two : namely, the similarities, which are very clear and certain, can be explained by a common source, and, secondly, are used in contexts which manifest a totally different 'spirit'.

At first sight, some of the resemblances are very striking. Like Paul, the Teacher of Righteousness declares that no man is just before God (1QH 4 : 30-31; 7 : 16; 12 : 19; 16 : 11); every man, and he himself first of all, is by nature a sinner (1QH 1 : 22 and *passim*). Even the Pharisee admitted that man was a sinner; but

he also believed that the observance of the Law enabled him to
merit in the strict sense of the word, and that he would become
just in the end as long as his good works outweighed the evil.
The author of the Hodayoth does not share this optimism. He
certainly busied himself with the observance of the Law, for that
was his main preoccupation; but, he did not seek from it a
justice which would be his own work. Rather it was from the
mercy and justice of God that he hoped to obtain the power
to carry out the commandments (e.g. 1QH 16 : 9-18). We have
here a point of contact with Paul, even though it is rather
negative; for the Teacher of Righteousness did not attack the
Law itself; he accepted its value and knew of nothing else which
could be more pleasing to God, yet he was certain that he could
only observe it through the pardon and grace of God.

For this pardon he trusted to the goodness of God (1QH 6 : 9;
7 : 27, 30; 13 : 16ff.). Such a doctrine is thoroughly traditional;
the mercy of God tempers his justice and restrains his decision to
take vengeance, or, at least, modifies it and turns the penalty
into medicinal suffering, which purifies the sinner. The theme
of God's vindictive justice and its interplay with his mercy is
too well attested in the bible (Jer 10 : 24; 30 : 11; Ps 6 : 2) to
demand any special treatment from the Teacher of Righteousness
(1QH 5 : 5ff.; 9 : 9-10, 33; cf. 1QS 1 : 26-2 : 1). What is unusual,
and what seems to connect him in a special way with Paul, is
the way in which he makes this gratuitous pardon and mercy
the fruit of the 'justice' of God. God is just in forgiving the sinner,
for it is by his justice that he purifies the sinner (1QH 4 : 37;
11 : 30). Here appears the notion of 'salvific justice', which
transcends mere 'vindictive justice', and is one of the striking
elements of Paul's doctrine. At the same time, we should not
think of it as something completely new, and, having attributed
it to Paul in the past, now claim that he must have received it
from Qumran. In fact, this idea is already present in the bible,
not as frequently as some have thought, but really there,
especially from the Exile on (Ps 143 : 1-2, 11; Ezra 9 : 13-15;
Dan 9 : 16). It would appear that after that event, groups of
pious Jews, brought together by their love of Yahweh, were

aware that it was sin that had brought so many calamities on their people, and yet were sure that God needed them to preserve his truth in the world; therefore, they believed that he would pardon them and save his remnant, not merely despite his justice (vindictive), but even because of his justice (salvific). God's way of being truly just, which is to be faithful to his Covenant, would be to wipe away all their sins and save them by grace alone for love of his Name. This is the doctrine we find in the writings of the Teacher of Righteousness, who considers himself to be sent by God to re-establish the Covenant, and is certain that both he and his disciples have been chosen by God to be the sons of light, who are to conquer the sons of darkness; God, therefore, must, even by reason of his justice, pardon and purify them, and make them really holy (1QH 7: 19ff., 28-31).

But how and when will this triumph of the justice of God over the sin of man be achieved? The answer they give to this question highlights the fundamental differences between the Teacher of Qumran and Paul.

First of all, it is clear that for the Teacher of Righteousness this justice will not be granted to the sinner before the eschatological judgment, which is still future. While they await it, he and his disciples only advance towards 'the ways of justice' (1QH 7: 14). They are 'just', 'perfect of way' (1QH 1: 36), only in vocation, as the 'elect of justice' (1QH 2: 13). The just will be distinguished from the sinner only at the eschatological judgment, (1QH 7: 12), if one may speak in this way at all (1QH 7: 28; 9: 14ff.)! We may agree with Luther that this represents Paul's point of view too, but only on condition that we remember that for Paul the eschatological judgment has already taken place in Christ. And that changes everything. The Christian remains subject to sin only because he still belongs to the old world. In so far as he belongs to the new order 'in Christ', which is so much more real, he possesses the new justice, that of Christ. Already he is 'justified' by the historical act of the cross and by baptism (1 Cor 6: 11; Rom 3: 24; 5: 1, 9, etc.). It should be noted that at Qumran the sinner is never said to be 'justified'. With due deference to certain translators, *mishpaṭ* of 1QS 11 : 2ff. is not 'justification', but the efficacious judgment of God on the conduct of man in virtue of his *sedaqah*, which is his righteousness. It is a merciful, even salvific, judgment, which preserves the sinner from damnation and enables him to remain in the service of God, but it does not effect his 'justification' in the Pauline sense. In 1QH 13 : 17 it is not stated that man 'is justified', but that he 'will be just'. While it is true that man receives a spirit from God, which purifies him and helps him to make his conduct perfect (1QH 4 : 31ff.; 16 : 9-12), this sharing in the spirit of truth is not the effect of any new act of God in the history of salvation. For Paul, the Spirit is the Spirit of Christ, which, after having raised Christ from the dead (Rom 1 : 4; 8 : 11; 1 Cor 15 : 45; 1 Tim 3 : 16), is given to those who believe in him as the gift of the eschatological age (Rom 8 : 2-4; 2 : 11; 1 Cor 6 : 11; 2 Cor 5 : 5; Gal 4 : 6; 5 : 5). Once again, a complete change has taken place, for, in passing from Qumran to Paul, we pass from one epoch of the history of salvation to another; we exist in the time after the decisive event and not before it. If same themes are still used, it is in a completely new context. They are in fact completely dated by the new situation which God has created in Christ Jesus.

The Christian attains to his new justice through faith in Christ (Rom 3 : 22ff.). There is nothing comparable to this in Qumran, where it is not even conceivable. The Teacher of the Hodayoth never proclaims belief in his own person which would bring salvation to his disciples. Certain scholars have made much of the appeals for belief in his teaching found in 1QpHab 2 : 6-8; 8 : 2ff.; CD 20 : 28, 32. But these are concerned with nothing more than the normal obedience of a disciple to the teaching of his master, and cannot be compared with that total commitment to the very person of Another as the source of salvation. The faith in Christ, which saves a Christian, is not merely faith in his teaching, but faith in his death and resurrection, or, more accurately, it is faith in the crucified and risen Christ (Rom 3 : 25; 4 : 25; 5 : 1, 9; Col 2 : 12). There is no possibility of such faith at Qumran, for despite some theories the Teacher of

Righteousness is neither the Christ, nor crucified, nor risen from the dead.

When we examine Paul more closely, we find in his writings an ambivalent use of the idea of justice which one would describe as the work of a genius were it not rather 'revealed' by God himself : the triumph of the salvific justice of God by means of the satisfaction of his vindictive justice. We have deliberately emphasized the salvific aspect of the justice of God in St Paul, and correctly so; but it would be a mistake to think that Paul was ignorant of its vindictive, or, if one prefers, retributive, aspect, which was quite as traditional, more deeply rooted in the bible, and still a vital force in Pharisaism. On the contrary, Paul integrates both aspects very cleverly. Like the Teacher of Qumran, and a whole religious movement of pious Judaism on which both depended, Paul speaks of the transcendent justice, whereby God is faithful to his Covenant despite the unfaithfulness of the sinner, whom he saves by grace alone, without works of which he is in any case incapable. However, at the same time he takes account of the Pharisaic position and the strong traditional view, both of which required that the justice of God should reward good and punish evil. But, Paul has the solution of God himself : the free sacrifice of a victim, who through his death takes on himself the punishment for sin demanded by the Law (Gal 3 : 13; Rom 8 : 3; Col 2 : 14), and through his resurrection merits the justice, which he will communicate to those who believe in him (2 Cor 5 : 21). This is an inspired answer to the problem, because it is a divine one. Salvific justice, in pardoning, does not suppress but fully satisfies vindictive justice, for the expiation that the latter demands is effected through the voluntary sacrifice of a divine victim. We may be sure that the Teacher of Righteousness could have said nothing like this, nor even conceived of such a doctrine. Like so many religious leaders in Israel, he was certain that God was too just to abandon his chosen ones to perdition; but, while he believed in the final triumph of divine justice, he never suspected such a mystery as this *coup d'état*. Paul obtained the key to it through the revelation on the road to Damascus; the Crucified, who was despised and persecuted by Paul, is he who by his free sacrifice has redeemed all men, and made it possible for God to be just while giving to the new man a justice which is both merited in Christ and a pure gift of grace in all the faithful (cf. Eph 5 : 24).

The above observations, to which we could add many others, are intended as a warning against an error of historical method noticeable in many disciplines. It occurs when an early stage of some movement is interpreted in the light of a later stage, for this inevitably leads to the beginnings of the movement being incorrectly presented and erroneously understood. This mistake is made in textual criticism when recently discovered ancient documents are judged in function of a subsequent period, and are forced into the categories of documents more recent than they, e.g. an attempt to classify a third century papyrus using the categories 'Alexandrian', 'Caesarian', 'Western', all of which describe more recent manuscripts. In the study of heresy this error occurs, when an early author is condemned in the name of theological developments and dogmatic declarations subsequent to his time, and he is charged with error for holding opinions which, in fact, were matters of free debate during his lifetime and therefore perfectly excusable. Again, this error appears when Paul or John is read in the light of a systematic Gnosticism, which belongs to the second century, and when certain themes in their writings are declared to be 'gnostic'. This, of course, is without foundation, since their writings existed before Gnosticism, and, far from drawing from it, were used by it. Surely the same mistake is made in the study of the writings of Qumran, when a Christian mind discovers in them doctrines that had not yet come into being? Read in this false light, doctrines or expressions which are still purely Jewish are understood to possess a new meaning, which they received in fact only after the work of Christ had been completed. Led astray by an undeniable similarity of 'mentality' some have come to believe that the 'spirit' is also the same. Unconsciously (we believe) some have transferred the image of Jesus, the Messiah who was crucified and rose from the dead, to the Teacher of Righteousness, and then have stood amazed at the resemblance between the two. Once aware of this danger, we must guard ourselves against it by a rigorous care to explain the writings of Qumran by earlier or at least contemporary sources. In this way they will preserve their true nature as the writings of a thoroughly Jewish sect, influenced by syncretism, but, like the whole of Judaism of that period, preoccupied with the proximate coming of the eschatological crisis, yet in its own way preparing for it by a conscious return to the past of the Chosen People.

In itself this is of immense importance. This attitude reflects the mentality of Judaism as it was immediately before Christianity; and this is why it is so important to understand it correctly today. There is no doubt that the literature of Qumran is an inestimable help to us in our effort to study primitive Christianity. Yet, we must keep comparisons within correct limits, and sometimes the comparison may turn out to be a contrast. In the New Testament we find the same themes and similar expressions, yet everything has been transformed from within and endowed with a new significance. The stage scenery may be the same, but the entry of a new character has revolutionized the drama. Jesus' essential role was not to be the last of a long line of teachers, but to effect by his life and work a total renewal of the whole universe. His essential work was to come into the world in the Name of God and to die and rise again. In Christ, all the tendencies embryonic in the old economy are now brought together, perfected and fulfilled. We should not be surprised, then, to find many of the older beliefs of Judaism, also found at Qumran, on the lips of Jesus and in the writings of early Christianity. He unites all of them in himself, but changes and renews them in the living synthesis of his own person. This suffices to change the world. Finally, at Qumran nothing new has taken place, except the enlightenment and fervent conversion of a deeply religious person, a leader of men. In the New Testament something has happened : the death and the resurrection of Jesus Christ. It would be unfortunate if this new and sovereign intervention of the Word of God were not recognized because of certain similarities of human language.

2

A FEATURE OF QUMRAN ANGELOLOGY AND THE ANGELS OF 1 Cor 11: 10*

Joseph A. Fitzmyer, S. J.

THE Qumran texts have brought to light a feature of Jewish thought about angels which helps us to interpret the meaning of the phrase *dia tous angelous* 'on account of the angels' in 1 Cor 11 : 10. This phrase has been the subject of many inter-pretations from the time of Tertullian on. The evidence from Qumran, however, does not just add another interpretation to the many that have already been given; rather it adds a detail to one interpretation already rather common, thus supporting it and rendering the other interpretations less probable. It is our purpose in this study to indicate the bearing of the new evidence from Qumran on this Pauline expression.

In vv. 3-16 of ch. 11 in the first epistle to the Corinthians, Paul is dealing with an abusive practice that had arisen in the Church of Corinth. It had been reported to him that women were praying and 'prophesying' in the liturgical gatherings with heads uncovered. It has been asserted that Greek women were accustomed to wear a veil on the streets and often even at home, if they were married, but usually removed it in religious assemblies.[1] This custom is supposed to have been imitated by

---

* Published in *NTS* 4 (1957-58) 48-58.

[1] E. B. Allo, *Saint Paul, Première Épitre aux Corinthiens*, Paris (1956), p. 258; see also p. 263. The chief source of evidence for Greek women taking part in a religious ceremony with uncovered head is the Andania Mysteries inscription. See W. Dittenberger, *Sylloge Inscriptionum Graecarum*, Leipzig, vol. II, 1917, no. 736, 4. Also important is the Lycosurae lex sacra (*ibid.* III (1920), no. 999). For the bearing of these inscriptions (and others) on

the Christian women of Corinth in their religious assemblies. Though it is not certain just how the abuse arose, we are certain from the way Paul speaks about it that he looked upon it as such, especially because it was contrary to the custom of other Christian communities. In this regard the Church of Corinth was not in conformity with the *paradosis* 'tradition' which Paul had passed on to them (v. 2).[2] So he writes to correct the abuse.

Four reasons may be distinguished in the course of Paul's remarks why a woman should veil her head in assemblies of public prayer. (1) Theologically, the order of creation found in the Genesis story shows that woman is subordinated to man; she is destined to be his companion, helper and mother.[3] Hence she should manifest that subordination by wearing a veil. (2) Philosophically (or sociologically), natural decency would seem to demand it. (3) As a matter of ecclesiastical discipline, the 'churches of God' recognize no other practice in worship. (4) 'On account of the angels' (v. 10). The last reason causes a difficulty, because it is abruptly added to a verse which is the conclusion of the theological reason set forth in vv. 3-9. As several commentators have remarked, it is a surprise to find it there.[4] More-

---

1 Cor 11 : 10, see S. Lösch, 'Christliche Frauen in Corinth (1 Kor 11, 2-16). Ein neuer Lösungsversuch', *Theologische Quartalschrift* 127 (1947), pp. 230-51. Though many details about the wearing of the veil in antiquity, both by Jewish and Greek women, have been preserved for us, none of them bears directly on the problem of the Church in Corinth. We do not know the exact nature nor the origin of the abuse that Paul was trying to handle. Was it a reaction against a custom that he was trying to introduce? G. Delling, *Paulus' Stellung zur Frau und Ehe*, Stuttgart, 1931, p. 98, seems to think so; likewise A. Schlatter, *Die korinthische Theologie*, Beiträge zur Förderung christlicher Theologie, 18/2; Gütersloh, 1914, pp. 23, 54. On the use of the veil in antiquity see R. de Vaux, 'Sur le voile des femmes dans l'Orient ancien', *RB* 44 (1936), pp. 397-412; A Jeremias, *Der Schleier von Sumer bis heute* (Der Alte Orient 31/1-2), Leipzig, 1931.

2 S. Lösch (*op. cit.* pp. 225-30) rightly rejects the idea that there was a movement in Corinth in favour of the emancipation of women, which Paul was trying to combat.

3 Paul is obviously speaking in vv. 3-9 of the order of creation; cf. 1 Tim 2 : 13. Further on, however, in v. 11 he introduces another point of view, namely, *en kuriō* 'in the Lord'. Under this aspect Paul says, in Gal 3 : 28, *ouk eni arsen kai thēlu* 'there is neither male or female'.

4 So P. Bachmann, *Der erste Brief des Paulus an die Korinther*, 4. Aufl., Leipzig, 1936, p. 356; J. Sickenberger, *Die Briefe des hl. Paulus an die Korinther und Römer* (Bonner Bibel, 6), Bonn, 1932, p. 51; J. Héring, *La première épître de Saint Paul aux Corinthiens*, Neuchâtel, 1949, p. 94.

over, it is added without any explanation, and all the attempts that have been made to integrate it with the preceding argument have not succeeded. Hence it is best to regard it as a subsidiary reason stated succinctly.

Because the context of this verse will be necessary for our interpretation, we shall give the translation of the entire passage. Goodspeed's translation,[5] which is being used, is a good example of the way modern translators have wrestled with v. 10.

'I appreciate your always remembering me, and your standing by the things I passed on to you, just as you received them. But I want you to understand that Christ is the head of every man, while a woman's head is her husband, and Christ's head is God. Any man who offers prayer or explains the will of God with anything on his head disgraces his head, and any woman who offers prayer or explains the will of God bareheaded disgraces her head, for it is just as though she had her head shaved. For if a woman will not wear a veil, let her cut off her hair too. But if it is a disgrace for a woman to have her hair cut off or her head shaved, let her wear a veil. For a man ought not to wear anything on his head, for he is the image of God and reflects his glory; while woman is the reflection of man's glory. For man was not made from woman, but woman from man, and man was not created for woman, but woman was for man. That is why she ought to wear upon her head something to symbolize her subjection, on account of the angels, if nobody else. But in union with the Lord, woman is not independent of man nor man of woman. For just as woman was made from man, man is born of woman, and it all really comes from God. Judge for yourselves. Is it proper for a woman to offer prayer to God with nothing on her head? Does not nature itself teach you that for a man to wear his hair long is degrading, but a woman's long hair is her pride? For her hair is given her as a covering. But if anyone is disposed to be contentious about it, I for my part recognize no other practice in worship than this, and neither do the churches of God.'

The Greek text of v. 10 reads as follows : *dia touto opheilei hē gunē exousian echein epi tēs kephalēs dia tous angelous.*

The words *dia touto* 'that is why' indicate the conclusion to the preceding theological argument. Because of them the un-

⁵ In J. M. P. Smith (ed.), *The Complete Bible, an American Translation*, Chicago, 1951, New Testament section, p. 162.

expected addition of *dia tous angelous* 'on account of the angels' has made some commentators think that this phrase was a gloss.[6] But Robertson and Plummer have pointed out that it cannot be dismissed so lightly : 'Marcion had the words, and the evidence for them is overwhelming. An interpolator would have made his meaning clearer.'[7] Nor is it possible to admit any of the many purely conjectural and often far-fetched emendations, such as *dia to euangelion* 'on account of the gospel'; *dia tas agelas* 'on account of the crowds'; *dia tous agelaious* 'on account of the men who crowded in'; *dia tous andras* 'on account of the vulgar' or 'gazing men'; *dia tous engelastas* 'on account of the mockers'; *dia tous ochlous* 'on account of the mobs'; *dia tēs angelias* 'throughout [the whole of] her [divine] message'.[8] Consequently, we must try to understand the words as they stand.

v. 10 contains another difficult expression that has tormented interpreters and no satisfying solution has really been found for it—the word *exousian*. Since this is actually the key-word in the verse, we must indicate briefly the main attempts to interpret it, as its meaning affects the phrase *dia tous angelous*. Four interpretations are currently proposed and unfortunately no new light from Qumran has been shed on this problem.

In itself *exousia* means 'power, authority, right to do something; ability; dominion'.[9] But what is its meaning when Paul says, 'That is why the woman should have *exousian* upon her head'?

(1) Most commentators understand *exousia* today in a figura-

[6] C. Holsten, *Das Evangelium des Paulus*, Berlin, 1880, pp. 472-4, eliminates the whole verse. J. M. S. Baljon, *Novum Testamentum Graece*, Groningen, 1898, p. 525; A. Jirku, 'Die "Macht" auf dem Haupte (1 Kor 11 : 10)', *Neue kirchliche Zeitschrift* 32 (1921), p. 711, consider *dia tous angelous* a gloss.

[7] *First Epistle of St Paul to the Corinthians* (International Critical Commentary), Edinburgh, 1911, p. 233.

[8] See R. Perdelwitz, 'Die *Exousia* auf dem Haupt der Frau', *Theologische Studien und Kritiken* 86 (1913), pp. 611-13; A. P. Stanley, *Epistles of St Paul to the Corinthians*, 3rd ed., London, 1865, p. 186.

[9] See W. Bauer, *Griechisch-Deutsches Wörterbuch zu den Schriften des Neuen Testaments*, 4. Aufl.; Berlin, 1952, 502; Liddell-Scott-Jones, *A Greek-English Lexicon*, 9th ed.; Oxford, 1925-40, vol. I, p. 599; C. Spicq, 'Encore la "Puissance sur la tete" (1 Cor 11 : 10)', *RB* 68 (1939), pp. 557-62. Fr Spicq has studied the uses of *exousia* especially in Ben Sira and the Greek papyri and has shown that the word was used specifically of the authority of a husband over his wife or of a father over his children.

tive sense as a *symbol of the power* to which the woman is
subjected (by metonymy). Theophylact expressed it thus : *to tou
exousiazesthai sumbolon* 'the symbol of being dominated'.[10] It
must be admitted that this sense of the word fits the context well,
but the chief difficulty with this interpretation is a philological
one, since it attributes to *exousia* a passive sense, which is otherwise unknown. Apropos of this interpretation W. M. Ramsay
has remarked : '. . . a preposterous idea which a Greek scholar
would laugh at anywhere except in the New Testament, where
(as they seem to think) Greek words may mean anything that
commentators choose'.[11] *Exousia* should indicate a power that
the woman possesses or exercises (cf. Rev 11 : 6; 14 : 8; 20 : 6),
not one to which she is subjected or subordinated.[12] We may
rightly ask why St Paul says 'power' (or 'authority'), if he really
means 'subjection'. Then, too, the shift from an abstract idea like
power to the specific meaning of an article of feminine attire is
not an easy one to explain, even by metonymy.[13] Wendland asks

[10] *Expos. in Ep. I ad Cor.* (*PG* 124, 697C); the symbolical meaning has
been proposed by Theodoret (*PG* 82, 312D); Chrysostom (*PG* 61, 218);
A. Lemonnyer, *Épîtres de saint Paul, première partie*, Paris, 1908, p. 145;
R. Cornely, *Commentarius in S. Pauli apostoli epistolas, II: Prior epistola
ad Corinthios*, Paris, 1909, p. 319; P. Bachmann, *op. cit.*, p. 356; Strack-
Billerbeck, *Kommentar zum Neuen Testament aus Talmud und Midrasch*,
München, vol. III (1926), p. 436; J. Huby, *Saint Paul, Première épître aux
Corinthiens*, Paris, 1946, pp. 248-9; C. Spicq, *op. cit.*, p. 558; J. Kürzinger,
Die Briefe des Apostels Paulus, die Briefe an die Korinther und Galater,
Würzburg, 1954, p. 28; *et al.*

[11] *The Cities of St Paul. Their Influence on his Life and Thought*, London,
1907, p. 203.

[12] This is the weak point, in our opinion, in Spicq's study of *exousia* (see
above in n. 9). Granted that metonymy is a legitimate way to interpret the
word, and granted that *exousia* does mean in the papyri and Ben Sira the
authority of the husband over his wife or of the father over his children, the
fact remains that *echein exousian* in the New Testament is used in an *active*
sense of a power which one exercises. Even in the examples from the papyri
which Spicq cites the word *exousian* seems to us to have this meaning; thus
didonai exousian means to transfer the authority to another so that he can
exercise it.

[13] Allo (*op. cit.*, pp. 266-7) cites the use of a similar expression in Diodorus
Siculus (1, 47, 5), who reports that the statue of an ancient Egyptian goddess
bears *treis basileias epi tēs kephalēs*, that is, three diadems, signs of a triple
royalty. But there is an important difference to be noted : 'here it is question
of the power of its wearer and not of the power of someone else' (J. Héring,
op. cit., p. 95); see also J. Weiss, *Der erste Korintherbrief*, Göttingen, 1910,
p. 274.

what evidence there is for the veil as a sign of subordination to a man.[14] Consequently, if this interpretation of *exousia* is to be retained, one must say that Paul has created the figurative meaning to suit his context.

(2) Because of this philological difficulty, some commentators have preferred to interpret *exousia* rather as a symbol of the power, the honour and the dignity of the woman. 'The woman who has a veil on her head wears authority on her head: that is what the Greek text says.'[15] The woman who veils her head exercises control over it and does not expose it to indignity; if she unveils it, everyone has control over it and she loses her dignity.[16] Such an interpretation has the advantage of giving to *exousia* an active meaning, but it seriously forces the context, since Paul is not speaking of the dignity of woman nor of her dignified actions. The context treats rather of woman's subordination to man according to the Genesis account of creation.[17]

(3) A fairly common interpretation of *exousia* today explains the word in the sense of a *magical power* that the veiled woman possesses to ward off the attacks of evil spirits. Since woman is the secondary product of creation, she requires this additional force 'as the weaker sex' against the fallen angels.[18] She needs this magic force, which is the veil, especially in times of prayer and ecstasy, when the angels draw near, for her natural frailty is not sufficient to protect her. The advantage of this interpretation is that it preserves the active meaning of *exousia* and provides a closer connection with what precedes for the phrase *dia tous*

---

[14] *Die Briefe an die Korinther* (Das Neue Testament Deutsch, 7), Göttingen, 1954, p. 83.

[15] W. M. Ramsay, *op. cit.*, p. 203. E. B. Allo, *op. cit.*, p. 267, combines this interpretation with the first one: Paul is stressing not only the subordination of the woman, but also strives to bring out her dignity. See Delling, *op. cit.*, p. 99, n. 4.

[16] Robertson and Plummer, *op. cit.*, p. 232.

[17] J. Huby, *op. cit.*, p. 248.

[18] Thus O. Everling, *Die paulinische Angelologie und Dämonologie*, Göttingen, 1888, p. 37; M. Dibelius, *Die Geisterwelt im Glauben des Paulus*, Göttingen, 1909, pp. 13-23; J. Weiss, *op. cit.*, p. 274; H. Lietzmann, *An die Korinther I-II*, 4. Aufl.; Tübingen, 1949, p. 55; R. Reitzenstein, *Poimandres*, Leipzig, 1904, p. 230, n. 1; J. Héring, *op. cit.*, pp. 90, 94-5; E. Fehrle, *Die kultische Keuschheit im Altertum* (Religionsgeschichtliche Versuche und Vorarbeiten 6), Giessen, 1910, p. 39; *et al.*

angelous. But the major difficulty with this opinion is the lack of evidence showing that a woman's veil was ever thought of as having such a function in antiquity. J. Héring believes that M. Dibelius proved this very point. Yet H. Lietzmann, whose commentary made this interpretation popular, admits the difficulty : 'Freilich ist bisher die Vorstellung von einer apotropäischen Wirkung des Schleiers nicht nachgewiesen.'[19]

(4) In 1920 G. Kittel proposed a new interpretation of *exousia* which has been adopted in some quarters. He pointed out that an Aramaic word, *šltwnyh*, meaning a 'veil' or an 'ornament of the head', occurs in the Jerusalem Talmud.[20] It is given there as the equivalent of the Hebrew *šbys* of Is 3 : 18. Now the root of this word is *šlt*, and is identical with the common Aramaic verb meaning 'to have power, dominion over'. Hence, either by a mistranslation or by a popular etymology, the Greek *exousia* was taken as the equivalent of the Aramaic *šltwnyh*. The proponents of this explanation of *exousia* point out that an ancient variant reading in 1 Cor 11 : 10 is *kalumma* 'a veil',[21] found in Irenaeus (*PG* 7, 524B), which is supported by *velamen* of Jerome (*PL* 25, 439A) and a codex of the Vulgate. Origen (*PG*, 13, 119B) combined the two readings, *velamen et potestatem*. Though we cannot rule out the possibility that the reading *kalumma* or *velamen* is an interpretation of the text or an attempt to eliminate a difficulty of the original text,[22] nevertheless it does show that the word was understood in antiquity in the sense of 'a veil'. This interpretation has been adopted by W. Foerster and M. Ginsburger and seems to underlie the translation given

---

[19] *Op. cit.*, p. 55. W. G. Kümmel's added note on p. 184 is scarcely pertinent.

[20] Sabbath 6 : 8b, commenting on Is 3 : 18 : *hšbysym: šltwnyh kmh d't 'mr šbys šl sbkh*. 'Was die *šᵉbisim* anlangt, so sind damit gemeint die *šaltonayya*, wie du sagst: der *šabis* des Kopfnetzes.' ('Die "Macht" auf dem Haupt (1 Kor 11 : 10)', *Rabbinica* (Arbeiten zur Vorgeschichte des Christentums, 1/3; Leipzig, 1920), p. 20. Though this opinion is usually ascribed to G. Kittel, he was actually anticipated by J. Herklotz, 'Zu 1 Kor 11 : 10, *Biblische Zeitschrift* 10 (1912), p. 154. See Levy, *Wörterbuch über die Talmudim und Midraschim*, IV, 562a.

[21] Treated as a variant by Nestle, Merk. But is it certain that the text of Irenaeus offers nothing more than a paraphrase of our verse?

[22] See J. Héring, *op. cit.*, p. 95.

in the *Revised Standard Version*.[23] The main difficulty with this meaning of *exousia* is that the Greeks of Corinth would never have understood what Paul meant by it.[24] We must admit that this is a real difficulty, but the presupposition on the part of those who propose it usually is that the Church of Corinth was wholly, or almost wholly, Greek. It is, however, beyond doubt that there were *Jewish* elements in the Corinthian community who would have understood the word *exousia* in the sense of *šlṭwnyh*.[25] Consequently, until a better suggestion is made for the sense of *exousia* we prefer to go along with Kittel.

Having given a survey of the main interpretations of *exousia* we can turn to the phrase *dia tous angelous*. The figurative meanings that have been given to the phrase can be dismissed immediately, as it is obvious that they are 'last-resort' solutions. For instance, St Ephraem thought that *angelous* meant *sacerdotes*,[26] while Ambrosiaster commented : *angelos episcopos dicit, sicut in Apocalypsi Ioannis*.[27] But though the word *angelos* is found in the New Testament in the sense of a human messenger (Luke 7 : 24; 9 : 52; Jas 2 : 25), it is never used thus by Paul.

Likewise to be rejected is the interpretation, 'in imitation of

[23] Foerster proposes it only as a conjecture in *TWNT*, vol. II, p. 571. Ginsburger's discussion ('La "gloire" et l' "autorité" de la femme dans 1 Cor 11 : 1-10', *RHPR* 12 (1932), p. 248) was apparently written independently of Kittel's study. G. Delling (*op. cit.*, p. 105, n. 68) regards this interpretation as 'die annehmbarste Lösung'.

[24] Thus Strack-Billerbeck, *loc. cit.*, p. 437; Allo, *op. cit.*, p. 264.

[25] According to Acts 18 : 1-5 Paul on his first arrival in Corinth was given hospitality by 'a Jew named Aquila, a native of Pontus, who had recently come from Italy with his wife Priscilla. . . . Every Sabbath he would preach in the synagogue, and try to convince both Jews and Greeks'. When he turned in anger from the Jews to preach to the heathen, 'he moved to the house of a worshipper of God named Titus Justus, which was next door to the synagogue. But Crispus, the leader of the synagogue, believed in the Lord and so did all his household. . . .' See Allo, *op. cit.*, pp. 12-13; J. Holzner, *Paulus*, Freiburg im B., 1937, p. 206.

[26] *Commentarii in Epistulas D. Pauli, nunc primum ex Armenio in Latinum sermonem translati*, Venice, 1893, p. 70. This was likewise the opinion of Pelagius, (*PL* 30, 781B) and of Primasius of Adrumentum (*PL* 118, 532D).

[27] *PL* 17, 253. Similarly D. Bornhäuser, ' "Um der Engel willen", 1 Kor 11 : 10', *Neue kirkliche Zeitschrift* 41 (1930), pp. 475-88; P. Rose, 'Power on the head', *Expository Times* 23 (1911-12), pp. 183-4.

the angels', or 'because the angels do so'. Support for this opinion has been sought in Is 6 : 2, where the angels covered their faces and loins with their wings in the presence of the Lord. So a woman in prayer should cover her head. Just as the angels, who are subordinate to God, veil themselves in his presence, so should woman 'as a subordinate being'[28] follow their example. But we may ask, with J. Huby, why this imitation of the attitude of the angels during divine worship should be prescribed for women only.[29] Moreover, what evidence is there for understanding *dia* in this sense?

In mentioning above the third interpretation of *exousia* we indicated a meaning of *angelous* that is fairly common among that group of commentators, namely, *fallen angels*. As far as we know, Tertullian was the first to suggest this meaning for *angelous* in this passage. In *De virginibus velandis*, 7, he says, *propter angelos, scilicet quos legimus a deo et caelo excidisse ob concupiscentiam feminarum.*[30] Tertullian's suggestion has been illustrated by reference to Gen 6 : 2, 'the sons of the gods' (*b^{e}ne ^{e}lohīm*) noticed that the daughters of men were attractive; so they married those whom they liked best'. Lietzmann adds that this passage in Genesis often excited the fantasy of later Jewish writers, for whom bad angels preying on weak, defenceless women were a literary commonplace.[31] He refers, in particular, to the *Testament of Reuben*, 5, where women are warned *hina mē kosmōntai tas kephalas kai tas opseis autōn* because the

---

[28] W. Meyer, *I. Korinther 11-16 Leib Christi*, Zurich, 1945, p. 26. Similarly K. Roesch, ' "Um der Engel willen" (1 Kor 11 : 10)', *Theologie und Glaube* 24 (1932), pp. 363-5; Robertson and Plummer, *op. cit.*, pp. 233-4 (as a suggestion 'worth considering'); J. Mezzacasa, 'Propter angelos (1 Cor 11 : 10)', *VD* 11 (1931), pp. 29-42; S. Lösch (*op. cit.*, p. 255, n. 80) labels K. Roesch's *exposé* as 'die einzig richtige, von den Kirchenvätern übereinstimmend vertretene Deutung'.

[29] *Op. cit.*, p. 251.

[30] *PL* 2, 947A; cf. *Contra Marcionem*, 5, 8 (*CSEL* 47, 597); *De cultu feminarum*, 2, 10 (*CSEL* 70, 88).

[31] *Op. cit.*, p. 55. He refers to W. Bousset, *Die Religion des Judentums im neutestamentlichen Zeitalter*, Berlin, 1906, p. 382. See also L. Jung, *Fallen Angels in Jewish, Christian and Mohammedan Literature*, Philadelphia, 1926, pp. 97ff.; W. Weber, 'Die paulinische Vorschrift über die Kopfbedeckung der Christen', *Zeitschrift für wissenschaftliche Theologie* 46 (1903), pp. 487-99. See n. 18 above for others who hold this opinion.

women before the Flood bewitched the angels in that way.[32] But J. Héring thinks that, since it is not certain that the Corinthians were *au courant* with such Jewish beliefs, it is preferable to suppose with M. Dibelius an allusion to Hellenistic ideas, according to which a woman in a state of ecstasy (as in sleep) was by her weakness particularly exposed to the attacks of certain spirits.[33] Hence *exousia* gives her a magic protection against such attacks.

Against this opinion we may point out that the *weakness* of woman is a notion that the interpreters have introduced. Paul speaks of woman's subordination to man; he says nothing of her weakness. Hence woman's need of an added protection introduces into the context a consideration that is quite foreign to Paul's argumentation. But the most decisive reason against this interpretation is that *angeloi*, used with the article, never designates bad or fallen angels in the Pauline writings.[34] Moreover, sensuality is never attributed to any of the good angels in any of the Christian or Jewish writings of the period.[35] One of the other problems that are met in interpreting this verse is visualizing just what kind of veil Paul has in mind. It is far from certain that he means a veil that covers the face after the fashion of the oriental women in modern times (at least until fairly recently); he speaks of a covering for the head. If it is merely a head-covering, is that sufficient protection against the fallen angels? Consequently, we believe that this opinion must be abandoned, especially since the new evidence from Qumran rules it out.

The most common opinion has always regarded *angelous* as meaning good angels. Theodoret specified this view, by under-

---

[32] Compare *Enoch* 6 (Charles, *Apocrypha and Pseudepigrapha of the Old Testament in English*, 2, p. 191); 19: 1 (2,200); *Jubilees* 4: 22 (2, 19); *Apocalypse of Baruch*, 56: 12 (2,513); *Tobit* 6: 14; 8: 3.

[33] *Op. cit.*, p. 94; cf. M. Dibelius, *Die Geisterwelt*, pp. 18ff.

[34] Compare 1 Cor 13: 1; Mt 13: 49, 25: 31; Lk 16: 22; Heb 1: 4, 5. See Bachmann, *op. cit.*, p. 357.

[35] See Allo, *op. cit.*, p. 266. J. Héring (*op. cit.*, p. 95) thinks that he can weaken this point made by Allo by pointing out that the angels of Gen 6 were also good, 'before permitting themselves to be seduced'. This is hardly *ad rem*.

standing the word of guardian angels.[36] J. Moffatt expands this notion : 'Paul has in mind the midrash on Gen 1 : 26f., which made good angels not only mediators of the Law (Gal 3 : 19), but guardians of the created order. Indeed, according to one ancient midrash, reflected in Philo, when God said, "Let us make man", he was addressing the angels.'[37] Consequently, a woman should wear a veil on her head out of respect for the angels who are guardians of the order of creation (to which Paul alludes in vv. 8-9).

But Moffatt adds another function of the angels, which some commentators either give as the only one, or join, as he does, to their task as guardians of the created order. This second function is their assistance at gatherings of public worship.[38] We separate this function from the former for two reasons. First, it is supported elsewhere in the Old and New Testament. In Ps 137 (138) : 1 we read *enantion angelōn psalō soi* (LXX). In Rev 8 : 3 an angel is the mediator of the prayers of the saints.[39] Secondly, two passages in the Qumran literature so far published mention the presence of angels in sacred gatherings.

In column 7 of the *War Scroll* the physical requirement of those who would take part in God's war, an eschatological war, are set forth.

'No one who is lame or blind or crippled or who has a permanent blemish in his flesh, nor any person afflicted with a disease in his flesh—none of these shall go with them to war. All of them are to be men who volunteer for battle, perfect both in spirit and in body and prepared for the day of vengeance. Nor shall any man go down with them who is not yet cleansed from his bodily discharge on the day of battle, for holy angels accompany their armies' (1QM 7 : 4-6).[40]

[36] *PG* 82, 312D-313A. So too E. Zolli, *Christus*, Rome, 1946, p. 88; Strack-Billerbeck, *loc. cit.*, p. 437; Kittel, *op. cit.*, p. 26, regards the angels rather as guardians of the woman's chastity.

[37] *The First Epistle of Paul to the Corinthians*, London, 1947, p. 152. See also L. Brun, ' "Um der Engel willen" 1 Kor 11 : 10', *ZNW* 14 (1913), pp. 298-308.

[38] See G. Kurze, *Der Engels- und Teufelsglaube des Apostels Paulus*, Freiburg im B., 1915, p. 12.

[39] See further Tobit 12 : 12; 1 Cor 9 : 9; Eph 3 : 10; 1 Tim 5 : 21; Heb 1 : 14 for functions of the angels that are similar.

[40] *'Ôṣar hammᵉgillôt haggᵉnûzôt*, Jerusalem, 1954, Milhemet . . . lûᵃḥ 22.

The Hebrew of the last clause reads as follows: *ky' ml'ky qwdš 'm ṣb'wtm yḥd*. The same reason is given in the so-called 'Rule of the Congregation' for the exclusion of similar cases of physical unfitness from assemblies of the 'congregation'.

'Nor shall anyone who is afflicted by any form of human uncleanness whatsoever be admitted into the assembly of God *(bqhl 'lh);* nor shall anyone who becomes afflicted in this way be allowed to retain his place in the midst of the congregation. No one who is afflicted with a bodily defect or injured in feet or hands, or who is lame or blind or deaf or dumb, or who has a visible blemish in his body, or who is an old man, tottering and unable to stand firm in the midst of the congregation of the men of renown, for holy angels are (present) in their [congre]gation. If anyone of these persons has something to say to the holy council, let an oral deposition be taken from him; but let him not enter, for he is contaminated' (1QSa 2 : 3-11).[41]

The Hebrew for the clause we are interested in is, *ky' ml'ky qwdš [b'd]tm*.

In these two passages we see that every sort of bodily defect, affliction or discharge was considered a thing unworthy of the sight of the angels, who were believed to be present at the gathering of the army for the eschatological war and at the meeting of the congregation or the assembly of God. The volunteer for the holy war had to be perfect not only in spirit but also in body. One gathers from the expression *lr'wt 'ynym* (1QSa 2 : 7) that bodily defects offend the sight of the angels who are present.

It is interesting to note in this connection that similar bodily defects excluded descendants of Aaron from service in the Temple, according to Lev 21 : 17-23.

'Say to Aaron, "None of your descendants, from generation to generation, who has a defect, may draw near to offer his God's food; for no one who has a defect may come near, no one who is blind, or lame, or has any perforations, or has a limb too long; no one who has a fractured foot, or a fractured hand, or is a hunchback, or has a cataract, or a defect of eyesight, or scurvy, or scabs, or crushed testicles—no one of the descendants of Aaron, the priest, who has a defect, may come near to offer the Lord's

[41] D. Barthélemy, J. T. Milik, *Discoveries in the Judaean Desert—I, Qumrân Cave I*, Oxford, 1955, 110.

sacrifices; since he has a defect, he may not come near to offer his God's food. He may eat his God's food, some of the most sacred as well as the sacred; only he must not approach the veil nor come near the altar, because he has a defect in him, lest he profane my sanctuaries".'

There is no mention of angels in this passage of Leviticus, but we see that a bodily defect was considered in ancient Judaism as a source of irreverence toward that which was *qōdeš*, even independently of any moral culpability. In the two passages from the Qumran literature the angels are specified as *ml'ky qwdš*, and the exclusion of bodily defects from their sight is put on the same basis of reverence. From this notion we may interpret the meaning of *dia tous angelous* in 1 Cor.

The context shows that it is a question of a sacred assembly, for men and women are praying and 'prophesying'.[42] In v. 16 Paul refers to the 'custom' which is current in the 'Church of God' (the resemblance of this last expression to *qhl 'lh* in 1QSa 2: 4 should be noted).[43] In such an assembly, Paul says, the woman is to wear upon her head a veil *dia tous angelous*. We are invited by the evidence from Qumran to understand that the unveiled head of a woman is like a bodily defect which should be excluded from such an assembly, 'because holy angels are present in their congregation'.

Furthermore, the Pauline context supports such an interpretation. 'Any woman who prays or "prophesies" with uncovered head disgraces her head, for it is just as though she had her head shaved. For if a woman will not wear a veil, let her cut off her hair too. But if it is a disgrace for a woman to have her hair cut off or her head shaved, let her wear a veil' (v. 6). 'Does not nature itself teach you that . . . a woman's long hair is her pride? For her hair is given her as a covering' (vv. 14-15). In Paul's view there is no difference between the unveiled head of a woman and the shaven head of a woman; and the latter is an unnatural condition. This is not much different from saying that the un-

---

[42] This is the common interpretation of the situation in this passage; see Allo's remarks (*op. cit.*, p. 257) against Bachmann's understanding of the context.

[43] On *qhl* and *ekklēsia* see Kittel's *TWNT* 3, pp. 350ff.

veiled head of a woman is like a bodily defect. Hence *dia tous angelous* should be understood in the sense of 'out of reverence for the angels', who are present in such sacred gatherings and who should not look on such a condition.

Though this evidence from Qumran has not solved the problem of *exousia*, it has, we believe, made the interpretation of *dia tous angelous* as 'fallen angels' far less plausible, and consequently the interpretation of *exousia* as a magical power loses much of its force.

One last remark. It may be asked whether it is valid to cite evidence from the Qumran texts to interpret a passage in the epistles to the Corinthians. These letters have always been looked upon as the special preserve of those who would point out 'Hellenisms' in Paul's thought or language. Influence from the Greek world on the Apostle's writings cannot be denied, given his background as a Jew of the Diaspora and his vocation as the missionary to the Gentiles. It is to be expected that the Epistles to the Corinthians will continue to be better understood as our knowledge of their Hellenistic background increases. But Paul was a Jew and his chief education was rabbinical, based on a thorough study of the Old Testament and saturated with the ideas of contemporaneous Judaism. Hence it is not surprising that some of the background should appear even in the most Greek of his letters.[44]

We do not know *how* the theological ideas of the Qumran sect influenced Paul. That they *did* so is beyond doubt. M. le chanoine Coppens, in an early article on the relation of the Qumran scrolls to the New Testament, stated that the influence of the sect was more apparent in the later writings of Paul than in the 'great epistles'.[45] As the Qumran texts continue to be published, we see this influence appearing abundantly throughout Paul's letters. Consequently, if our suggestion that *dia tous angelous* of 1 Cor 11 : 10 is to be explained in terms of Qumran

[44] In the same vein writes S. Lyonnet ('L'étude du milieu littéraire et l'exégèse du Nouveau Testament', *Biblica* 37 [1956], pp. 1-3), apropos of the results of J. Dupont's researches into Pauline gnosis.

[45] 'Les documents du Désert de Juda et les origines du Christianisme', *Analecta Lovaniensia Biblica et Orientalia*, ser. 2, no. 41 (1953), p. 26.

angelology were an isolated case of such influence in the Epistles to the Corinthians, we might suspect its validity. But a glance at the list of rapprochements between Qumran and the New Testament writings recently published by R. E. Murphy[46] will show that it is not alone. And that list is far from complete, as its author admits. Consequently, we should not be surprised to find a detail of Qumran angelology shedding light on a passage of the Pauline Letters which is otherwise heavily 'Hellenistic'.

Postscript. Since my arrival in Jerusalem I have found that there are two other passages in the Qumran Cave 4 material that support the interpretation set forth in this article. One is in an unpublished fragment of the Damascus Document (provisional abbreviation 4QD[b]). A translation of it appears in J. T. Milik, *Ten Years of Discovery in the Wilderness of Judea,* London, 1959, 114: 'Les gens stupides, les fous, les sots, les déments *(mšwgh)*, les aveugles, les estropiés *(ḥgr)*, les boiteux, les sourds, les mineurs, nul d'entre eux entrera au sein de la communauté, car les anges saints (se tiennent au milieu d'elle).' The second passage was pointed out to me by Dr Claus-Hunno Hunzinger, who has found it in a Cave 4 fragment of the *Milḥamah,* which he is preparing for publication (4QM[a]). Enough of the context has been preserved to show that bodily defects were to be excluded from the presence of the angels. In the immediately preceding lacuna reference was most probably made to a nocturnal pollution. The text reads: *[ly]lh hh'wh l[w' yṣ]' 'tmh l[mlḥ]mh ky' ml'ky qwdš bm'rkwtmh* ('for the holy angels are among their battle-lines'). In all of these passages the force of *ky'* should not be overlooked; it gives the reason for the exclusion of the defects in the camps, the battle-lines and the assemblies. It parallels the Pauline use of *dia.*

Postscript (1966): The interpretation of 1 Cor 11 : 10 which I have proposed in the above article finds support in the independent study of H. J. Cadbury, 'A Qumran Parallel to Paul', *Harvard Theological Review* 51 (1958), pp. 1-2. It has been

---

[46] 'The Dead Sea Scrolls and New Testament Comparisons', *CBQ* 18 (1956,) pp. 263-72.

favourably adopted by K. H. Schelkle, *Die Gemeinde von Qumran und die Kirche des Neuen Testaments* (Patmos: Düsseldorf, 1960), p. 82.

Criticism of my interpretation can be found in J. Héring, *The First Epistle of Saint Paul to the Corinthians* (tr. A. W. Heathcote and P. J. Allcock; London: Epworth, 1962), p. 108; H. Braun, 'Qumran und das Neue Testament: Ein Bericht über 10 Jahre Forschung (1950-1959)', *Theologische Rundschau* 29/3 (1963), 213-14; J. C. Hurd, Jr., *The Origin of 1 Corinthians* (Seabury: New York, 1965), p. 184, n. 4.

Both Braun and Hurd have noted my omission of a reference to Col 2 : 18 in the discussion of the Pauline use of *hoi angeloi*. It should certainly have been included in footnote 34. But I am not too sure that they are right in saying that the omitted reference militates against my thesis at that point. Is it certain that the angels mentioned in Col 2 : 18 are 'fallen' or 'bad' angels? It seems to me that the argument in Colossians (whether this is genuinely Pauline or not) does not depend on whether the angels are good or bad. The 'worship of angels' (Col 2 : 18) is apparently to be understood in terms of the other references to spirits in that letter, i.e. to those beings, good or bad, whom certain Christians in the Colossian church were venerating and whose cult was jeopardizing the cosmic role of Christ. The author's opposition to this cult is just as intelligible if the angels be good or bad.

Braun further criticizes the interpretation of both Cadbury and myself, maintaining that its main point is forced, viz. that the uncovered or shorn head of a woman is comparable to a bodily defect. I probably would never have made such a comparison personally, nor have I found any ancient data to support it. But it should not be overlooked that it is Paul who (at least implicitly) suggests this comparison. He equates the unveiled head of a woman with the shaven or shorn head (1 Cor 11 : 5-6); again it is Paul who regards such a condition as disgraceful *(aischron)*. Is his attitude toward the uncovered head of the woman so radically different from that of the Qumran author who would exclude bodily defects from the sight of the angels?

Lastly, Braun asserts that 'the magically protective effect of a headcovering *is* attested in b. Shabbat 156b' (p. 214 [his italics]). He refers to W. G. Kümmel's revision of Lietzmann's commentary on 1 Cor (*HNT* 9 [1949], p. 184). When, however, one checks this reference, one sees how far-fetched the parallel is, as far as the Pauline passage is concerned. We shall quote Kümmel's note in Braun's own language: 'In einer späten talmudischen Erzählung (*Schabbat* 156b, s. W. Foerster, *ZNW* 30 (1931), pp. 185f.) wird ein Rabbi zum Dieb, als ihm das Kopftuch vom Haupt gleitet: da ist das Kopftuch deutlich ein magischer Schutz gegen den "bösen Trieb" (die Stelle kann unmöglich auf die Kopfbedeckung als "Unterordnung unter Gott" gedeutet werden, so W. Foerster, *TWNT*, vol. II, p. 571, Anm. 72). Damit ist, wenn nicht die apotropäische, so doch die magisch beschützende Wirkung einer Kopfbedeckung deutlich belegt.'—But is the head-covering which protected the rabbi against his 'evil impulse' to steal really a parallel to Paul's 'veil' on a woman's head in a sacred assembly? Is the 'böser Trieb' *(ysryh)* comparable to a bad angel? Finally, is this 'late Talmudic narrative' of the Babylonian tractate *Shabbat* (156b; ed. Goldschmidt, 1. 717) a tale that might have been known to Paul? After all, it is told of R. Naḥman bar Isaac who belonged to the fourth generation of Babylonian Amoraim and died *ca.* A.D. 356 (see H. L. Strack, *Introduction to the Talmud and Midrash* [Philadelphia: Jewish Publication Society of America, 1931], p. 130). In short, none of the above mentioned points of criticism seems to be serious enough to invalidate the interpretation.

Hurd speaks of the Qumran parallels as being 'rather distant'. I am fully aware of this difficulty and know no more to say about it than what has already been said on pp. 44-5 of our original article. But until a better solution to this *crux interpretum* comes along, the Qumran parallel seems to shed most light on the problem. For a recent discussion of the passage which makes no reference to Qumran or my interpretation, see M. D. Hooker, 'Authority on Her Head: An Examination of 1 Cor 11: 10', *NTS* 10 (1964), pp. 410-16.

3

2 Cor 6: 14-7: 1 IN THE LIGHT OF THE QUMRAN TEXTS AND THE TESTAMENTS OF THE TWELVE PATRIARCHS*

Joachim Gnilka

'Seek not to associate yourself with unbelievers under an alien yoke! For what form of union (can there be) between righteousness and lawlessness? Or of communion between light and darkness? What harmony (does) Christ (find) with Belial? Or what has a believer to do with an unbeliever? What accord has God's temple with idols? For we are a temple of the living God, as God hath said, "I will dwell and walk about among them, and I will be their God and they shall be my people. Wherefore come out from among them and be separate!" saith the Lord. "Touch no unclean thing, and I will receive you, and be a Father to you, and ye shall be my sons and daughters," saith the Lord, the Almighty. Having therefore these promises, beloved, let us cleanse ourselves from all that would defile flesh and spirit, fulfilling (the) consecration in the fear of God!' (2 Cor 6: 14-7:1)

THIS brief, parenetic portion, written in an elevated style, poses various questions. It disturbs the continuity of the Epistle just where Paul is trying to win the love of the church at Corinth, by introducing the new concept of the Christian's relationship to the heathen. If the portion is removed, verse 2 of Chapter 7 follows without a break on verse 13 of Chapter 6. Furthermore, considered in itself, it contains a series of thoughts, images,

* Originally delivered as a lecture in the Oriental Institute in Vienna on 13 April 1962, and published in *Neutestamentliche Aufsätze* (Festschrift J. Schmid), e. J. Blinzler *et al.*, Regensburg, 1963, pp. 86-99.

concepts and words which seem out of character for Paul. These difficulties have been obvious for quite some time and attempts have been made to clear them up by declaring the passage to be non-Pauline[1] or by ascribing it to another Pauline epistle.[2] Particularly during the last century a very popular theory was that 2 Cor 6 : 14-7 : 1 was a fragment of the Apostle's so-called pre-canonical Letter to the Corinthians mentioned in 1 Cor 5 : 9 but which has disappeared.[3] Finally, attempts were made to prove the passage to be part of 2 Cor, merely transposing some sections of Chap. 5-7.[4] Since the discovery of the Qumran texts various authors have noticed the terminological and theological affinity of our passage and the Dead Sea Scrolls. One suggestion has been that Paul is here quoting a more ancient precept from the traditions of the Early Church, which in its turn testified to the ideas of the Qumran Church which lived on in it.[5] Another was that Paul reproduces here an Essene text to which he has merely given a Christian form.[6] J. A. Fitzmyer advocates a 'non-

[1] R. Bultmann, *Theology of the New Testament*, London, 1965, p. 205; G. Bornkamm, 'Die Vorgeschichte des sogenannten Zweiten Korintherbriefes', *Sitzungsberichte der Heidelberger Akademie der Wissenschaften, Phil.-hist. Klasse*, 1961, p. 32. [idem, 'The History of the Origin of the so-called Second Letter to the Corinthians', *NTS* 8 (1961-62), pp. 258-64—Ed.].

[2] E. Dinkler, 'Korintherbriefe', *RGG³*, vol. IV, p. 22, would place 2 Cor 6 : 14-7 : 1 before 1 Cor 5 : 9-11; O. Pfleiderer, *Das Urchristentum, seine Schriften und Leben*, vol. I, Berlin, 1902, p. 134, note, after 1 Cor 6; H. D. Wendland, *Die Briefe an die Korinther (NTD 7)*, Göttingen, 1954, p. 187, before 1 Cor 6 : 3.

[3] Most recently, R. H. Strachan, *The Second Epistle of Paul to the Corinthians* (Moffat NT Comm.), London, 1935, p. xv. Cf. the synopsis of various attempts at an explanation in E. B. Allo, *Seconde épître aux Corinthiens*, Paris, 1956, pp. 190-3, and in H. Windisch, *Der zweite Korintherbrief*, Göttingen, 1924, pp. 18-20.

[4] H. Windisch (*op. cit.*, pp. 211-20) suggests the following arrangement : 5 : 14-6 : 2; 6 : 14-7 : 1; 6 : 3-10. Cf. W. Schmithals, *Die Gnosis in Korinth*, Göttingen, 1956, p. 21; H. Leitzmann, *An die Korinther I-II*, Tübingen, 1931, p. 129 does not rearrange the text, but contents himself with the assumption of a considerable break in the dictation of the letter before 6 : 14. A. Plummer, *A Critical and Exegetical Commentary on the Second Epistle of St Paul to the Corinthians*, Edinburgh, 1915, p. 207 makes an allusion to Paul's versatility.

[5] G. Molin, *Die Söhne des Lichtes*, Wien, 1954, p. 179.

[6] K. G. Kuhn, 'Les rouleaux de cuivre de Qumran', *RB* 61 (1964), pp. 193-205, especially p. 203, note 2; idem 'Die Schriftrollen vom Toten Meer. Zum heutigen Stand ihrer Veröffentlichung', *EvTh* 11 (1951-52), pp. 72-5, especially pp. 74f.

Pauline interpolation' but forgoes any suggestions as to how it came to be inserted in 2 Cor.[7] On closer examination the problem shows itself to be really involved, and so for the sake of clarity we shall proceed as follows: I. a brief exegesis of the passage, consciously disregarding the context; II. an examination of terminology used; and III. a study of the theological concepts with a view to seeing if the same or similar terms and concepts can be identified in the Corpus Paulinum and in the Qumran literature. We shall also take into consideration the Testaments of the Twelve Patriarchs. In conclusion, IV. we shall attempt, on the basis of the knowledge thus gained, to clarify the history of the origin of the passage.

I

The actual theme of the section is sounded right at the beginning: a prohibition against consorting with unbelievers, with the heathen. This admonition is presented in the form of an easily remembered metaphor, familiar to Jews from the O.T. Just as the Kilajim Law forbids the harnessing of different types of animals under one common yoke (cf. Deut 22 : 10; LXX Lev 19 : 19),[8] so the Christians—for we have to consider those being addressed, as such—should not let themselves be forced together with the heathens under an alien yoke. Although this demand for separation from the heathen environment does not forbid all contact or communication with a heathen, it does go quite far by contesting the wisdom of a Christian and a heathen uniting to work together for a common goal. The introductory imperative is substantiated by five rhetorical questions. These questions contain five sets of antithesis, aimed at illustrating the impossibility of a Christian allying himself with a heathen. In doing so, the contrasts have been chosen in such a way that they are appropriate for denoting the particular spheres to which the Christian

[7] J. A. Fitzmyer, 'Qumran and the Interpolated Fragment in 2 Cor 6 : 14-7 : 1', *CBQ* 23 (1961), pp. 271-80.

[8] On the Kilajim law cf. H. L. Strack-P. Billerbeck, *Kommentar zum NT aus Talmud und Midrasch*, vol. III, München, 1926, p. 521 *in loc.*; Philo, *Spec. Leg.*, 4, 203; Joshepus, *Ant.*, 4, 228; *P.Cair.Zen.*, 38, 12.

or heathen belongs. Righteousness, light, Christ point to the sphere allocated to the believer, whilst lawlessness, darkness, Belial pertain to the unbeliever. In the fourth question the contrasts refer specifically to the particular situation in so far as mention is made of *pistos* and *apistos*. With the statement (contained in the question) that a *sunkatathesis* is not possible between a believer and an unbeliever (v. 15),[9] this train of thought is rounded off to a certain extent. The following question, the fifth, forms the climax and transition, for here we have the confrontation between God's Temple and idols, thus demonstrating the secret dignity of the Christian and the essential abomination of the heathen. The study now concentrates on the Christians, not the heathens. Their dignity, as 'temples of the living God', is so considerable that it requires detailed scriptural proof. The sudden change to the plural *(hēmeis . . . esmen)* means that the honour of being a spiritual sanctuary does not pertain to an individual but to the community.[10] The scriptural proof is just as artistically constructed as the preceeding question-verses, for it contains at least four O.T. scriptural phrases which are skilfully combined and adapted to form a harmonious unit. God has said—and it is important here that God's name is expressly mentioned—that he will dwell and walk among his people.

The first scriptural proof comes from Lev 26 : 11f. or Ezek 37 : 27, but the former is preferable since Ezekiel does not mention God's 'walking'. Apart from the change from second to third person plural the text agrees to a great extent with LXX, although God's 'dwelling' is not mentioned there. The close relationship between God and people made manifest in the characterization of God as the God of his people, and of the people as God's people, forms the basis for the summons (joined on by *dio*) to separate themselves, and to abstain from any unclean thing.

---

[9] For the idea *sugkatathesis*, cf. Ex 23 : 32f. 'Thou shalt make no covenant with them (the inhabitants of the land) nor with their Gods (LXX: *ou sugkatathēsē autois . . . diathēkēn*). They shall not dwell in thy land, lest they make thee sin against me'.

[10] The plural reading *naoi* in v. 16. (Aleph* 1739 81 Clement of Alex.) corresponds to 1 Cor 6 : 19 and is definitely secondary.

This summons, somewhat modified and abridged, is to be found in LXX Is 52 : 11. An allusion to Jer 51 : 45 is unlikely. In the Isaiah text the summons goes out to the people in captivity to leave Babylon; the departure is not seen as a hasty flight but as a holy procession in which only those may participate who have cleansed themselves according to the levitical laws. For the sacred vessels of the Temple are to be carried along with this procession and Yahweh himself will go before the people as he did in the past during the Exodus from Egypt.[11] Applying it to the situation in our passage, this O.T. background means that God himself sanctions and guides the separation of the Christians from the heathen, although it is not clear, from the passage considered in itself, whether this Exodus is meant in a real or moral sense. A decision can only be reached in this matter when it has been established if our section of the Epistle is an Essene or Christian (or Pauline) document.[12] The prohibition against touching any unclean thing can refer to an unclean man and an unclean object.

The third quotation is very brief. It says that on account of their readiness to go forth, or on account of their already completed departure, God will receive those departing (with pleasure); it comes either from Ex 20 : 34 or from Soph 3 : 20, more probably from Exodus where the point at issue is God's bringing the people out of the land of captivity into the wilderness of the peoples. Here we must note that the use of the Greek verb *eisdechomai* as opposed to the Hebrew equivalent (Ezek *qbsty*; Zeph *'by'*) has given rise to a by no means inconsiderable change in sense. Whereas the Hebrew verbs merely signify a simple gathering together of the people by God, *eisdechomai* means that God graciously receives his people.

This serves as a neat link with the last quotation in which God

[11] Cf. Ex 13 : 21f; 14 : 19 and J. Ziegler, *Das Buch Isaias* (Echter-Bibel), vol. III, Würzburg, 1958, pp. 172f.

[12] It is noteworthy that Rev 18 : 4 evokes Is 52 : 11 or 48 : 20, so does the first citation in the fragment of 2 Cor, Lev 26 : 11f., or Ezek 37 : 27 in Rev 21 : 3, the latter certainly going back to the text of Ezek. Apart from these common quotations there is the use of the title *pantokratōr*, which links the fragment with the Apocalypse.

declares himself to be Father, and the members of the people
to be his sons and daughters. It comes from 2 Sam 7 : 14, the
blessing on the house of David, which extends the promise made
to the seed of David to all members of the chosen people. This
was easily done, since the O.T. had, at various times, already
referred to the Israelites as the children of God.[13] The statement
concluding the quotation *legei kurios pantokratōr* is to be
regarded as a quotation from 2 Sam 7 : 8, or as a spontaneous
creation on the part of the author, who here makes use of a divine
title which is particularly frequent in the Apocalypse.[14]

A final admonition calls upon those addressed, who possess
the promises, to cleanse and sanctify themselves. The 'flesh and
spirit' which are subject to defilement[15] refer, corresponding to
popular linguistic usage, not to higher and lower parts of man,
but to man in his entirety.[16] With this summons the passage again
alludes back to the concrete situation by means of a concrete
imperative similar to that with which it began.

II

Does the phraseology in 2 Cor 6 : 14-7 : 1 correspond to Paul's
or not? Does it correspond to someone else's, and if so, whose?
The first thing that strikes us is that seven words occur in these
six verses which are not to be found anywhere else in the whole
N.T. These are: *heterozugountes, metochē, sumphōnēsis, Beliar,
sugkatathesis, enperipatēsō,*[17] *molusmos.* Furthermore *pantokratōr* is not found in the Pauline literature. When Allo[18] states
that some of these words only occur in the Epistle because the
five parallel questions necessitate the choice of new terms
(*metochē, sumphōnēsis, sunkatathesis* beside *koinōnia* and *meris*)

---

[13] Jer 31 : 9; Is 43 : 6; Hos 2 : 1. Cf. also 1QH 9 : 35f.; 4 : 32f.; 11 : 9;
1QM 17 : 8; Jub 1 : 24, etc. 2 Sam 7 : 11-14 is understood in 4QFlor 1 : 10
of the Davidic Messiah.
[14] Rev 1 : 8; 4 : 8; 11 : 17; 15 : 3; 16 : 7, 14; 19 : 6, 15; 21 : 22.
[15] For *molusmos*, cf. 2 Macc 5 : 27.
[16] Cf. R. Bultmann, *Theology* . . . , vol. I, p. 205; E. Schweizer, art. *Sarx,*
in *TWNT*, vol. VII, p. 125; H. Leitzmann, *op. cit.*, p. 130.
[17] This word is found in the quotation from Lev 26 : 12.
[18] E. B. Allo, *op. cit.*, p. 190.

one can counter that Paul does not otherwise use this poetic style or a series of comparisons.

Nevertheless some of the terms mentioned do have definite cognates in the Pauline epistles. Schlatter[19] emphasizes that Paul uses the verb *metechein* precisely in conjunction with *koinōnia*, which evokes the association of *metochē* and *koinōnia* in v. 14 (1 Cor 10 : 16f., cf. 20f.). He further uses the adjective *sumphōnos* (1 Cor 7 : 5) and the verb *molunesthai* (1 Cor 8 : 7). Nonetheless the large number of new words is impressive.

The proper name Belial seems strangest of all. The term Belial, used here as an antipode to Christ and meaning a personal incarnation of the powers of evil, has a peculiar history.[20] In the O.T. the word *Blyʿl* does in fact occur (or more frequently *ish* and *bny hblyʿl*) and connotes worthlessness, wickedness, perdition, but the idea of Belial as a person is not found there. Thus our author cannot have found the devil-name 'Belial' in the O.T., nor in the LXX, for the latter always translates the Hebrew expression : it is only seldom that individual manuscripts retain it in isolated passages (e.g. Judges 20 : 13 A-Text). Belial does not become a popular name for the incarnation of the powers of Satan until the period of the later Jewish literature.

This transition can be clearly observed in the Qumran literature.[21] Belial is still an impersonal concept in the *Hymns*, representing falsehood, worthlessness, perdition. The *Rule* does not show clearly if it has advanced beyond the interpretation given in the *Hymns*, but Belial appears in the *War Scroll* and the *Damascus Document* as the supreme incarnation of the powers of evil who, however, has been constituted by God as the tempter of Israel and of the just, and head of the evil spirits. 'Thou hast made Belial for perdition, (to be the) angel of persecution, in the da[rkness] . . . his ways are ways of wickedness, creating sin, and all the spirits of his lot are angels of perdition.'

---

[19] A. Schlatter, *Paulus der Bote Jesu. Eine Deutung seiner Briefe an die Korinther*, Stuttgart, 1956, pp. 580f.

[20] Cf. W. Foerster, art. *Beliar*, in *TWNT*, I, 606; P. Joüon, 'Bélial', *Biblica* 5 (1924), pp. 178-83.

[21] Cf. H. W. Huppenbauer, 'Belial in den Qumrantexten', *TZ* 15 (1959), pp. 81-9.

(1QM 13 : 11f.; cf. CD 4 : 13; 5 : 18; 12 : 2; 4QFlor : 8f.). In the Qumran texts Belial is always the adversary of God, never the adversary of the Messiah. Just as in 2 Cor, we find the name Belial in the *Test. XII Patriarchs*, the *Oracula Sibyllina* and the *Book of Jubilees*.[22] The *Testaments*, in which Belial plays a very important role, offer us two different concepts of the position of the adversary, in unharmonious juxtaposition. On the one hand Belial appears as the adversary of God, thus e.g. TSim 5 : 3, 'Lewdness is the mother of evil, separating us from God and leading to Belial'; TLev 19 : 1 'Choose between light and darkness, either the law of the Lord or the works of Belial!', and TIss 6 : 1 'They will abandon the commandments of the Lord and follow Belial.'[23] On the other hand Belial appears as the counterpart of the Messiah who vanquishes him. Thus we read in TLev 18 : 12 'And Belial will be bound by him [the "new priest", i.e. the priestly Messiah] and he will give his children power to tread on evil spirits.' On account of its similarity to Mark 3 : 27 and par. and Luke 10 : 19 this passage seems to be of Christian inspiration.[24] Also TDan 5 : 10f. 'And from the race of Judah and Levi the salvation of the Lord will come upon you. For he himself will wage war against Belial . . . , he will take captivity from Beliar.' According to De Jonge[25] this passage is a patched-up job in which a so-called Levi-Judah passage is clumsily linked to one dealing with the Messiah. De Jonge considers the latter to be the Christian revision of a Jewish original. TSim 6 : 5f., and TZab 9 : 8 also seem questionable to me. Here

[22] For example TDan 5 : 1; TNph 2 : 6; TRub 2 : 2; 4 : 11, etc.; Or Sib 2 : 167; 3 : 63, 73; Jub 1 : 20. In 2 Cor 6 : 15 the reading 'Beliar' is the best supported. The Vulgate and some Fathers read 'Belial'. The variants 'Belian' and 'Beliab' are obviously secondary. Beliar here designates Satan (cf. R. H. Charles, *Revelation of St John* (ICC), II, Edinburgh, 1920, p. 80; W. Foerster, *loc. cit.*; H. Windisch, *op. cit.*, p. 215) not Antichrist (W. Graf Baudissin, 'Belial', *Realencyklopädie für protestantische Theologie*, vol. II, pp. 548f.; cf. E. B. Allo, *op. cit.*, p. 185).

[23] Cf. TDan 4 : 7; 5 : 1; TNaph 2 : 6; 3 : 1; TJos 20 : 2.

[24] M. de Jonge, *The Testaments of the Twelve Patriarchs*, Assen, 1953, pp. 90f. regards TLevi 18 in its present form as a hymn to Jesus Christ, but Jewish material has been worked into it. It is impossible to separate the Christian from the non-Christian elements.

[25] M. de Jonge, *op. cit.*, p. 92.

it is not the Messiah who is actually mentioned *expressis verbis*, but the Lord, who will appear on earth or rise like the shining light of justice. However, the result he achieves, and particularly his power to trample under foot false spirits, does give the impression of a Christian interpolation seeking an allusion to the actions of Christ. The complicated problem of the history of the origin of *Test. XII Patriarchs* has not yet been finally solved, but here it seems certain that Jewish and Christian materials have been used together, or that more or less Christian entries have been inserted into a passage which was originally Jewish.[26] If Belial appears in the *Test. XII Patriarchs* as the adversary not only of God but also of the Messiah, this probably cannot be attributed to one and the same author but to the use of various sources. The dualism God-Belial is older. It is Jewish and found, of course, in Qumran. The dualism Christ-Belial, on the other hand, does not seem to have originated in Jewish but in Christian circles influenced by the traditions which are also found in Qumran. For the Qumran traditions also play an active part in the original text of the *Test. XII Patriarchs*.[27] These findings are not without importance for our study of 2 Cor 6 : 14-7 : 1. They suggest that it cannot be an Essene document, but a document penned by the hand of a Christian author.

However, rather than concentrating on *hapaxlegomena* it would seem more fruitful to concentrate on words which also occur elsewhere in the Pauline epistles. It would be significant if some of them were used with a meaning other than that usually accorded to them by Paul.

---

[26] De Jonge regards the Testaments as the work of a Christian author, who, however, has made use of Jewish material. In the opinion of M. Philonenko, 'Les interpolations chrétiennes des Testaments des Douze Patriarches et les manuscrits de Qumran', *RHPhilRel* 38 (1959), pp. 14-38, it is a Judaeo-Essene work and entirely free of Christian interpolations. Philonenko's interpretation is unfounded for there are obvious Christian interpolations. Cf. J. Gnilka, 'Die Erwartung des messianischen Hohenpristers in den Schriften von Qumran und im NT', *RdeQ* 2 (1959-60), pp. 395-426, especially pp. 407f. On this problem: M. de Jonge, 'Christian Influence in the Testaments of the Twelve Patriarchs', *NT* 4 (1960), pp. 182-235; F. M. Braun, 'Les Testaments des XII Patriarches et le problème de leur origine', *RB* 67 (1960, pp. 516-549.

[27] K. G. Kuhn considers the *Test. XII Patr.* to have originated in Qumran: cf. below, p. 115.

If *dikaiosunē* is attributed to the Christian and *anomia* to the heathen, *dikaiosunē* does not have the meaning here of grace and justice given by God to man, which is the sense in which Paul uses this term, but connotes, as an antithesis to *anomia*, a practical manner of living in accordance with the commandments and will of God.[28] This practical meaning is discernible in some Pauline texts (cf. Rom 6 : 13-19; 2 Cor 6 : 7), but it can also be verified again and again in the Qumran literature and *Test. XII Patr.* For example the summons directed to the member of the community : 'To keep aloof from all evil and adhere to all good works, *to do* truth, *justice* and righteousness. . . .' (1QS 1 : 4f.). This means justice as expressed in one's manner of living, which plays a decisive part in the Qumran texts and, as in our section of the Epistle, is opposed to evil, to *anomia*, i.e. a manner of living which disdains and denies God's will.[29] An obvious parallel is to be found in TDan 6 : 10, 'Refrain from all injustice and adhere to the justice of God!'

When opposed to *apistos* in 2 Cor 6 : 15, *pistos* used absolutely carries the technical connotation of 'believer' in the sense of a 'believer in Christ'.[30] Paul does in fact use *apistos* in the sense of 'heathen' (cf. 2 Cor 4 : 4; 1 Cor 6 : 6; 7 : 12-15; 10 : 27; 14 : 22-4) but *pistos* still retains for him the original meaning of 'worthy of belief, reliable, faithful'. Thus *pistos* can be applied equally to God (e.g. 1 Cor 10 : 13; 2 Cor 1 : 18) and to man (1 Cor 4 : 17). The later connotation appears first in the preface to Eph (1 : 1 *pistois en Christō Iēsou*) and is clearly defined in the Pastoral letters. Here the *pistoi* (without any further qualification) are the believers in Christ (1 Tim 4 : 10-12; 5 : 16). This change in meaning, reflecting a later development, is already in evidence in 2 Cor 6 : 15. The opposition between believer and unbeliever is only possible in a Christian document, for this contrast was of no importance to the Essenes. As was the case with the antithesis Christ-Belial, the mention of believers and unbelievers points to a Christian author, whose frame of reference

---

[28] G. Schrenk, art. *Dikaiosunē*, in *TWNT*, vol. II, p. 214.
[29] Cf. 1QH 1 : 26f.; 14 : 15f.
[30] R. Bultmann, *Pisteuō*, in *TWNT*, vol. VI, p. 215.

is close to the traditions prevalent in the Qumran community. It is not easy to imagine that these two dualistically inclined statements (Christ-Belial; believer-unbeliever) were introduced into an originally Essene document at a later date, for they contain a statement which significantly advances the thought of the whole passage.

The unusual formula introducing the scriptural quotation 'as God hath said' (2 Cor 6 : 16) has indeed a parallel in 4 : 6 (though there it is not followed by a literal quotation), but it is also to be found in the *Damascus Document*. Here ordinances of the community are, as occasion offers, substantiated by O.T. scriptural quotations, which are expressly characterized as the Word of God by the formula 'God hath said' (CD 6 : 12f; 8 : 9; cf. 19 : 22).

The absolutely untheological use of 'flesh' and 'spirit' in the concluding admonition of 2 Cor 7 : 1 has always been suspect to exegetes, and was often given as the reason for the un-Pauline character of this portion of the epistle. Though it is characteristic of Paul to view 'flesh' as intimately related to sin, it is 'not impossible'[31] that he should here conform to the popular idea that man is formed from 'flesh' and 'spirit', and that the two together mean simply man. This idea appears, for example in 1 Cor 5 : 3 and 7 : 34. However, nowhere does he speak of the 'defilement of flesh and spirit', or of the need for purification from such defilement. The dissection of man into flesh/spirit is found in the Qumran literature (cf. 1QS 3 : 8f; 1QH 13 : 13f; 15 : 21f; 17 : 25) as well as in the *Test. XII Patr.* (TJud 18 : 4). This in itself is not especially remarkable, but in Qumran we find the urgent summons to be irreproachable in spirit and flesh : 'All should be men, willing for war, faultless in spirit and flesh and ready for the day of wrath. Every man who is not pure from his source on the day of battle may not go with them, for the holy angels are with their armies' (1QM 7 : 5f).—The purification called for here is not only Levitical purity but also includes the inner purification from sin. One without the other is

---

[31] E. Schweizer, *TWNT*, vol. VII, p. 125.

meaningless.[32] 'By subjecting his soul to all the commandments of God he purifies his flesh.' (1QS 3 : 8).—A distinction is indeed made here between soul and flesh but probably in the sense that both terms apply respectively to the whole person.[33] The purification of the flesh resulting from the voluntary acceptance of God's commandments becomes much more graphic through the selection of the same words as are used in 2 Kings 5 : 10 for purification from leprosy.[34] The purification and sanctification apportioned to the Qumran-Essenes are so wonderful that they can be compared to the joy experienced by a leper on being healed of his disease. Purification is regarded, then, in 1QS 3 : 8f. as well as in 2 Cor 7 : 1 as the personal achievement of a willing, striving man. The goal is 'to perfect holiness'. It is true that Paul, elsewhere uses the words *epitelein* and *hagiōsunē* (although the latter only once in 1 Thess 3 : 13), but their association is new, and harmonizes perfectly with the concepts of the Essenes, who know themselves to be 'men of perfect holiness' (1QS 8 : 20) or 'those walking in perfect holiness' (CD 7 : 5).

In this connection brief reference must be made to the scriptural quotations used in 2 Cor 6 : 16-18, where four quotations (Lev 26 : 11f.; Is 52 : 11; Ezek 20 : 34; 2 Sam 7 : 14 [2 Sam 7 : 8]) have been artistically linked to form a chain.[35] In other contexts Paul forms similar scriptural combinations (Rom 3 : 10-18) but in many cases he takes care to distinguish the individual quotations from one another and to identify the author (Rom 9 : 25-29; 10 : 18-20; 15 : 9-12). However, the biblical texts used here are not to be found in the Pauline Epistles. This observation alone would naturally not warrant further deductions,

---

[32] On the concept of sanctity at Qumran, cf. F. Nötscher, 'Heiligkeit in den Qumranschriften', *RdeQ* 2 (1959-60), pp. 163-81; 315-44.

[33] Cf. R. Meyer, *Sarx*, in *TWNT*, vol. VII, p. 110.

[34] Cf. P. Wernberg-Moller, *The Manual of Discipline*, Leiden, 1957, p. 64, note 25.

[35] J. A. Fitzmyer, *art. cit.*, pp. 278f., refers to 4QTest. This document consists of a series of scriptural passages of messianic importance. It does not belong to a scroll, but is a single page, written on one side, perhaps for private rather than public use. Cf. J. Maier, *Die Texte vom Toten Meer*, vol. II, München-Basel, 1960, p. 165.

but it is interesting to note that a scriptural quotation used here figures quite prominently in the Dead Sea Scrolls. In 1QM 1: 2f. reference is made, as in 2 Cor 6: 17, to Ezek 20: 34 or 35. The introduction to the *War Scroll* mentions the return of the sons of light who have gone into exile, 'out of the wilderness of the peoples[36] to camp in the wilderness of Jerusalem.'[37]

According to Ezek 20: 34f. God gathers the exiles out of the nations to bring them into the wilderness of the people. Before commencing the time of salvation they will be judged by God in the wilderness; all the rebels against God are forbidden entry into the land of salvation. If the sons of light are the exiles in the wilderness of the people this means, in the light of Ezek 20, that they as God's chosen people have come close to the time of salvation, but have been called upon to keep themselves for God alone and to resist the evil seductions during their sojourn in the wilderness, so that they will not be judged by God. Belial is still at work, his followers will be judged only when the time of salvation that is imminent has finally arrived (1QM 1: 5). If we apply this background to the understanding of our passage the withdrawal required of Christians is viewed in the perspective of the imminent hour of salvation, and appears as primarily directed to excluding as completely as possible any danger of backsliding or infidelity arising out of their association with their pagan fellow-citizens.

Our study of the terminology of 2 Cor 6: 14-7: 1 leads to the conclusion that on account of the profusion of *hapaxlego-mena*, and of the change in meaning of various words used by Paul in another sense, this passage cannot have originally been

---

[36] In *La règle de la guerre*, Paris, 1958, p. 6, J. Carmignac interprets the 'wilderness of the peoples' as symbolic of the difficult period in which the just man is susceptible to the allurements of sin. With greater probability J. Maier (*op. cit.*, pp. 112f.) understands it of a real desert in which man rests at God's command to prepare for the time of salvation. Cf. 1QS 8: 12-16; 4QpPs 37 2: 1.

[37] To J. Carmignac (*loc. cit.*) the 'wilderness of Jerusalem' suggests the devastation of the city, but to J. Maier (*loc. cit.*) it evokes the deserted state of the city before the beginning of the time of salvation. It is noteworthy that in 1QM Jerusalem appears as a military base and the departure point of the army of the Sons of Light. Cf. J. van der Ploeg, *Le rouleau de la guerre*, Leiden, 1959, p. 112, and 1QM 7: 3f.; 2: 1-6.

written by Paul. The contrasting pairs Christ-Belial, believer-
unbeliever (with the established meaning of Christian believer-
heathen) compel us to assume that the author of this fragment
was a Christian. But he has been considerably influenced by
traditions which are active in Qumran and the *Test. XII Patr.*,
as is proved by a number of parallel concepts and ideas. Paul or
someone else inserted the already existent fragment into 2 Cor.

The question as to whether the transference of this cento-like[38]
portion entailed any additions, and whether the latter were made
by Paul or someone else, is difficult to determine on the basis of
terminology alone. *Agapētos, tautas oun echontes tas epangelias*,[39]
en phobō theou could be additions, but offer too weak a basis
for a definite conclusion. We shall return later to this question.
But now we must devote special attention to the basic theological
ideas of this passage, the study of which will reveal their affinity
with certain doctrines of the Essenes.

III

There are three basic theological concepts : (1) the community
as God's temple; (2) separation from a godless environment;
and (3) dualism. All three are closely linked together.

K. G. Kuhn has already pointed out that, of all the documents
contemporaneous with the N.T., only the Essene writings apply
the metaphor of the temple to a community.[40] In the Qumran
texts we find this idea expressed clearly and emphatically in the
Rule. While the *Damascus Document* designates the community
as the 'House of the Law' (20 : 10, 13), though not yet thinking
of a spiritual temple, 1QS 5 : 6 says ' . . . to absolve all who are
volunteers for the holiness of Aaron and for the house of truth
in Israel'. A careful distinction is made here between priests and
laymen, since special functions are allotted to the priests in the
sanctuary as in the community conceived as a spiritual temple.[41]

---

[38] This simile is used by J. Cambier in *Introduction à la Bible*, ed. A.
Robert—A. Feuillet, vol. II, Tournai, 1959, p. 443.
[39] Cf. A. Schlatter, *op. cit.*, p. 581.
[40] K. G. Kuhn in *RB* 61 (1954), p. 203, note 1.
[41] Cf. J. Maier, *op. cit.*, vol. II, p. 46.

According to 1QS 8 : 5f. the 'Council of the community' which
is firmly based on truth is 'a holy house for Israel and a community of infinite holiness for Aaron' (cf. 8 : 8f.). The community
is furthermore the 'precious corner stone' (8 : 7)[42] foretold in
Is 28 : 16. Perhaps 1QS 9 : 5f. best reveals how the men joined
together in common life regarded themselves as a spiritual
dwelling-place of God : 'They shall separate the members of the
community (into) the house of holiness for Aaron that infinite
holiness may be assembled together, and (into) the house of
community for Israel for those that walk in perfection.' The
community was in opposition to the Temple at Jerusalem[43] and
this confrontation may have helped contribute to its transferring
the spiritual dignity of the sanctuary, which had fallen into the
hands of unworthy rebels, to itself. And at this point the special
feature of the understanding of the metaphor community/temple
in the Qumran texts becomes apparent. For it is linked with
the call to separation from the other sinful people who have
turned away from God. The men are to separate a holy house
for Aaron (cf. 1QS 9 : 5f.). Thus, before 'sanctuary in Aaron'
and 'house of truth in Israel' are mentioned (line 6), the summons
goes out (1QS 5 : 1f.) to withdraw 'from the council of sacrilegious men'. This connection between spiritual temple and
separation throws some light on the background of 2 Cor 6 : 14-
7 : 1. Paul is also aware of the Christian's dignity as a 'temple
of God' (1 Cor 3 : 16f.); the same thought is presupposed in
Eph 2 : 20-22. But in our fragment, just as in the Qumran texts,
the dignity of being a spiritual temple is linked with the idea of
separation. This brings us to the second basic theological concept : separation from a godless environment.

Separation from the rest of the nation, who, in the eyes of
the Essenes, have become unfaithful to God and disdain his
commandments, forms the basis of the existence of Qumran.

---

[42] Is 28 : 16 is always used christologically, never ecclesiologically, in the
N.T. Cf. J. Maier, op. cit., vol. II, p. 93, and Rom 9 : 33; 10 : 11; I Pet
2 : 4, 6.
[43] Cf. O. Cullmann, 'L'opposition contre le Temple de Jérusalem. Motif
commun de la théologie johannique et du monde ambiant', NTS 5 (1958-59),
pp. 157-173.

They have departed into the wilderness mindful of the word of Is 40 : 2, to prepare the way of the Lord, who is expected in the near future.[44] This preparation of the way consists in the study of the Torah and other holy scriptures in order to live according to the true, pure will of God as praised in the scriptures, and to which they knew themselves bound as the possessors of revelation. The separation from men of injustice, which is constantly emphasized and recalled, extends to the affairs and tasks of everyday life. 1QS 5 : 13-20 forbids the sharing of table, work and possessions with outsiders. Nor may there be dealings with them in questions concerning law and justice. This separation is justified by the fact that the others despise the Word of God and thus are vain. They can only expect the dreadful vengeance of God. 'Impurity is in all their wealth' (line 20). The holy member of the community should be removed from the danger of being made unclean himself as a result of contact with the unclean. The community understands uncleanness not merely in a cultic-levitical sense but principally in an ethical sense, because priestly cleanliness and the fact of being pleasing to God merge for it into one inseparable unit.[45]

The call in 2 Cor 6 : 14-7 : 1 for a radical separation from a heathen environment does not seem to harmonize with the Pauline concept of the relationship heathen/Christian. Paul tolerates the marriage of a believer with an unbeliever provided that the unbelieving partner is prepared to live in peace with the believer, for, as a result of the belief of one partner, their offspring are holy, whereas they were formerly (before one partner became a believer) unclean (cf. 1 Cor 7 : 12-15). He considers speaking with tongues to be a sign for the unbelievers (1 Cor 14 : 22-24) and permits the believer, if invited to a meal by an unbeliever, to eat everything put before him (10 : 26f.). He knew that if all forms of contact with lascivious, covetous men, thieves and idolators should be broken off, then it would be necessary to withdraw from this world (5 : 9f.). Of course the possibility must be considered that a special situation in Corinth

---

[44] Cf. S. V. McCasland, 'The Way', *JBL* 77 (1958), pp. 222-30.
[45] Cf. F. Nötscher, *loc. cit.*

could have caused Paul to make a special appeal for separation, but the terms and imperatives used in 2 Cor 6 : 14-7 : 1 belong to another pattern of thought which is not found elsewhere in 2 Cor. 'Go out from among them!',[46] 'Be separate!', 'Touch no unclean thing!' are the same demands as are made in the Qumran texts. The Qumran mentality becomes tangible in these imperatives. However this call does not originate from an Essene but from a Christian. This is why we should understand the required exodus not in a literal, but in a moral sense; the concept of uncleanness leads from the outset to ethics without implying any detour via levitical impurity. The Christian is called upon to separate himself spiritually from the godless and heathen so as not to participate in their works. There is a notable parallel to this thought in Eph 5 : 7ff. : 'Have naught to do with them (the sons of disobedience)! Once you were darkness, now you are light in the Lord. Walk as children of the light! . . . Do not consort with the unfruitful works of darkness!' In the same context the 'unclean person' (verse 5 : *akathartos*) is one having no inheritance in the kingdom of Christ and of God.

At Qumran, separation from the godless is, in the last analysis, based on a strictly dualistic form of thought. This Qumran dualism does not—as has already been frequently emphasized[47]—employ Gnostic substantial categories in which matter is sharply differentiated from God's world of light, but insists on the contrast between two forms of existence, which are revealed in good and bad actions. Mankind is divided into two groups : the sons of light under the sway of an angel of light, and walking in the paths of light, and the sons of darkness, under the sway of an angel of darkness, and following the paths of darkness. (cf. IQS 3 : 19-24). Between these two groups there is an insuperable opposition, which is as exclusive as light and darkness.

The same acute contrast can be seen in the question : 'What

---

[46] The aorist imperative *exelthate* emphasizes the necessity and swift decisiveness of the withdrawal. Cf. A. Plummer, *op. cit.*, p. 209. For the idea of withdrawal, cf. Ass Moses 9 : 6; Syr Apoc Bar 2 : 1.

[47] K. G. Kuhn, 'The Epistle to the Ephesians in the light of the Qumran Texts', pp. 122-3, below.

communion have light and darkness?' (2 Cor 6 : 14), referring here to the Christian attitude to the heathen. Paul, too, is acquainted with the dualism of light-darkness. He uses dualistic statements to impress upon his followers that they now belong to light, to salvation, and may no longer serve darkness, the evil one; or to define the former as contrasted with the present status of his converts. Thus he writes in Rom 13 : 12 : 'Let us cast off the works of darkness, let us put on the armour of light!' (cf. 1 Thess 5 : 4f.; the passage in Eph 5 : 7-14 which has already been quoted, and Col 1 : 12-14, which is also perhaps an inter-polated fragment, are particularly close to statements found in the Qumran texts.)

Apart from light-darkness, other antitheses are used in the Qumran literature to describe the separation of the chosen community from its corrupt environment. We can limit ourselves to those which also play a role in 2 Cor 6 : 14-7 : 1. The opposition of *dikaiosunē* and *anomia* (or their corresponding Hebrew equivalents) is met with frequently in the Scrolls. 'I know that thou hast established the spirit of the *just* man *(rwh ṣdyq)* . . . and the soul of your servant abhors all works of *injustice (kwl m'sh 'wlh)'* (1QH 16 : 10f.; cf. 1QS 5 : 1-4). This tension-filled opposition will persist until the end of time, because only then will all injustice be abolished. 'And all *injustice (kwl 'wlh)* . . . you will destroy for ever, and your *justice (ṣdqtk)* will be revealed before all your works' (1QH 14 : 15f.). Since justice, for Qumran, is based on the Law and its commandments, and injustice is, thus, the result of denying the Law,[48] these concepts remain within the framework of Judaism, which regards justice as being peculiar to the Jews, while injustice is characteristic of the situation of the heathen. By stressing obedience to the Torah, to which the community has committed itself, justice is here restricted to the small circle of the chosen. Paul uses the contrast *dikaiosunē-anomia* in Rom 6 : 19 to bring home to his readers the fact that

[48] Cf. perhaps 1QS 8 : 13-15 'They shall be separated from the midst of the habitation of the men of iniquity to go into the desert to prepare the way of the Lord . . . that is the study of the Law'. Cf. also B. Otzen, 'Die neugefundenen hebräischen Sektenschriften und die Testamente der zwölf Patriarchen', *ST* 7 (1954), pp. 125-57, esp. 128.

frequent good deeds lead to salvation, while a chain of injustice results in *anomia*.[49]

The opposition God-Belial (or Beliar) is typical of the Qumran texts and of the *Test. XII Patriarchs*, and reveals here in all its bitterness the animosity of the opposition between the two camps. The antitheses light-darkness, and justice-injustice, do not in themselves enable us to mark off a more narrowly defined area of tradition, but the association of the two pairs light-darkness and God-Belial (or Beliar) indicates the Jewish circles to which exegetes have constantly had recourse for parallels. The *Test. XII Patriarchs*, in particular, link God with light and Belial with darkness very closely : 'Choose between light and darkness, either the law of the Lord or the works of Belial' (TLevi 19 : 1); 'Then is the Lord with you in light, and Belial in darkness with the Egyptians' (TJos 20 : 2; cf. TNeph 2 : 6f.).

The conjunction of the contrasting pairs light-darkness, Christ-Belial, believer-unbeliever, which sounds the main theme of 2 Cor 6 : 14-7 : 1 points clearly to a traditional association also to be found in the Qumran texts. However, in 2 Cor this tradition has already been subjected to Christian revision, but the reviser was not able to disguise the basically Essene character of the fragment, which is still evident.

IV

If 2 Cor 6 : 14-7 : 1 is a Christian exhortation in the Essene tradition, whose author is not Paul, but some unknown Christian, the question must be raised as to how these verses got into 2 Cor. Is it possible that Paul himself inserted this section into the epistle?[50] In this perspective it is conceivable that the Apostle would have effected certain stylistic modifications[51] *(agapētoi,*

---

[49] Cf. W. Gutbrod, '*Anomia*', *TWNT*, vol. IV, p. 1708, and Heb 1 : 9 (= LXX Ps 44 : 8).

[50] Cf. E. Dinkler (art. 'Korintherbriefe', in *RGG³*, vol. IV, p. 22) would prefer to place the fragment before 1 Cor 5 : 9-11.

[51] Cf. A. Schlatter, *op. cit.*, pp. 575-81; P. Bachmann, *Der zweite Brief des Paulus an die Korinther*, Leipzig, 1922, pp. 290-2. Both, however, consider 2 Cor 6 : 14-7 : 1 to be Pauline.

tautas oun echontes tas epangelias, en phobō theou). Against
this there is the difficulty that the incorporation was carried out
so clumsily as to disturb the continuity of the passage by introducing a new idea that is not really relevant in the context. It
cannot be denied that if this section is omitted 2 Cor 7 : 2 follows
smoothly and logically on 6 : 13. Why should Paul have chosen
such an unsuitable place to make such an insertion? The
hypothesis that there were people in the church at Corinth
(whose concrete situation is rather obscure), who in a questionable
way were again drawing closer to the heathen, is not satisfactory,
because a thorough discussion of the Christian's relation to the
heathen really seems out of place here.

There is another explanation for the introduction of this
section into 2 Cor, which is more convincing and therefore preferable. It is based on the assumption that 2 Cor was not originally
a unit, but represents a collection of Pauline letters, or letter-
fragments. This is no place to go into the various theories, the
detail of which is sometimes debatable, but it seems certain that
2 Cor is in fact a collection of letters.[52] It was most probably a
member of the Corinthian church, who, fearing that the still
existing letters and fragments of letters were in danger of disap-
pearing into oblivion, began at a very early stage to collect the
various missives (apart from 1 Cor) which Paul had sent to the
church. In the course of this process 6 : 14-7 : 1 won a place
in the collection because the editor believed it to be a fragment
of a Pauline letter.[53] It is not clear what caused him to place the
fragment in its present context, because the majority of exegetes
who support the collection-theory consider 2 : 14-7 : 4 (excluding
6 : 14-7 : 1) to be one epistle.

That the editor of 2 Cor, and not Paul, is to be regarded as
the interpolator is strongly suggested by the use of *pistos* (v. 15)
in the sharply defined sense of 'believer in Christ'. This indicates

---

[52] On the various divisions proposed in recent times, cf. especially, E.
Dinkler, *loc. cit.*, pp. 17-23; G. Bornkamm, *loc. cit.*; W. Schmithals, *op. cit.*,
p. 21; R. Bultmann, *Exegetische Probleme des zweiten Korintherbriefes*
(Symbolae Bibl. Upsaliensis 9), 1947.

[53] Cf. C. Clemen, *Paulus, sein Leben und Wirken*, vol. I, Giessen, 1904,
p. 77.

a later period, subsequent both to the Great Epistles, and to the letters and portions of letters collected in 2 Cor. It cannot be stated with certitude that our fragment was independent or that it belonged to another letter antecedent to its inclusion in 2 Cor, but the former seems more likely.

In conclusion we would like to emphasize once again the correspondence of the theme of the fragment with some ideas found in Eph. Both lay stress on keeping oneself spiritually aloof from the heathen, and on the dignity of the spiritual temple. The opposition to *akathartos*, and the sharply defined light-darkness dualism are common to both. There is apparently no further terminological affinity.[54] The traditions found at Qumran are also in evidence in Eph.[55] They influenced the Church through various channels, and it is thus easy to understand how a document like 2 Cor 6: 14-7: 1, so reminiscent of the statements and ideas of a letter endowed with apostolic authority, could have been unhesitatingly included in a Pauline letter, or in the collection of 2 Cor.

This investigation of a small portion of 2 Cor has revealed associations in the history of religions, leading us finally to question the literary unity of the epistle. The light thrown by the texts discovered at Qumran illuminates not only the great process of the growth of Christianity, but also such petty problems as are posed by the fragment of 2 Cor 6: 14-7: 1.

[54] Eph does not use the terms *apistos, anomia, koinōnia, meris, eidōlon, aphorizein, epitelein. Epangelia* is never used in the plural as in 2 Cor 7: 1. *Katharizein* in Eph 5: 26 is an allusion not to self-purification, but to Christ who through his devotion cleanses the Church. On the affinity of Eph to the thought-patterns and terminology of the Scrolls, cf. K. G. Kuhn, 'The Epistle to the Ephesians in the light of the Qumran Texts', below, pp. 115ff.
[55] Cf. K. G. Kuhn, *loc. cit.*

4
THE COURTS OF THE CHURCH OF CORINTH AND THE COURTS OF QUMRAN*

Mathias Delcor

I

SAINT PAUL'S mood is often one of anger as he writes to the faithful of the church of Corinth, for these recent converts are not all that they should be. At the start of Chapter 6 in the first Epistle to the Corinthians, Saint Paul complains that the Christians of Corinth, the saints, as he calls them, dare to bring their law-suits before pagan judges, the *adikoi*, when some dissension occurs among them. This is probably not because the pagan courts were incompetent to pass judgment on such disputes. On the contrary, everything suggests that the Apostle wishes especially to prevent the private scandals of the community from being known by judges who did not share their faith. So Paul requests the faithful to have their own affairs judged among themselves in their own courts. To make them aware of this obligation, the Apostle in v. 2 appeals to belief in the eschatological judgment: 'Do you not know that the saints will judge the world?' If, then, you are to judge the world, you can *a fortiori* deal with matters of less importance. In v. 3 he goes further and again recalls the doctrine of the eschatological judgment: 'Do you not know that we are to judge angels? And

* Published in *Studiorum Paulinorum Congressus Internationalis Catholicus 1961*, Rome, 1963, II, 535-548.

if the world is to be judged by you, are you incompetent to try trivial cases?'[1] And he adds: 'If then you have such cases, set up judges who are acceptable to the church.'[2]

This passage, then, leads one to presume that the church of Corinth had instituted courts for the benefit of the faithful. Saint Paul seems to be saying that it is more natural to have such courts, just as it would be quite extraordinary if at Corinth there could not be found a man of experience to mediate between his brethren.

Naturally we would like to know something of the structure and procedure of these first courts of the Church, about which the N.T. writings unfortunately give little information. This is not surprising, since the two Epistles to the Corinthians were written for particular purposes, and are clearly not treatises of canon law, still less systematic expositions of theology.

Some modern commentators have tried to interpret this passage by making use of what we know of the Jewish courts from the rabbinical writings, as for example, such competent experts as Strack and Billerbeck.[3] Commenting on v. 5, these authors suppose that Paul had in mind certain procedures derived from rabbinical law. They give the example of cases concerning money, where there should be three judges, who need not be professional, but may be lay people. Furthermore they say that in some cases, even one man of experience could pass judgment alone, if he was the only competent person available.

These legal procedures may be a very valuable illustration of those of the church of Corinth. Unfortunately, the texts attesting these procedures date from the middle of the second century A.D.,

[1] Allo translates *kritēria* in verses 2 and 3 by 'courts'. This is one of the possible meanings of the word; however, it may also mean 'dispute', cf. Weiss, *Der Erste Korintherbrief, in loco.*

[2] Here we are following the interpretation of the older Fathers (John Chrysostom, Saint Augustine, Theodoret, Pelagius) and the majority of the modern exegetes: Allo, Huby, Osty, Spicq, Lightfoot, etc., who make *kathizete* an imperative rather than an indicative. *Kathizein* has a very precise technical meaning: 'to constitute judges' cf. *Ant. Jud.*, XX, § 200: *kathizein sunedrion kritōn* 'to constitute an assembly of judges': Polybius, IX, 33, 12, and Eph 1: 20.

[3] *Kommentar zum Neuen Testament aus Talmud und Midrasch*, vol. III, p. 354.

and we have no proof that they were in use during the middle of the first century A.D.

However, it seems to me that today a more adequate idea of the probable organization of the courts of the primitive Church can be obtained by studying those of the community at Qumran, rather than those of the rabbinical writings; as is well known, the organization of Qumran shows many similarities with that of the Christian communities.[4] Lately J. Schmitt has emphasized these similarities in a field close to ours, namely, that of penitential practice.[5]

Yet it must be clearly acknowledged that it would be extremely conjectural to transpose without modification the institutions which we see functioning in the Jewish community of the Essenes beside the Dead Sea in Palestine to the Greek world of Corinth.

The problem is made more complicated by the fact that the community of Corinth was not composed exclusively of Jews, who had recently come to Christianity from the local synagogue, but also of Greeks[6] and, apparently, Romans, if we may judge by the Latin names found in the two Epistles.

In any case we know that the Jews of the Diaspora, even Roman citizens, had their own courts for civil cases, which possessed a particular jurisdiction. This was true for the Jews of Sardis in 50/49 B.C., as Josephus reports. (*Ant.J.*, xiv, x, 17).[7]

It would appear that Paul was following Jewish custom, when he requested the Corinthian Christians to set up courts to try their own cases. He was extending a special privilege of the Jews

---

[4] J. Schmitt, 'L'organization de l'Eglise primitive et Qumran', *La secte du Qumran et les origines du Christianisme* (Recherches bibliques, IV), Bruges, 1959, pp. 217-31.

[5] 'Contribution a l'étude de la discipline pénitentielle dans l'Église primitive à la lumière des textes de Qumran', *Les manuscrits de la Mer Morte (Colloque de Strasbourg, 25-27 May 1955)*, Paris, 1957, pp. 93-109.

[6] J. Dauvillier has been able to show that the marriage law as it appears in the first Epistle to the Corinthians can be explained in terms of Greek law: cf. 'Le droit du mariage dans les cités grecques et hellénistiques d'après les écrits de Saint Paul', *Revue Internationale des Droits de l'Antiquité*, 7 (1960) pp. 149-64.

[7] Schürer, *Geschichte des jüdischen Volkes im Z.A. Jesu Christi*, Leipzig, 1909, vol. III/4, pp. 74, 114.

to the new community, which numbered also non-Jewish members. Yet it should be remembered that the Greek confraternities also possessed their own jurisdiction and courts to judge disputes, quarrels, or crimes which took place among their members; in some places when one of their members appealed to the city court, he was punished by a fine.[8] Paul's way of acting would have surprised neither the Jews nor the Greeks who belonged to the community.

Lastly, we must point out that while we may compare the courts of Qumran and those of Corinth and establish some similarities, this does not imply any dependence. At the most it points to a certain resemblance between the legal institutions of two religious groups, a resemblance also verified in other fields.

Before describing the judicial organization at Qumran, let us see if it was also forbidden to the members of the sect beside the Dead Sea to have recourse to pagan courts.

The text of CD 9: 1

Some have tried to find this prohibition in a difficult passage of the *Damascus Document*, 9 : 1, for which very different translations have been suggested. Vermès translates : 'Quiconque fera vouer à l'anathème un membre de l'humanité par la justice des nations, qu'on le mette à mort.'[9] Del Medico : 'Tout homme qui fera vouer a l'anathème un homme d'entre les hommes, selon les dispositions des "peuples" (mecréants) est à mettre à mort.'[10] Molin's translation, which agrees with the two above mentioned authors, should be included : 'Jedermann, der irgendeinen Menschen verurteilt nach den Gesetzen der Heiden, der soll sterben.'[11] According to these translations, the passage forbids, under pain of death, citing a person before a pagan court on a charge carrying the death penalty.

[8] Cf. San Nicolo, *Zur Vereinsgerichtsbarkeit im hellenistischen Ägypten*, (*Epitymbion*, Heinrich Swobodo dargebracht), Reichenberg, 1927, pp. 255-300; and recently H. Bardtke, 'Die Rechtstellung der Qumran-Gemeinde', *TLZ*, 1961 (no. 2), col. 98.

[9] *Les manuscrits du désert de Juda*, Paris, 1954, p. 174.

[10] *L'énigme des manuscrits de la Mer Morte*, Paris, 1957, p. 568.

[11] *Die Söhne des Lichtes*, Wien-München, 1952, p. 50.

However, those translators who follow Rabin, the best commentator on the *Damascus Document*, present quite a different rendering. 'As for every case of "devoting", namely that a man be devoted so that he ceases to be a *living* man, he is to be put to death by the ordinances of the Gentiles.' Rabin obtains this meaning by replacing the first *kl 'dm*, which he considers corrupt, by *kl ḥrm*, by making *m 'dm*, which is translated by 'ceases to be a living man' the accusative of result of *yḥrym*, and then by connecting 'by the ordinances of the Gentiles' with the following verb instead of the preceding one.[12]

This translation has been accepted by Dupont-Sommer, and in almost every detail,[13] by Bardtke,[14] and by Gaster.[15] Our final translation is: 'In every case where anathema shall have been pronounced against a man, he shall be put to death according to the laws of the Gentiles.' The translation favoured by Vermès, de Medico and Molin should be abandoned, because it is very hard to grant that the sect of Qumran was able to inflict the death penalty and this is demanded by their hypothesis. It is more likely that the sect, having in mind Leviticus 2 : 29, should rule that the execution of a death sentence rendered by a Jewish court should be carried out by pagans, not Jews. Moreover, this procedure would agree with what we know from John 18 : 31.

We must, therefore, accept the fact that there is no prohibition against recourse to pagan courts in the *Damascus Document*. On the other hand everything we know about the sect of Qumran suggests that such a prohibition did in fact exist. It is almost certain that the sectarians did not differ from other Jews on this matter.

The Courts in the Document of Damascus and the Epistles to the Corinthians

When the other passages of the Qumran writings which speak

---

[12] *The Zadokite Documents*, Oxford, 1954, p. 44.
[13] *Les écrits esséniens découverts près de la Mer Morte*, Paris, 1959, p. 163.
[14] *Die Handschriftenfunde am Toten Meer, Die Sekte von Qumran*, Berlin, 1958, p. 266.
[15] *The Dead Sea Scripture in English Translation*, New York, 1956.

of the judicial institutions are examined, it is immediately obvious on one hand that the documents themselves are not perfectly clear (or at least are not always as detailed as we might desire), and on the other hand that they suggest that variations existed.

A passage in the *Damascus Document* supplies us with a number of indications about the choice of judges in the congregation. (CD 10 : 4-11.) There must be ten, four belonging to the tribe of Levi and Aaron, and six from Israel. Not less than twenty-four years of age, not more than sixty, they should be well versed in the mysterious book of *Hagu* and the 'teachings' or 'principles' of the Covenant *ywsdy bryt* (cf. the same expression in CD 7 : 5). But why ten? Rabin immediately connected this practice with the ten judges of the temple courts (Mishnah, *Sanhedrin*, 1, 3; cf. *b. Sanhedrin*, 7b) and the custom of the ancient Karaites.[16] But, since these judges also had administrative duties, he considers that they could be better related to the *dekaprōtoi* of the Hellenistic cities. It is well known that one of their duties was to collect taxes.[17] We find for example these *dekaprōtoi* at Tiberias (Josephus, *Vita XIII*), at Palmyra with the archontes (the Aramean '*srt*' is translated by *dekaprōtous* in the bilingual Tariff of Palmyra).[18]

Now, according to another passage in the *Damascus Document* (14 : 13f.), the judges are elected with the mebaqqer and exercise an administrative role, as did most magistrates of the ancient world, in both the Phoenician and the Greek cities, the Roman world, and earlier as did the Judges of Israel. They had the duty of providing for charitable works, for which they received certain funds gathered through taxation.[19]

The *Damascus Document* is neither very explicit nor positive

---

[16] *The Zadokite Documents*, Oxford, 1954, p. 49.

[17] Cf. Schürer, *Geschichte des jüdischen Volkes im Z.A. Jesu Christi*, Leipzig, 1907 (4th ed.), vol. II, p. 218, and note 529 with the earlier bibliography.

[18] *Tariff of Palmyra*, I, 8. Cf. Cooke, *North-West Semitic Inscriptions*, Oxford, 1903, 313ff.

[19] It is a modern conception, inspired by Montesquieu's *l'Esprit des Lois*, to think of judicial power as a separate power, distinct from governmental or administrative power, as from the legislative. In the ancient world things were different.

about the length of the tenure of office of the judges, the manner of their election, and even the type of cases that come before them. The document actually says that they were elected *lpy h't*. Gaster and Dupont-Sommer translate this by 'periodically', Bardtke by 'for the occasion' and Rabin hesitates between 'for the occasion' and 'for a determined time'. In fact, it is very probable that the judges only remained for one period and were changed at regular intervals, in order to avoid any temptation to negligence or even corruption in the fulfilment of their office.

It would be interesting to know how they were nominated, but, here also, the text is ambiguous. They were chosen *brwrym*, but who made the choice? Was it the congregation? *Brwrym mn h'dh* could mean this, and it is translated by Burrows, Dupont-Sommer as 'chosen by the community', but others propose 'chosen from the community' (cf. Rabin with hesitation, Vermès, Bardtke, Molin, Gaster, del Medico). It is, in fact, possible to take *mn* in a passive sense (cf. Carl Brockelmann, *Hebräische Syntax*, 1956, p. III) as well as in a partitive sense, which is more usual. However, it seems to me that the most natural and least complicated translation is 'chosen from the community'. Lastly, while we know that these judges also had administrative duties, these writings give no certain indications about the type of cases submitted to them.

In our opinion there is no resemblance between the settlement of disputes of a temporal nature in the *Damascus Document* and the practice of the Church of Corinth. For in the one there are real judges, in the other mere arbitrators. In both communities it was accepted as the general principle that the settlement of disputes should be done within the community and should not pass outside. To suppose that 1 Cor 6 : 4 insinuates that the community of Corinth had appointed a number of arbitrators from whom disputing parties could choose is to force the text.

The *Damascus Document*, moreover, assigns to the mebaqqer of all the camps a judicial role, for the members of the congregation, when occasion demanded, could bring before him any matter of dispute or litigation *ryb wmspt* (CD 14 : 6-12). There are good grounds then, for believing that any person could have recourse to this Inspector General, who as supreme judge had jurisdiction over all the communities. In any case the requirements of age and character for the office of mebaqqer are more demanding than for the ordinary judges. In age he must be not less than thirty nor more than fifty, no doubt because of his heavy duties, involving continual travelling. But above all else, he must be 'a master in all human secrets and in all languages according to their families', which doubtless refers to supernatural qualities of the government of souls rather than to natural, even exceptional, talents. In the Epistle to the Corinthians this office of supreme judge has fallen on the Apostle himself; far from Corinth he heard of the serious disorders in the community there, where there was a case of incest, and he pronounced a sentence of excommunication against the incestuous man (cf. 1 Cor 5 : 3), even though the whole community had been at fault. We shall return to this later.

The Second Epistle to the Corinthians clearly implies that Paul himself will personally judge the serious disputes of the community on the testimony of two or three witnesses according to the prescription of Deuteronomy 19 : 15. Now this passage is very well illustrated by a complete section in the *Damascus Document*, which is formally concerned with how the statements of witnesses should be made before the mebaqqer (CD 9 : 16-23).

Let us turn once again to 1 Cor 6. We should remember that Paul wished the judges whom the community were to appoint to be men of wisdom : 'Can it be that there is no man among you wise enough to decide between members of the brotherhood?' he asks them. To whom is the Apostle referring in this passage? We have already seen the explanation of Strack and Billerbeck, an explanation theoretically possible only if it is proved that the practices spoken of by the late rabbinical writings existed in the first century of the Christian era. But this remains to be proved. We have noted the existence of ten judges in the *Damascus Document* but, unfortunately these passages make no mention of arbitrators, and it is to private arbitrators rather than real judges that the community of Corinth must appeal. Further, we do not find any references in the writings of the Dead Sea sect to the *beth din*, which in Jewish law should be composed of three judges. At most, it is a question in these texts—and this is a totally different matter—of the obligation of fraternal correction in front of witnesses before bringing an accusation against a brother in the plenary assembly : the many (cf. 1QS 5 : 24-6 : 1 and CD 9 : 2-4).

Should the judges appointed by the community of Corinth be identified with the members of the hierarchy? It is most unlikely. Paul would certainly have been more explicit, because, even if the presbyters are not mentioned by name in the epistles, we have indications that the basic features of a hierarchy existed, even though in its early stage (cf. 1 Cor 12 and 16 : 16). On the contrary, everything suggests that the Apostle desired that within the Christian community those who administered justice in temporal matters should be distinct from those who administered it in spiritual matters. Ideally the hierarchy should not be involved in disputes of a temporal kind. We have here a far clearer separation of the temporal and the spiritual than in later centuries, when the bishop, even in temporal affairs, was the normal mediator between Christians.[20]

We must admit, then, that the *sophos* spoken of by the Apostle was an ordinary Christian chosen by the parties as arbitrator, that he gave a verdict, being guided by civil law without being bound by it. Dauvillier investigated the standing of the verdict of an arbitrator in Corinthian law, and he admits that we do not possess the documents which would enable us to give a clear answer. But he considers that on this matter Corinthian law

[20] We owe these details to Prof. J. Dauvillier, the eminent historian of law, who is preparing a work on the law of the primitive Church. In the near future we shall have in this work most detailed studies of every mention of law in the N.T. It is possible, as J. Dauvillier suggested to me, that the incident in Luke 12 : 13-14 (which must have been familiar to Christians before the redaction of this gospel), when Jesus refused to act as arbitrator in a dispute between two brothers over the division of heritage, was the reason why the spiritual authorities of the community, the *presbuteroi*, refused to decide disputes, but left this to one or more arbitrators, not chosen from themselves.

would have been surely the same as Athenian law, which allowed recourse to one or more private arbitrators *(hairetoi diaitētai)*.

It would also be desirable to have some details about the types of cases which the Corinthians were to bring before the judges whom they were to establish. The epistle tells us that they were disputes of a temporal nature *(biōtika)*. Everything suggests that the directives of Paul were normally concerned with civil lawsuits between two Christians, for example, a suit over the division of inheritance, litigation about property or debts, but excluding all strictly religious matters, which were doubtless judged by the whole community, as we shall see immediately.

The Office of Judge according to the Rule of the Community and the Epistles to the Corinthians

Whereas in the *Damascus Document* judicial functions are exercised by a number of judges, endowed with certain required qualities, the *Rule* attributes this office to the whole community acting as a college: *mwsb hrbym*, 'the assembly of the Many', a term equivalent to the English 'session' and German 'Sitzung'. For this assembly the order of precedence is given: first the priests, then the elders, and lastly, the rest of the people; next its powers are described: 'they shall be questioned *(ys'lw* understood as a nifal) concerning the law *(mspt)* and every kind of counsel *(kwl 'sh)* and business' (1QS 6 : 8-9). The passage is clear then: the full assembly will make a judicial decision, offer recommendations, and express its opinion on every matter. The two Hebrew words *mspt* and *'sh* are equivalent in practice, as has been pointed out for *krisis* and *boulē* in Ecclesiasticus 25 : 4 by Wernberg-Møller.[21] The exercise of this judicial power at Qumran by the full Assembly corresponds exactly with what Josephus tells us about the Essenes *(B.J.* II; xii, 9). When they judge, there are no less than one hundred members present, and so, he adds, their verdict is final.

We must say something about a passage in 1QS 8 : 1-4, which speaks of a college of fifteen members, 'perfect in all that has been revealed in the entire Torah' etc. This passage, which has

[21] *The Manual of Discipline*, Leiden, 1957.

been sometimes cited in connection with another passage in the *Damascus Document* speaking of a college of ten judges, does not contradict in any way what we have already stated about the judicial powers of the *mwsb hrbym*. This passage of the *Rule* in fact does not affirm that the college of fifteen members administers justice. On the contrary, the whole context seems to indicate that theirs was a doctrinal role, 'to maintain the faith on the earth' *(lsmwr 'mwnh b'rs)* (8 : 3).

Whatever the solution of this problem, it seems to me that the full assembly of Qumran with its judicial powers supplies us with a better understanding of another passage of Paul, when he calls on the Corinthian community to gather in full assembly and condemn the incestuous man (1 Cor 5 : 4).

St Paul does not say, as Allo, for example, suggests (p. 122), that the court should consist of a number of leaders assisted by a few deputed by the Church, but he addresses himself to the whole community of the Saints, *sunachthentōn humōn.* This is the equivalent of the *mwsb hrbym* of Qumran and, when Paul required the whole community to assemble to publicly pronounce the sentence which he himself had already given (v. 3), his purpose, as at Qumran, was doubtless to give greater weight to the sentence.

Another passage in the Second Epistle to the Corinthians speaks also of a penalty inflicted by the majority of the community *(tōn pleionōn)* on one of its members for a serious fault (an injustice or an injury), the nature of which is hard to decide (2 Cor 2 : 5-8).[22] Paul asks the community to forgive the unfortunate man, as he has already done, fearing that excessive suffering would overwhelm him. This passage is interesting for more than one reason. It manifests, first of all, the democratic nature of the judicial verdicts of the community, which were reached by a majority. This was surely agreeable to the Corinthians. Now this was also the practice of the Essenes, as Josephus expressly says : 'It was a point of honour with them to submit to the elders *(presbuterois)* and to the majority *(tois pleiosin)* ;

---

[22] The different hypotheses proposed on this point may be found in Allo, *Seconde épître aux Corinthiens*, Excursus III, pp. 56ff.

when ten were sitting together, no one spoke if the other nine desired silence' (*Jewish Wars*, II, 146).[23]

Secondly, this passage shows Paul making use of his judicial power of 'loosing' and asking the church to do the same. Unfortunately the parallel at Qumran, which one might be tempted to advance, is not convincing. According to the directives set forth in the *Damascus Document* for the mebaqqer, a real pastor of his flock, 'he will loosen all the chains that bind them, so that there will be no one oppressed or crushed in his congregation' (CD 13 : 10). The expression bind-loose should not be understood in a juridical sense, which it normally had in the rabbinical writings[24] but rather in a pastoral and disciplinary sense as reform and correction.

II

Through the *Rule* especially we know what type of cases were judged by the assembly of the many. There the articles of the penal code are stated in detail; in it no distinction is made between the breaches of the Rule of the sect and violations of the Law, both of which the community gathered in full assembly must judge (cf. 1QS 6 : 24-7 : 25).

Compared to the *Moshab harabbim*, it would seem that the first Christian communities enjoyed more restricted judicial power and that it was limited to spiritual matters.

The 'saints' will judge the world

We have attempted to understand the judicial institutions, which were in existence in the community of Corinth; we must now learn the nature of the eschatological doctrine on which the Apostle claimed to base them. To convince the 'saints' of Corinth to stop going before pagan courts to have their disputes judged, and to persuade them to make use of the judges established within the community, the Apostle explicitly refers to an

[23] It is probably a question here of the ten judges mentioned by CD. 'To sit' has a juridical connotation here. Cf. CD 14: 3 and Ex 18: 13.

[24] Cf. under *deō (luō)* in Kittel, *TWNT*, and J. Schmitt, *Colloque de Strasbourg*, p. 98.

eschatological doctrine, which must have been common knowledge in the community : 'Do you not know that the saints will
judge the world?' In their explanation of this passage, some
exegetes (Allo, among others) have been content to say that
Paul here is extending to all the faithful the promise made by
Christ to his Apostles. But whereas the Apostles were to judge
only the twelve tribes of Israel, i.e. the chosen people, here the
saints are to judge the whole world, that is, every intelligent
creature : angels (v. 3) and men.

Other exegetes, such as Weiss[25] and Strack-Billerbeck, have
tried to trace the the Old Testament or apocryphal sources on
which this doctrine is based. They bring forward Dan 7 : 22
which appears in the well-known chapter about the vision of
the Son of Man. There it is clearly stated that the saints of the
Most High, i.e. Israel, will exercise judgment and will possess
the kingdom, or rather sovereignty. The whole context suggests
that it concerns sovereignty over the fourth empire, symbolized
by the fourth beast. It is a question here, then, of a limited
judgment.

Further on, in v. 27, the sacred author states simply that the
kingdom, the dominion and the greatness of all kingdoms under
heaven shall be given to the people of the saints of the Most
High. It is not actually said that they shall judge all the kingdoms, although the concepts of 'dominion' and 'judgment' are
very close to each other in the Semitic mentality.

Wis 3 : 8, another often cited passage, considers that the
' "just" will govern nations and rule over peoples'. This passage
is placed after the promise of a blessed life made to the just.[26]
On the contrary, according to the passages in Henoch (1 : 9;
95 : 3; 96 : 1, etc.), the judgment of the just will be exercised
on the sinners, probably Israelites.

All these passages habitually cited by the authors are of value,
but they do not deal with a judgment on such a vast scale as

[25] *Der Erste Korintherbrief*, in *Kritisch-exegetischer Kommentar über das
Neue Testament*.
[26] On the meaning which should be given to this judgment of the just,
cf. especially Rudolphe Schutz, *Les idées eschatologiques du Livre de la
Sagesse*, Strasbourg, 1935, pp. 85ff.

that considered by Paul. In all these passages, the eschatological judgment will be exercised over a limited field; even when the just will judge the peoples, as in Wisdom, Israel would seem to be excluded from this judgment. Actually what we have here is a trace of that Messianic expectation which promised the Jews domination one day over the other peoples. If the context of Wisdom 3 recalls Obad 18, it should be recognized that a nationalistic idea has been transposed and spiritualized, for, instead of the Israelites, it speaks of the just.

In my opinion a Hymn of Qumran better illustrates not only the doctrine of Paul but also that of Jesus. First of all we should take note of a point of phraseology which is in itself significant. The phrase *krinein ton kosmon* 'to judge the world', found in 1 Cor 6 : 2; Jn 3 : 17; 12 : 47; Rom 3 : 6, does not belong to the language of the LXX. The closest parallel there is *krinein oikoumenēn*, Ps 95 : 13; 97 :9, which translate *spt h'rs*. Strack-Billerbeck report that the corresponding phrases in Hebrew and Aramaic *dyn 't h'wlm* and *lmdn yt 'lm'* are rare in rabbinical literature, where 'to judge the peoples of the world' is preferred. But since these writings are late it should be admitted that the New Testament expression stands alone. Yet if, following Carmignac,[27] one connects the Hymn fragments 1QHf. 15 : 6 and 18 : 6, then we have expression *s[p]t tbl,* which is equivalent to *krinein ton kosmon.* It is also found in the Concordance of Kuhn.[28] Unfortunately, these texts are too fragmentary for anyone to determine their context.

In any case, the vocabulary in itself appears to suggest that we look to Qumran in order to understand the Pauline text. This is also true for the themes. Mt 19 : 28 (cf. Lk 22 : 28-30) relates Jesus' promise to his Apostles that they would sit on thrones as the judges of the twelve tribes of Israel. For Matthew and Luke, this unique promise is inserted after Jesus has spoken of the fidelity of the Apostles in following him even in his sufferings : 'You who have followed me' (Mt), 'You are those who

---

[27] 'Localisation des fragments 15, 18 and 22 des Hymnes', *RQ* 1 (1959), p. 425.

[28] *Konkordanz zu den Qumrantexten*, ed. K. G. Kuhn, Göttingen, 1960.

have continued with me in my trials' (Lk). Now a very similar doctrine is to be found in one of the Hymns of Qumran, where the context is much the same. The complete text reads :

> You have not covered with shame the faces of all my disciples who assemble for your Covenant.
> They hear me, those who walk in the way of your heart and who are ranked for thee in the assembly of the Saints.
> You will give everlasting victory to their cause and truth according to justice.
> You will not permit them to stray in the power of the reprobate according to the scheme which they have devised against them. On the contrary you will place their fear upon your people together with destruction for all the peoples of the lands to cut off, by the judgment, all who transgress your word.
>
> (1QH 4 : 23-27)

This text demands a few preliminary remarks. The expression 'you will place their fear' seems ambiguous, for the suffix can be understood as referring to the reprobate or to the disciples. We consider that the first explanation should be rejected, since the psalmist in line 25 prays that the reprobate, i.e. the enemies of the sect, may not lead into error the members of the community. *Wttn* has an adversative meaning ('On the contrary, you will place') and introduces the idea that the faithful disciples of the Master will inspire a religious fear among the other saintly members of the community of Qumran. 'Your people' here does not mean the whole of Israel, but the faithful Israel, the *verus Israel*, that the sectarians claimed to be. (For the same meaning of 'your people', cf. 1QH 4 : 6, 11, 16; 6 : 8.) On the other hand, the faithful disciples of the Master will without pity sentence to destruction 'all the peoples of the lands' *'my h'rswt*, i.e. the pagans (cf. Neh 10 : 3) and 'all those who transgress thy word', i.e. sinful Israel.

Now if we are correct, the psalmist, who is surely the Teacher of Righteousness, asks God to give victory to the cause of his disciples who have followed and heard his words and to make them one day judges, not only of the sinful Israelites (the transgressors of the word), but also of the Gentiles.

In the gospels, where the context is so similar to that of the hymn, the judgment to be exercised by the Apostles is limited to the twelve tribes of Israel; but in the Epistles to the Corinthians, it embraces the whole world: Jews and pagans. So the magnificent perspectives of this judgment are very like those of our Hymn. Yet, there is one aspect lacking in the Hymn: the judgment of the angels, by which is meant either all the fallen angels or the whole angelic world. This problem could by itself be the subject of another paper.

Let us briefly sum up. We find that in the courts of Corinth as well as at Qumran, there exists apparently the same judicial system, whether it is a case of the community judging in full assembly, or of a number of individuals chosen for this purpose, or, finally, of recourse being had to a supreme judge, with jurisdiction over several communities. Yet, we must go deeper than superficial appearances, because there are important differences. Real judges appear in the Document of Damascus, but at Corinth those selected by the community are merely arbitrators, whose existence is shown by Athenian law, but about whom, as far as is known, there is not the smallest reference in the writings of Qumran. Far more enlightening, on the other hand, is the comparison between the community gathered in full assembly at Qumran and Corinth. At Qumran its powers seem to be wider that at Corinth, where the 'saints' only judge cases of a spiritual nature. Lastly, St Paul's doctrine of the eschatological judgment exercised by the saints, which he uses to support his proposals, is the element in his teaching which is best illustrated by that of Qumran. In any case, these examples serve to show how much attention to the Qumran texts can contribute to Pauline studies.

5
THE TEACHER OF RIGHTEOUSNESS OF QUMRAN AND THE QUESTION OF JUSTIFICATION BY FAITH IN THE THEOLOGY OF THE APOSTLE PAUL*

Walter Grundmann

In his presentation of the scholarly discussion of the question connected with the discoveries at Qumran, Millar Burrows states : 'From my first acquaintance with the Dead Sea Scrolls in 1947, what has most surprised and impressed me is the agreement of some aspects of Qumran theology with the most distinctive doctrines of the apostle Paul'. Burrows brings out two points : 'The point at which the very roots of Paul's theology and that of the Dead Sea Scrolls are intertwined is the experience of moral frustration, with the resulting conviction of man's hopeless sinfulness. . . . The affinity of Paul's doctrine and that of Qumran goes beyond the conviction of human corruption. The Thanksgiving Psalms and the concluding psalm of the Manual of Discipline express also a profound sense of the righteousness of God, by which man is given a righteousness he could never attain for himself.'[1] This raises important questions for the structure of Pauline theology and its relation to contemporary Jewish doctrinal formation, matters which have been much discussed.[2]

* This essay is a revised version of the study published in the *RQ* 2 (1960), pp. 237-59.

[1] M. Burrows, *More Light on the Dead Sea Scrolls*, New York, 1958, pp. 119-20. Burrows refers to his first study, *The Dead Sea Scrolls*, New York, 1955, pp. 333-6.

[2] Cf. H. Braun, 'Römer 7: 7-25 und das Selbstverständnis des Qumran-Frommen', *ZTK* 56 (1959), pp. 1-18, and also a study which appeared at the same time as the first version of this paper, S. Schulz, 'Zur Rechtfertigung aus Gnaden in Qumran und bei Paulus. Zugleich ein Beitrag zur Form- und Überlieferungsgeschichte der Qumrantexte', *ZTK* 56 (1959), pp. 155-85.

In his latest book on St Paul, Hans Joachim Schoeps agrees with Albert Schweitzer in regarding Paul's doctrine of justification as a mere fragment of his teaching on salvation. Schweitzer had spoken of the doctrine of justification as a subsidiary crater in the main volcanic crater of the mystique of existence in Christ.[3] But in view of the situation at Qumran the question of the significance of the doctrine of justification by faith in Paul must be raised again. General formulations and summary judgments are not sufficient; they cry out for more precise conclusions. The discovery of the Dead Sea manuscripts has made us familiar with one of the most significant figures in pre-Christian Jewish religious history, and he turns out to be a teacher of justification through grace. From the documents containing his teachings and from the statements of Paul we shall try to determine how each of them understands human existence from the point of view of the justice of man in the sight of God, and where the differences between their doctrines lie.

I

A. Dupont-Sommer begins his short characterization of the 'Teacher of Righteousness' with the sentence: 'The Teacher of Righteousness is certainly the most amazing revelation of the Dead Sea Scrolls.'[4] In his thorough investigation of the Teacher of Righteousness, Gert Jeremias describes him as 'the greatest personality of later Judaism known to us'.[5] We learn of him in the Damascus Document and in the Explanations of Habakkuk and Nahum and of Ps 37. We come upon traces of him in the Hymns of Thanksgiving (Hodayoth), which Hans Bardtke calls 'the most typical and richest part of the writings of Qumran. . . . There is nothing similar in later Jewish literature or in the rest of the writings of Qumran. Here we are face to face with the

[3] H. J. Schoeps, *Paulus. Die Theologie des Apostles im Lichte der jüdischen Religionsgeschichte*, Tübingen, 1959, p. 206. For the discussion of Schweitzer's thesis, cf. my study 'Rechtfertigung und Mystik bei Paulus', *ZNW* 32 (1933), pp. 52-65, the conclusions of which are still valid.

[4] A. Dupont-Sommer, *The Essene Writings from Qumran*, trans. by G. Vermes, Cleveland-New York, 1962, p. 358.

[5] Gert Jeremias, *Der Lehrer der Gerechtigkeit*, Göttingen, 1963, p. 351.

great creative religious spirit which formed the community of Qumran.'[6] More careful investigation has led to these poems being distinguished into different literary categories;[7] among poems of a fairly conventional stamp some stand out which can be attributed with a fair degree of certainty to the Teacher of Righteousness himself.[8] These above all are significant for the understanding of this important figure.

If Bardtke is correct, the Hymns of Thanksgiving form a meditation book whose goal is 'to have the spiritual effect of penetrating and thereby dominating the will and mentality of the individual members of the community'.[9] In this case their significance is increased, because in them the individual has also the character of a type. In this individual we find the spiritual personality of the Teacher of Righteousness. First of all we must realize what this personality is. The poems which can be ascribed to the Teacher of Righteousness himself contain a series of statements where expressions of his own lowliness and of vivid awareness of his mission are inseparably joined. They constantly exalt the content of his message, and attest the fierce oppositions and enmities into which the fulfilment of his mission brings him.[10] The author describes himself as 'potter's clay'; he regards mankind as being 'in sin, in guilty evil-doing from mother's womb to old age'; he turns in upon himself and speaks of the reproaches which await him at God's judgment: 'Fear and trembling take hold of me; my knees knock like water falling from a mountain cliff, for I thought of my misdeeds and the guilt of my fathers'

[6] H. Bardtke, *Die Handschriftenfunde vom Toten Meer, II; Die Sekte von Qumran*, Berlin, 1958, pp. 141f.

[7] G. Morawe, *Aufbau und Abgrenzung der Loblieder von Qumran. Studien zur gattungsgeschlichtlichen Einordnung der Hodajoth*, Berlin, 1961.

[8] On the basis of work done under the direction of K. G. Kuhn in the Arbeitsgemeinschaft über die Qumran-texte, Heidelberg, G. Jeremias attributes the following parts to the Hymns to the Teacher of Righteousness: 1QH 2: 1-19, 31-39; 4: 5-5: 4; 5: 5-19; 5: 20-7: 5; 7: 6-25; 8:4-40 (*op. cit.*, pp. 171-173).

[9] H. Bardtke, *op. cit.*, pp. 138f., also 'Das "Ich" des Meisters in den Hodajoth von Qumran', in *Wissenschaftliche Zeitschrift der Karl-Marx-Universität Leipzig* 6 (1956-1957), *Gesellschafts-sprachwissenschaftliche Reihe 1*, pp. 94-104.

[10] Our translations of the Qumran texts follow those of Gert Jeremias, H. Bardtke, and J. Maier (*Die Texte vom Toten Meer*, München Basel), 1960, vol. I, pp. 70-121.

D

(1QH 4 : 29-35). Not only his own sins but also those of his fathers and of his fellow-men move his heart and drive it to grief and despair. He knows that 'no man is just, no son of man is perfect' (1QH 4 : 30). This despair finds expression in austere words and images : it leaves him forlorn, his soul sinks 'down to the underworld,' 'restless night and day' while his body is sick in every limb.[11]

Against this background the affirmations of salvation and illumination shine in vivid contrast. Through his holy spirit God has given light to the erring, reconciled the guilty to himself, given stability to the waverer, and granted health and wholeness to the sick. 'I will praise you, Lord, for you have held me up in your strength and poured out over me your holy spirit; you have given me strength and I do not waver' (1QH 7: 6f.). The Teacher is, then, prophet in virtue of the gift of God's holy spirit. Of the highest significance is the difference between this claim and the Jewish doctrine that no prophet had risen up since Malachi, and that the holy spirit had disappeared from Israel (1 Sota 13, 2),[12] a doctrine which is foreshadowed in Ps 74 : 9 and 1 Macc 9 : 27 and in the prayer of Azariah 13f.; it is found in *syr. Bar.*, 85 : 3, and attested for Judaism by Origen (*contra Cels.*, 7, 8). One must not forget that this doctrine was developed and strengthened by the Teacher's opponents with the object of denying his prophetic character. In another passage he proclaims : 'I praise you, Lord, for the light of your covenant has lit up my face; I seek you, and sure as the glow of morning have you appeared to give me perfect light' (1QH 4 : 5f.). In all this he praises God's action; it is clear from the background of these confident claims that God's action is upon an unworthy subject. God's action to him is conditioned by his mercy. If he had been 'cast out from your alliance', he now proclaims 'as I thought of

---

[11] Cf. 1QH 1 : 21-23, which, even if it cannot be attributed with certainty to the Teacher himself, nevertheless shows clearly his influence on the imagery used by his friends and disciples, cf. also 1QH 3 : 23-25. Both passages are at least confessional statements of the Teacher's community, which was directly influenced by his teaching.

[12] Cf. H. Strack-P. Billerbeck, *Kommentar zum Neuen Testament aus Talmud und Midrasch*, München, 1922, vol. I, p. 127; W. Foerster, *Neutestamentliche Zeitgeschichte*, Hamburg, 1955 (2nd ed.), pp. 16f.

the strength of your hand and the multitude of your mercies, I could hold myself erect again, and I stood, my spirit firm against the plague, for I relied on the evidence of your mercy and the greatness of your pity. For you forgive sins, in order to cleanse mankind through your justice' (1QH 4 : 35-7). Salvation, health, enlightenment, wisdom, standing erect through God's spirit and mercy, all this the Teacher has experienced.[13]

In this connection he makes express mention of man's cleansing from sin through God's justice.[14] This justice of God, is, as in the Old Testament, the expression of his fidelity to his covenant; it is at once the gift which cleanses men and the power which brings men under his dominion in the alliance.[15] It is this experience of God's justice as his fidelity to his covenant which constitutes the Teacher of Righteousness a prophet and teacher of the community which listens to his words. This he confesses when he says: 'Your justice has brought me into the service of your alliance; I rely on your truth' (1QH 7 : 19f.).[16] This truth is no other than the Torah, by whose proclamation he receives his enlightenment and wisdom, in which he experiences God's strength and mercy, whose exposition is the prophetical office which makes him a unique Teacher. He who has been chosen out and granted the revelation of the holy spirit has become a 'sign which shall be contradicted' (cf. Luke 2 : 34), 'a scandal for evil–doers and a physician for all who have turned away from sin'; he has been made 'wisdom for fools and firmness for all broken hearts', 'mockery and contempt for the wicked, a foundation stone of truth and understanding for the honest'; a 'laughing-stock for evil doers', a 'container for the elect of justice and a herald of the knowledge of wonderful secrets' (1QH 2 : 8-13). He proclaims of himself: 'you constituted me father to

[13]Cf. the passages formed in his community under his influence, and which clearly echo his doctrine, viz. 1QH 3 : 23-25, and 9 : 29-35, which, unlike Jeremias (op. cit., p. 141), I am strongly inclined to attribute to the Teacher himself.

[14] On the meaning and origin of this concept, cf. A. Oepke, 'Dikaiosune Theou bei Paulus', TLZ 78 (1953), pp. 257-64.

[15] Cf. E. Käsemann, 'Gottesgerechtigkeit bei Paulus', ZTK 58 (1961), pp. 367-78.

[16] Cf. also two passages which betray the influence of the Teacher, 1QH 3 : 19-23; 14 : 17-18.

the sons of your favour, to care for the men of your miraculous sign' (1QH 7: 20-21), and he shows full gratitude: 'Through me you have brought light to many eyes, have shown your might immeasurable, for you have made known to me the secrets of your marvels' (1QH 4: 27-28). His mouth has become a spring of living water: 'And you, God, have put in my mouth . . . a spring of living water, which does not deceive when it opens up the heavens' (1QH 8. 16-17).

By his doctrine, then, he brings salvation to others, for these claims are tantamount to saying: the Teacher has become, through his election and his enlightenment, the founder of a community which listens to and depends upon his teaching; its members 'open their mouths like sucklings . . . rejoice like a baby on its mother's bosom' (1QH 7: 21). The historical situation of this community is clear from the allegory of the Hymn 1QH 8: 4-40: it speaks of water-plants in the midst of which are hidden 'trees of life at mystic springs' whose purpose is 'to sprout forth shoots for an eternal planting'. The water-plants which grow, but have no roots in the water and must therefore pass away, represent Israel's desertion of God's covenant, while the trees of life indicate the Hasidim, from whose midst comes forth the 'shoot for an eternal planting', viz: the Qumran community,[17] which constitutes the heavenly Jerusalem, built on a rock beyond the waters of Hades (1QH 6: 24-28).[18] Since the factor which decides whether one belongs to the eternal planting and the heavenly Jerusalem or not is one's attitude to the doctrine of the Teacher, it is by this criterion that the just and unjust are differentiated. It is this doctrine, then, which plays the decisive part in the fate of Israelites. Here is a claim to importance whose like has not yet been found in later Judaism. It is clearly expressed in the Teacher's characterization of himself as 'container for the elect of justice' and immediately afterwards 'herald of the knowledge of wonderful secrets', a claim which alludes to the juncture in his doctrine of Law and Apocalyptic: 'enemy of all who proclaim error', 'Lord of peace for all who contemplate

[17] Cf. G. Jeremias, op. cit., pp. 257-61.
[18] Cf. G. Jeremias, op. cit., pp. 245-9.

truth' and 'a spirit of Zeal for all who live by flattery' (1QH 2 : 13-15). Zeal for Israel, the enlightenment of an apocalyptic writer, and the earnestness of a teacher of the Law, all enter into his consciousness of his mission and go to form his claim to importance.

It is not surprising that this claim and this consciousness encounter opposition. The Hymns of the Teacher show clearly the struggles in which he is involved. Opposition springs up in his own community; opposition rises from outside. 'I have brought . . . strife and battle to my friends, anger and opposition to all who enter my covenant, murmuring and unwillingness to those who gather about me. Even those who ate my bread have kicked out against me, those who joined my company have cursed me, my followers are refractory and murmur on every side, and blasphemously peddle the secrets you have revealed to me among the sons of perdition' (1QH 5 : 22-25). His Rule imposes stern discipline upon the community, and this opposition raised to it results in defection. This weighs upon him all the more heavily because he sees in his community the holy remnant announced by the prophets. He says he has been consoled from 'the din of nations and turmoil of kingdoms as they gathered against my poor folk whom you have raised to be some slight life-force in your people. And a remnant remained in your heritage, and you cleansed it thoroughly from guilt, so that all its works should be done in your truth and show forth your praise' (1QH 6 : 7-9). So he founds a community which is the holy remnant of Israel, harassed by the mass of the people, and their chiefs and the adherents of their chiefs. It is to this community that he gives a rule of life. Its mission extends beyond Israel : 'All peoples shall recognize your reliability and all nations your glory' (1QH 6 : 12). Here universalist aspects of the older prophetic preaching, which were suppressed in Israel after the exile, come to life again. But for Israel itself the appendices of the Rule of the Community sketch a model for the future eschatological way of life, in which the Teacher's community remains the nucleus.

The Teacher of Righteousness and his community are

harassed also from outside : 'I praise you, Lord; your eyes watch over my soul, and you have rescued me from the zeal of those whose message is lies; from the community of those who act treacherously you have rescued the soul of the poor they planned to destroy, shedding their blood at your services. Only they did not know that my path is in your sight. And they made me a despicable laughing-stock on the lips of all who traffic in deceit. But your help, my God, has freed the humble and wretched from the power of those who were stronger than he' (1QH 2 : 31-35). This passage mentions an attack on the Teacher of Righteousness aimed at his destruction. The attack failed, for the Teacher speaks of his rescue, calling himself humble and wretched.

Is this intended as an allusion to the events preserved in various passages of 1QpHab? Mention is made of two opponents of the Teacher, once of a sacrilegious priest, the other time of the man of lies, who, with his followers, is called a traitor 1QpHab 2 : 1-10).[19] This reflects the twofold oppression just mentioned. While the sacrilegious priest is the representative of the Temple high priesthood, from which the Teacher of Righteousness and his community have separated themselves, the man of lies is probably the leader of the opposition from Hasidim circles, i.e. members of his own community who have risen up against the Teacher and split off from him. Hab 1 : 12ff. refers to him : 'He sides with the house of Absalom and the men of their counsel, who were silent at the condemnation of the Teacher of Righteousness and did not help him against the man of lies who despised the Law in the midst of their gathering' (1 QpHab 5 : 9-12). Since the term 'condemnation' indicates a process between members of the community[20] we must suppose here conflict in the community which terminated in apostasy. The opponent of the Teacher who is termed the 'man of lies' opposed his interpretation of the Law, which had led to the separation from people and Temple, and gained—as we see especially in the later Damascus Document—a strong following.

---

[19] On the Evil Priest and the Man of Lies, cf. G. Jeremias, *op. cit.*, pp. 36-126.   [20] Cf. G. Jeremias, *op. cit.*, pp. 85f.

But the sacrilegious priest appears from outside to oppose the Teacher and his Way. He and his guilt, incurred 'from his action to the Teacher and his community', are mentioned in 1 QpHab 11 : 8–11 and 8 : 5-13. In a comment on Hab 2 : 15 we are told that the sacrilegious priest 'pursued the Teacher of Righteousness, to swallow him up in the fury of his rage. In the place of his exile and on the feast day of peace, the Day of Reconciliation, he appeared before them to swallow them up and to lead them astray on the fast-day, the Sabbath of peace' (1QpHab 9 : 4-8). This clearly refers to a persecution on the part of the high priest of Jerusalem for the purpose of annihilating the community. The Teacher of Righteousness himself admits : 'Indeed they have rejected me, and take no notice of me; when you show yourself clearly to me they thrust me forth from the land as a bird from its nest; all my friends and relations have deserted me and consider me a broken vessel' (1QH 4 : 8-9). So the Teacher has been driven out of the land, his relations and all his former friends (who are probably to be found in Hasidim circles and in his own community, since 1QpHab 5 : 9-12 calls them the 'House of Absalom') have deserted him. The high priest, who is called the sacrilegious priest, rises up against the Teacher who has opposed him; this has led to real attacks on the Teacher and to assaults on his person. The high priest has pursued him and his community even in their exile in Ein-Feshkha or Qumran; this occurred on the Day of Reconciliation, which they held according to a calendar different from that in Jerusalem; the high priest's attack was aimed at turning the Teacher from his way. It seems that the Teacher was forced to remain in hiding for some time. He says : 'You held closed the mouth of lions whose teeth were as a sword, and whose fangs are as lances. All their tendrils are serpents' venom, to plunder; though great in number they did not open their mouths against me, for you, my God, had hidden me from men's sight, and your Law had . . . gone into hiding until the time when your help was revealed to me; for you did not leave my soul in misery, but listened to my cries in the bitter trials of my soul. You have swept away and set to right my wretchedness because of my groanings, and rescued the soul of the poor from the den of lions' (1QH 5 : 9-13). In this paragraph the Teacher's consciousness of his mission is again to be seen. He is so closely linked to the Torah that when he is hidden the Torah is hidden too. To him alone is its meaning made clear, and therefore with his rescue the Torah too is revealed.

The conflicts point to opposition also from within. 'The light of my face has dimmed into darkness, my brilliance changed into blackness. You, my God, made a bulwark in my heart, but they carried it forth to oppress it, and built a barrier of darkness round me; sighs were my bread and endless tears my drink, for my eyes had grown weak with worry and my soul was daily in bitterness; sickness and misery surrounded me; derision was on my face, and my bread was transformed into conflict. . . .' (1QH 5 : 32-35). The opposition is even physical : 'All the foundations of my body were maltreated; my bones fell apart, my shoulders rose aloft like a ship in a fierce storm, and a tempest swallowed me up because of their destructive sins' (1QH 7 : 4-5). What was already alluded to in the earlier confession of opposition within is here explicit : it is connected with bodily maltreatment and suffering resulting in prolonged illness.

But amid this opposition the Teacher of Righteousness experiences assistance : 'I praise you, Lord, for supporting me with your strength and for sending down upon me your holy spirit', he says immediately after the above confession (1QH 7 : 6). 'Your action to the poor has been wonderful' (1QH 7 : 15-16); he has been refined as silver in a furnace. He confesses : 'My God, you convert tempest into calm, and have brought the soul of the poor into safety, rescued him (as a shepherd from the jaws) of lions' (1QH 7 : 18-19). In the attacks he gains the redeeming knowledge 'that there is hope for those who turn back from sin and evil-doing' (1QH 6 : 6).

Through the whole tale of the attacks on and opposition to the Teacher runs a passionate fury against his opponents; they are horned vipers; like snakes, they have designs on his life. Apocalyptic ideas of annihilation in battle and of their destruction in a fiery judgment come easily to him.

The Teacher of Righteousness is a man of deep humility and exalted consciousness of a mission based on a powerful religious experience, full of devotion to God's mysteries and commandments, full of warm affection for his community, full also of irreconcilable hatred for his opponents. He comes from a priestly, perhaps even Zadokite family. In 4QpPs 37, 2 : 15-16 we read : 'This is to be understood of the priest, the Teacher [of Righteousness whom God] ordained to build up for him the community [of truth]'. It is in virtue of prophetic authority, realized through knowledge of God's mysteries, that he builds up the community. In 1QpHab 2 : 6-9 there is question of those who violate the alliance, 'Who do not believe it when they hear everything which will come upon the last generation, from the mouth of the priest whom God has given to the community to interpret all the sayings of his servants the prophets'; and in 1QpHab 7 : 4-5 we read : to him has 'God made known all the secrets of the saying of the prophets'. Thereby he is characterized as the last of the prophets; the reason for this is to be found in his consciousness of his mission : he is the touchstone of salvation or damnation.

II

The name of this Teacher of Righteousness and the period of Jewish history in which he lived remain, now as before, open questions;[21] but his personality is coming more sharply into focus. We see a man who is hemmed about with conflict and persecuted for the sake of his doctrine and the attitude this compels him to adopt towards contemporary issues;[22] who founded an order of brethren and gave it a rule, a doctrine and a way of life; who may well be the architect of the much discussed buildings of the

[21] Cf. M. Burrows, *More Light on the Dead Sea Scrolls*, New York, 1958; also E. Stauffer, *Jerusalem und Rom*, Bern-München, 1957; H. Bardtke, *op. cit.*, pp. 184-98; G. Jeremias, *op. cit.*, pp. 64-78.

[22] Cf. the discussion in the works of Burrows and Bardtke mentioned in the previous note. It focuses especially on the question of the crucifixion of the Teacher of Righteousness; see also E. Stauffer, *op. cit.*, pp. 128-32, and J. M. Allegro. The arguments brought to prove the crucifixion of the Teacher are unconvincing and remain hypothetical. All that is certain is distress and persecution.

monastic settlement at Qumran;[23] who knows that all mankind is fallen and guilty, and who is made herald and minstrel of the mercy and grace of a saving God on which his life is based. These are the determining elements of his doctrine.

In the Hymns of Thanksgiving man's justice and God's mercy are directly linked. He bears witness: 'Only through your goodness can a man be just' (1QH 13: 16-17). For him man is 'guilty of infidelity from his mother's womb till old age. And I, for my part, have recognized that man has no justice and that the son of man is ever imperfect' (1QH 4: 29-31). This recognition leads him to seek refuge in God's mercy, through which he is raised up: 'for I rely on the favour and the fullness of the mercy you have shown, for you forgive sins, to cleanse man from guilt by your justice' (1QH 4: 36-37). It is this recognition which gives him his significance as Teacher of his order: 'your justice has set me up to further your alliance, and I rely on your truth . . . you made me a father to the sons of your mercy (1QH 7: 19-20); the Teacher styles himself father, as was customary in Israel;[24] what the sons learn from their father is: 'no man can subsist in the face of your anger, but you lead all the sons of your truth to forgiveness in your sight; you cleanse them from their sins through your great goodness and the fullness of your pity, to bring them into your presence for all eternity' (1QH 7: 29-31). So the Teacher of Righteousness knows that men may be just before their fellow-men, but are not just in God's sight: 'I know I rejoice in forgiveness and mourn freely my former sins. And I have recognized that all hope is in the proofs of your favour, and all expectation in the fullness of your strength, for no man can be just at your tribunal, nor (appeal against) your judgment. One man may be just before another, and one spirit the peer of another, but no strength equals your might. . . .' (1QH 9: 13-17). If the Hodayoth really are the meditation-book—which is the view supported by Hans Bardtke—then these sayings are not only significant for individuals, but determine the life of a community, 'a typical life

[23] Cf. especially H. Bardtke, *op. cit.*, pp. 25-82.

[24] Cf. W. Grundmann, 'Die *Nēpioi* in der urchristlichen Paränese', *NTS* 5 (1958-1959), pp. 188-205, especially 196-201.

of prayer in God's sight', 'a continuous exercising and practising of will and spirit in life and doctrine'.[25]

Various formulations contained in liturgico-hymnic sayings of the Rule of the Community confirm this conclusion. 'Indeed my own justification is God's work, and in his hands lie my blameless way of life and my heart's eloquence; through his justice have my sins been wiped out' (1QS 11 : 2-3). In another passage : '. . . if my sinful flesh brings me low, through God's justice will my justification endure for ever . . . his pity has brought me to himself, and the proofs of his favour have brought my justification. Through the justice of his truth has he made me just; he will forgive my sins in the fullness of his goodness, in his justice make me clean from the uncleanness of men and from the sins of the sons of men, to praise God for his justice' (1QS 11 : 12-15). In all these passages it is clear that the justice which man possesses in God's sight is beyond his own powers to gain; it is a gift from God's goodness and favour, his mercy and grace.

How does this relate to the undeniable fact that the brotherhood of Qumran received from the Teacher of Righteousness a rule in which a very strict interpretation of the Torah is given, and a conscientious attitude towards the Torah is encouraged and put into practice? In the Qumran Commentary on Habakkuk the passage of Habakkuk 2 : 4 (used often by Paul too) is interpreted : 'This means all who accomplish the Law in the House of Judah, [and] whom God will rescue because of their suffering and their fidelity to the Teacher of Righteousness' (1QpHab 8 : 1-3). Fidelity to the Teacher of Righteousness and accomplishment of the Law are put side by side. Salvation is won by faithful adherence to his person and teaching, by the suffering which the Teacher's followers endure, probably because of this fidelity, and by accomplishment of the Torah. To us it seems that the Teacher of Righteousness, in renewing the alliance of God with Israel for that remnant of Israel which gathers in his order as in an eschatological community, returns to the very core of the Old Testament conception of the alliance; for he renews the

[25] H. Bardtke, 'Das "Ich" des Meisters in den Hodajoth von Qumran', pp. 103f.

order of the alliance : election and alliance are acts of God's grace and free will, but they oblige the elect to observe the treaty of alliance given in the Torah; God's goodness makes the fallen and sinful men of Israel just through the renewal of the spirit of truth in them. This spirit overcomes the spirit of falsehood to whom they were subject; for this reason they are obliged to observe the Torah in the strict way in which the Teacher of Righteousness interprets it to them.

The attitude of Qumran, founded as it is on Old Testament bases, has its effect beyond their circle. In the Apocalypse of IV Ezra, conceived after the destruction of Jerusalem, we find the sentence : 'In truth, no man born of woman is without sin, no man lives without fault. For your justice and goodness, Lord, are revealed by your pardoning those who have a treasury of good works' (9 : 35f.). The author agrees with the Pharisees that : 'The just whose many good works are stored up with you receive their reward because of their own works'; but he knows : 'Precisely because we have no works of justice, will you, when it is your good pleasure to show us your mercy, receive the title of the merciful' (9 : 32f.). It is related of Rabbi Eliezer ben Hyrcanus at the end of the first century A.D. that he continually used and drummed in upon his pupils the sentence of Qoheleth 7 : 20 : 'No man on earth is just enough to do only good and not commit sin'—a confession which he applied even to the patriarchs.[26] It is related of Rabbi Shemaia, president of the synagogue, that he taught as early as the first century B.C. : 'Our father Abraham took possession of this world and the world to come only through the merit of the faith by which he believed in Yahweh, as it is written : 'He believed in Yahweh and he accounted it as justice to him' (Mekhiltha Exodus 14 : 14 [40b]).[27] The context in the tannaitic commentary from which the sentence is taken shows what significance faith had in rabbinic theology; there also we find the reference to Habakkuk 2 : 4 : 'It is this faith which will enable the Israelites to take possession of the land. It is referring to this faith that scripture says : "The

[26] Cf. H. J. Schoeps, *op. cit.*, pp. 210f.
[27] Cf. Strack-Billerbeck, *op. cit.*, vol. III, pp. 199f.

just man will live by his faith" (Hab 2 : 4).' This high estimation
of faith is shared by the whole of Hellenistic Judaism, and indeed
perhaps others too. For Philo faith is the queen of virtues (*De
Abrahamo*, II, 39). Rabbinic theology distinguishes justice
founded on faith and on the Law; they stand side by side (cf.
Midrash of Ps. 27, 13 and Ps. 94, 17), without possibility of
being played off against each other. Through faith one belongs
to the alliance; in the fulfilment of the Law one attests this
belonging. The same situation is to be seen in the Epistle of
James, though of course with the interpretation of Law which
is peculiar to this text of scripture applied to the Law of love
(cf. James 2 : 8-26).

III

The state of affairs which we have presented, and above all
the doctrine of the Teacher of Righteousness, compel us to direct
our attention to the question of Paul's precise meaning when he
speaks of 'justice of God from faith', which he defines more
precisely as 'justice outside the Law' (Rom 1 : 17; 3 : 21).
Albrecht Oepke has shown, in his important study on the history
of the concept,[28] that 'justice of God' is a Jewish formula which
Paul adopted while radically altering its sense. Justice of God
became in Judaism a concept which had no relation to the
attitude of God, but is rather connected with the activity of those
who accomplish it on earth. Justice of God meant 'man's justice
as recognized by God'. This is how the concept is understood in
the *Testament of the XII Patriarchs*, a document very close to
Qumran Theology, in which, no less than in Paul, we find the
expression *dikaiosunē tou theou* (Test. Dan 6 : 10).[29] Paul calls
this justice 'my own justice from the Law', and contrasts it with
'justice through faith in Christ, justice from God on the grounds
of faith' (Phil 3 : 9). The second expression clarifies the first.

The formulation 'justice of God' is itself used, and perhaps
coined, in Qumran. It is attested in 1QS 11 : 12; in 1QS 11 :
3, 5, 14, 15 there is mention in connection with God of 'his'
justice; in the Hymns the Teacher of Righteousness calls the

[28] Cf. A. Oepke, *op. cit.*   [29] Cf. A. Oepke, *op. cit.*, p. 262.

justice of God his own by speaking of 'your' justice (1QH 4 : 37; 7 : 19). Here, as we have already shown, the Teacher of Righteousness, as well as the pious of Qumran, are thinking of God's attitude as shown in his fidelity to his covenant, for they are familiar with Old Testament thought about God's attitude to the people of his alliance. This is especially clear in 1QS 9 : 14, where 'his true justice' is spoken of, and in 1QH 7 : 19f. with the parallelism between justice and truth (in the sense of fidelity or reliability) and with express reference to God's alliance.

For Paul, too, the 'justice from God on the grounds of faith', of which he speaks in Phil 3 : 9, is a pre-Christian reality. This is shown by his speaking of God's justice without the Law as of something 'attested by the Law and the Prophets . . . justice of God through faith in Christ for all believers' (Rom 3 : 21f.). This Paul discerns in Abraham (Rom 4) whom he entitles their father, in complete agreement with Jewish theology, as we have already seen. Here Gen 15 : 6 has the same significance for him as for the rabbis. He describes Abraham's faith thus : In God who had promised to make him father of many peoples 'he believed as in one who gives life to the dead, calls into being what does not yet exist' (Rom 4 : 17). So with his teaching on justice by faith Paul consciously returns to the Old Testament reality. But, unlike the Rabbis, the Teacher of Righteousness and (in a way to be more accurately defined later) the Epistle of James, he does not connect justice by faith with justice by the Law; rather he contrasts them, as mutually exclusive. This leads him, for example, to alter the quotation from Habakkuk—cf. Rom 1 : 17; Gal 3 : 11—from 'the just will live by faith' to 'he who through faith is just shall live'.

What factor determines this expression? The passage of Philippians which we have mentioned, where he contrasts his own justice from the Law with justice from God on the grounds of faith, comes in a context where Paul is led to speak of the significance of the event on the road to Damascus. For Paul the essence of Damascus consists in the encounter with Christ, who comes to him and enables him to rank himself as the last of the witnesses to the resurrection (1 Cor 15 : 1-11; 9 : 1).

4/112

What Damascus means for Paul as an encounter with Christ can be understood if one considers the two formulae which he contrasts in 1 Cor 12 : 3; 'No one who speaks in the spirit of God says "Jesus is accursed", and no one can say "Jesus is Lord" without the holy spirit'. The formula 'Jesus is Lord' is the primitive Christian confession of Jesus Christ's overlordship, which was probably called out at baptism as a proclamation over the neophyte, and taken up by him as an acclamation. Paul had battled against the overlordship of Jesus Christ. The formula 'Jesus is accursed' has the character of an abjuration; most probably Paul had demanded this abjuration from the Christians who professed Jesus' overlordship, for to him Christ is accursed, according to the sentence of the Torah : 'Accursed is he who hangs on the tree' (Gal 3 : 13). The scandal presented to Judaism by primitive Christianity consisted in the affirmation and profession of the overlordship of one whom the Jewish Sanhedrin, with the support of the Roman power, had had hung up on the cross, the gallows of the ancient world. That a man executed by crucifixion as Messiah should be granted the Kyrios-title used in the Greek bible[30] is insupportable for a man like Paul, 'a scandal to the Jews' (1 Cor 1 : 23), a curse according to the Law. Paul's experience on the road to Damascus consists in his being converted from the formula of abjuration to the formula of confession 'Jesus is Lord', by experiencing Jesus' overlordship in himself. But this does not alter the fact that the crucified Christ is accursed; only he is accursed no longer for himself but 'for our sakes' (Gal 3 : 13).

But what power is let loose, in this meeting with Christ on the road to Damascus, which converts Paul from 'Jesus is accursed' to 'Jesus is Lord', and makes him confess 'accursed for our sakes'? Paul leaves no shadow of doubt : it was not as one condemned by the Law that the Lord Jesus met him before Damascus. In Philippians he emphasizes, as he enumerates his

[30] The early Christian confessional formula 'God the Father and the Lord Jesus Christ' is a development of the formula in the Septuagint 'God the Lord *(Theos ho Kurios)'* and means : He whose Lord is Jesus has God for father. The application of Joel 3 : 5 to Jesus (cf. Acts 2 : 21; Rom 10 : 13) leads to the Christian community being entitled 'Those who invoke the name of the Lord' (cf. Acts 9 : 14, 21; 22 : 16; 1 Cor 1 : 2).

Lincoln Christian College

privileges as a Jew: 'according to the Law a Pharisee, according to zeal a persecutor of the community, according to justice founded on the Law faultless' (Phil 3 : 6). Similarly in Galatians : 'You have heard of my former way of life in Judaism, that I furiously persecuted and plundered God's community, and progressed further in Judaism than many of my contemporaries. for my zeal for our ancestral traditions was extreme' (Gal 1 : 13f.). This makes it clear that Paul was one of those Jews who held themselves above reproach in their fidelity to the Law, 'according to justice founded on the Law faultless'; he stands at the head of his contemporaries as far as his reliability as a Jew is concerned; the proof is his persecution of the Christian community, as a part of his fulfilment of the Law; for the Law prescribes the destruction of heretics, and the claim that the crucified Jesus is the promised Messiah is an affront and mockery to Jewish hope. Persecution of the community is a proof of his zeal for ancestral traditions, and attests his progress in Judaism.

In this connection the concept of 'zeal' has especial importance. Since the time of the Maccabees it had become a living reality again, orientated towards the figure of the priest Phinehas in Numbers 25.[31] Phinehas served as model for the priest Mattathias, the initiator of the Maccabean movement (1 Macc 2 : 26, 54; also the whole chapter 1 Macc 2, further Sirach 45 : 23-26; cf., also 1 Chr 9 : 20; Ps 106 : 29ff.). Paul is a zealot of the same kind as Phinehas. He strides forward, when the sanhedrin's hands have been bound by Roman religious policy and the delaying attitude of the Pharisees (cf. Acts 5 : 34-40), to spontaneous revenge on Jesus' followers, whose confession of the crucified Messiah he considers a sacrilegious blasphemy (cf. Gal 1 : 13f.; Phil 3 : 6; Acts 22 : 3-5; 1 Cor 1 : 23; Gal 3 : 13). His encounter with the glorified Christ overcomes by means of Jesus' own life the form of devotion shown in this zeal; so we read in 1 Cor 13 : 4 : love is not envious.

This means that precisely his most powerful evidence, zeal for God's Law, is revealed by the appearance of our Lord before

---

[31] Cf. M. Hengel, *Die Zeloten. Untersuchungen zur jüdischen Freiheitsbewegung in der Zeit von Herodes I bis 70 nach Christus*, Leiden-Köln, 1961, esp. pp. 151-234.

Damascus as enmity to God's community. His greatest zeal constitutes his deepest sin, his fulfilment of the Law constitutes his enmity to God. Paul is confronted with this situation before Damascus and puts to himself the question: Jesus Christ or the Law? From this experience of his springs the statement 'The end of the Law is Christ, for the justification of every believer' (Rom 10: 4). Whatever conceivable presuppositions this statement may have had in Jewish theology,[32] in Paul's case the experience before Damascus is decisive. That Christ is the end of the Law means not only that he puts a term to the validity of the Law, but also, and above all, that he takes the place of the Law. What the Law was for the Pharisaic Jew Saul-Paul, so is Christ for Paul the Christian. The Epistle to the Philippians bears witness that he gives up his whole proud past 'for the sake of the greater knowledge of my Lord Jesus Christ'; he considers it worthless, 'in order to win Christ and be found in him' (3: 8f.). Hence inevitably justice from faith in Christ is contrasted with justice from the Law.

This brings us to a crux of our consideration. In the First Epistle to the Corinthians Paul writes: 'Through God you are in Jesus Christ, who has been made for us God's wisdom and justice and rescue and salvation; so, as it is written, let him who wants to pride himself, pride himself in the Lord' (1 Cor 1: 30-1). Here it is made clear that the justice which comes from God is Jesus Christ; man wins justice by incorporation into Christ. First let us notice the remark: 'Christ has been made for us God's wisdom.' It may be reasonably assumed that Paul, during his stay in Damascus, had connections with those people from Qumran who—according to the document entitled 'The community of the new alliance in Damascus'—had found refuge in Damascus at about the beginning of our era.[33] They could have provided the occasion of his questions about justice, after his blameless justice according to the Law had been revealed to him

[32] Cf. H. J. Schoeps, *op. cit.*, pp. 177-83.

[33] Many scholars of course consider Damascus to be a symbolic expression for Qumran as a place of exile. But if Damascus was the refuge of people persecuted in Palestine it would account not only for the drift to Qumran but also for the unexplained appearance of Stephen's party in Damascus when they had been expelled from Jerusalen (Acts 8: 1, 4; 9: 2).

as enmity to God. But—and this is the novelty: Paul connects the justice of God, gift of grace to all believers, with Jesus Christ, who before Damascus had overcome him and become his Lord. Of him Paul confesses: 'Through the Law I am dead to the Law, to live to God. I am crucified with Christ. I live no more as myself, rather Christ lives in me; but in so far as I live in the flesh I live in faith in God's son, who has loved me and delivered himself up for me' (Gal 2 : 19-20). Justice of God is God's gift, bestowed on men in personal union with Jesus Christ. Thus, clearly, what is specific in the Christian faith is not original thoughts and ideas unattested elsewhere in the history of religions, nor is it a new theological system; there exist possible starting-points for this outside the Christian faith. What is specific is concerned with a person, the person of Jesus Christ. The factor which distinguishes the Christian faith from the rich and varied world of religion in antiquity, and which gives it a conquering strength, is Jesus Christ. For this reason Paul centres the whole religious world of ideas of Jewish and Hellenistic origin, as far as he uses it, strictly upon Jesus Christ and his overlordship. From him they receive their Christian content. Thoughts and concepts which lie ready outside Christianity, are somehow baptized. But what is the ground for this concentration on the person of Jesus Christ? In his confession in Galatians 2 : 20 Paul says: ' . . . Who has loved me and has delivered himself up for me'. It is the love of Jesus Christ, revealed above all in his offering of himself; but in this love of Jesus Christ is revealed God's love, so that Jesus Christ in his love becomes the representation of the reconciliatory power of God's love; cf. 2 Cor 5 : 14-19; Rom 5 : 5-11; 8 : 35, 38-39.

In the sentence of Paul which we have used are contained some expressions which the position we have established enables us to put in their proper context. First: Damascus is for Paul an apparition of the risen Lord which was granted to him and constitutes him apostle. 'Am I not an apostle? Have I not seen the Lord?' he asks his opponents (1 Cor 9 : 1). Hence he ranks himself among the witnesses to the resurrection, though as the last and least among the apostles, not worthy to be called apostle because of his persecution of the community (1 Cor 15 : 3-9). But the apparition to him of the risen Lord is an expression of grace, and makes him a 'figure of grace' (Paul Tillich). 'Through God's grace am I what I am, and his grace has not been wasted on me, for I have worked more than all of them, not I but the grace of God with me' (1 Cor 15 : 10). He lives from this grace of God; he hears the voice of God as he begs for the removal of that sting of the flesh which ever and again overthrows him : 'Let my grace be sufficient, for my power is perfected in weakness' (2 Cor 12 : 9). Grace determines his existence as an effective and uplifting force; the overpowering force of grace has become the centre of his theological thought; it meets him in the 'figure of grace', Jesus Christ.[34] Grace excludes self-praise, which had been characteristic of his life under the Law. In as much as man praises himself for his fulfilment of the Law, man praises himself for himself and his own achievement; the place of this self-praise is taken by that other praise which is based on the Lord (1 Cor 1 : 31). As one who praises himself for his own achievement Paul remained turned in upon himself and lived for himself. Through the revelation of Christ his life has gained a new centre; he lives no longer for himself, but for Christ, his Lord (Rom 14 : 79; 2 Cor 5 : 14f.). In living for the Lord he lives for God, for Christ sets men free from a life lived for themselves for a life lived for God (Rom 6 : 10f.).[35]

When Paul ranks himself among the witnesses of the resurrection and calls himself apostle in company with the other apostles, he gives himself a place in the story of Christ. At the same time he emphasizes his independence of a human call and of human instruction, and his immediate contact with the Lord Christ. He calls himself apostle 'not from men or through a man, but through Jesus Christ and God the Father who raised him from the dead' (Gal 1 : 1). He stresses : 'I would have you know, brethren, the gospel I preach is not according to human fashion,

---

[34] Cf. W. Grundmann, 'Die Ubermacht der Gnade. Eine Studie zur Theologie des Paulus', *NT* 2 (1957), pp. 50-72; O. Glombitza, 'Gnade—das entscheidende Wort. Erwägungen zu 1 Kor 15 : 1-11', *NT* 2 (1958), pp. 281-90.

[35] Cf. R. Bultmann, *TWNT*, vol. III, pp. 646-54; *Theology of the New Testament*, London, 1965.

since I also did not receive it from men or by instruction in it, but through the revelation of Jesus Christ' (Gal 1 : 11f.). The independence which results from his immediate contact with Christ has its effect in his message. Paul is aware of its distinctiveness with respect to the original apostolic witness to the event of Christ. This consists in a thorough and consistent reflection on the situation which arises from Jesus' crucifixion and resurrection; he regards it as the hidden but effective irruption of the world to come. This is why he relates Jesus Christ as the second Adam to the first Adam, and thereby makes clear that, with the crucifixion and resurrection of Jesus, the decisive turning point in the history of mankind, which affects all mankind, has occurred. To this all men are brought into relation under Christ's overlordship. This thorough and consequent thinking over of the situation created through Christ and of its universal character gives his preaching of the gospel, his missionary activity and his theological thinking a unique place in the history of Christianity. He himself realizes it to be a revelation of Jesus Christ, so that he can set himself beside the original apostles as an instrument of revelation, without disputing their office of witnesses.

Part of this change from one age to another lies in the fact that the Law loses its validity and Christ takes its place, so that there no longer exists a justice in God's sight which can be gained by the works prescribed by the Law; the only justice now is from faith in Jesus Christ. This faith is an answer to the call of Jesus Christ. Paul the apostle describes himself as 'called to be apostle' (Rom 1 : 1); he says in the great confession of Galatians : 'When it was pleasing to him who had set me apart from the womb of my mother and called me by his grace, when it was pleasing to him to reveal his son to me so that I should proclaim his message among the gentiles, then I did not proceed to parley with flesh and blood' (Gal 1 : 15-16). He listens to the call which comes to him and obeys it; that is the 'obedience of faith' in which he received 'grace and the task of being, for his name, an apostle among all nations' (Rom 1 : 5). So faith is not a common credulity, not one work and merit among other works and merits, as one work and merit can in Jewish theology have a character whis is especially stressed; faith is, in the present dispensation, clearly related to God who calls men through Jesus Christ, and is the answer to this call; this call calls into being what does not yet exist, and is thus God's word of creation; it calls the dead to life, and is thus God's word of resurrection; it acquits the sinner, and is thus the word of God's justification (Rom 4 : 17, 21, 25);[36] the answer to this call is faith, which gives God the glory, for faith is trust in God that he accomplishes what he promises; this is why man is justified in God's sight by believing.

Justification of sinners by faith without works of the Law (Rom 3 : 28) is based upon Jesus' cross and resurrection. Paul adopts the sentence, probably primitive in Christianity and formulated before him : 'He was delivered up for our sins and raised up for our justification' (Rom 4 : 25). On the cross of Jesus Christ the sins of man are condemned and sinful man judged; because the Law reveals and condemns sins (cf. Rom 3 : 20; 4 : 15; 5 : 13 etc.) therefore is condemnation of sin and judgment of the sinner the curse of the Law; Paul says : 'Christ has ransomed us from the curse of the Law by becoming accursed for our sakes' (Gal 3 : 13). Through Christ taking the place of men, sin is condemned and the sinner judged once and for all (Rom 3 : 25-26); by the crucified Christ rising again and being glorified he opens the freedom of a new existence for God to those men whose judgment he took upon himself. For Paul belief in Christ means : he has taken away my sins and allowed himself to be condemned on my behalf, so that I live a new life under his overlordship, free from the Law which condemned me, free from the sin which dominated me, free from death to which I was subject. For, if a man cries out : 'Wretch that I am, who will free me from such a death of my corrupt body?', Paul answers 'The Law of the spirit which is life in Christ has freed you from the Law of sin and of death' (Rom 7 : 24; 8 : 2). For such a faith God shows 'that he himself is just and that he

---

[36] Cf. 2 Cor 4 : 6 with its unmistakable reference to the event on the Damascus road, where word of creation and word of justification are so closely connected with each other.

justifies him who has faith in Jesus *(ek pisteōs Iēsou)*' (Rom 3 :
26). God is just because he condemns sin on Christ's cross; God
justifies because he gives justice to man anew, and by his power
incorporates him into the overlordship of Christ. This faith which
accepts the justice of God is faith in Jesus Christ, because he
merited this gift of God to men. So the genitive in *pistis Iēsou
Christou* is an objective genitive. This is confirmed by Gal 2 : 16 :
'we have believed in Christ Jesus in order to be justified by faith
in Christ *(ek pisteōs Christou)*.' The question is, however,
whether the genitive has not two senses, in so far as it has Christ's
faith in view, and so must be understood also as a subjective
genitive.[37] Paul speaks of the obedience of Jesus Christ, the
cause of our justification (Rom 5 : 19; cf. also Phil 2 : 8). But
Jesus' obedience is no other than his faith. In this case faith in
Jesus Christ is the imitation of Jesus' faith. For in faith man
lives from God's gift and from the grace which reaches him in
the call through the gospel, which provokes faith and to which
faith is the answer.

God's call in Jesus Christ inserts man into a new existence
which Paul expresses with his characteristic phrase, 'in Christ'.
We heard from Paul : 'Through God you are in Christ, whom
God has made justice for us. . . .' 'In Christ', i.e. the world to
come, which succeeds the present world and is hidden, but present
and effective in it since the resurrection of Jesus Christ. In order
to represent to ourselves what Paul means by 'in Christ' the best
image is one drawn from physics, that of a field of force, for
example an electro-magnetic field. G. R. Heyer has transferred
this concept to the psyche, and has ascertained that the psyche
no less than the external world is organized as a field of force.[38]
To be in Christ means to be in Jesus Christ's field of force. In
his capacity as head of the body Jesus Christ incorporates
organically into his field of force those who get there and makes
them members of his body (cf. 1 Cor 12 : 4-31; Rom 12 : 4-8).
Being 'in Christ' and the saying about the love of Christ belong

[37] Cf. H. W. Schmidt, *Der Brief des Paulus an die Römer*, Berlin, 1963,
esp. pp. 71f.
[38] G. R. Heyer, *Vom Kraftfeld der Seele. Zwei Abhandlungen zur
Tiefenpsychologie*, 1949.

together and are founded upon the expression 'Christ the second Adam'.[39] They define the existence of those who are justified by faith as existence in Christ. The invisible power of this field of force is the Holy Spirit. We had been told: 'No one can say "Jesus is Lord" without the Holy Spirit.' In Qumran too they know that the man who is justified by grace receives the Holy Spirit. The member of the order in Qumran is freed from the spirit of lies and of error, and receives the spirit of truth, the holy spirit. This is abundantly attested in the Rule of the Community and in the Hodayoth. The opinion that in Jewish theology the gifts of the Holy Spirit are an eschatological promise, and that post-pentecostal Christianity is the first to become aware of the reception of the Holy Spirit, cannot be maintained in this form. At least the Qumran community, which understood itself as the eschatological remnant of Israel, knows that it is endowed with God's holy spirit. This is the reason why prophecy occurs in the community. Once again Paul's originality lies where we have already pinpointed it: in the connection of the Holy Spirit with the person of Jesus Christ. For Paul the Holy Spirit is 'Christ in us', as the phenomenon which determines man's personal life. 'Now I live no more as myself, but Christ lives in me' (Gal 2: 20). What is in Gal a personal confession is expressed as a general principle in Rom 8: 9-11; there Paul interchanges and so inter-prets: Spirit of God, Spirit of Christ, Christ in us, Spirit of him whom Christ raises from the dead, his Spirit dwelling in us. This means that for Paul the holy Spirit is the glorified Lord: 'The Lord is the Spirit, and where the Spirit of the Lord is, there is freedom to be found' (2 Cor 3: 17).

The question before us now is: if God's call grafts man into 'existence in Christ', brings him into Jesus Christ's field of force, what is it precisely that occurs then, and how? Paul says: through baptism, which inaugurates incorporation in Christ, in that it grafts man into Christ, into union with Christ. 'Christ for me' in death and resurrection becomes my union with Christ, realized both in my being in Christ and in Christ's being in me.

[39] A. Oepke, *TWNT*, vol. II, pp. 534-9; F. Neugebauer, *In Christus. Eine Untersuchung zum paulinischen Glaubensverständnis*, Göttingen, 1961.

By receiving baptism the Christian recognizes his condemnation on the cross of Jesus Christ and dies the death demanded of the sinner by the Law, dying at the same time to the Law, since the Law has no dominion over the dead (Rom 7: 1-6). Hence Paul can say: 'Through the Law am I dead to the Law, to live to God. I am crucified with Christ' (Gal 2: 19). He who receives baptism has died with Christ, and at the same time has risen with him and has grown together with him (Rom 6: 3-11). Paul says: 'If someone is in Christ he is a new creation' (2 Cor 5: 17), and thereby with the expression 'new creation' takes up a concept of the Jewish theology of proselytism;[40] he also refers thereby to the event which is Christ. The new creation is really a creation into union with Christ. The man who dies with Christ rises to a new existence with him.[41] This new existence, a life for God in freedom from sin (Rom 6, 11ff.), by belonging to the world to come and by being hidden with it in the present world, is a suffering with Christ. Glorification with him is still to come and has its precondition in suffering with him (Rom 8: 17b); it is realized in Christ's parousia, in which he comes out from concealment with his own (cf. Col 3: 1-4). Christ shares the title of son with his own; with him they are sons of God (Rom 8: 14f.), and shall be co-heirs with him (Rom 8: 17). This means: the new existence of the believer is realized as existence with Christ, for God has ordained them to become 'formed into the image of his son, so that he be the first-born among many brethren'; to this end have they been called and acquitted (Rom 8: 29; also Phil 3: 21), so justification begins a process which is achieved in being formed with Christ into his image, and is completed in a common glorification (cf. also 2 Cor 3: 18). This glorification is described by Paul simply as eternal 'union with Christ' (cf. Phil 1: 23; 1 Thess 4: 17).

[40] Cf. K. H. Rengstorf, *TWNT*, vol. I, pp. 664-6; Strack-Billerbeck, *op. cit.*, vol. III, pp. 340f.; E. Sjöberg, 'Wiedergeburt und Neuschöpfung im palästinischen Judentum', *Studia Theologica* 4 (1950), pp. 44-85.

[41] E. Lohmeyer, *'Sun Christō'* in *Festgabe für A. Deissmann*, 1927, pp. 218-57; J. Dupont, *'Sun Christō'. L'union avec le Christ suivant St Paul*, Bruges, 1952; W. Grundmann, *TWNT*, vol. VII, pp. 766-98; 'Überlieferung und Eigenaussage im eschatologischen Denken des Apostels Paulus', *NTS* 8 (1961-1962), pp. 12-26.

The choice of the concept 'with Christ *(sun Christō)*' gives food for thought. Whereas the Greek Old Testament prefers *meta* with the genitive for statements with profound theological implications, Paul uses *sun* with the dative. This is doubtless the result of his development of 'with Christ' in a series of verbs compounded with *sun-*. The Greek language contains such verbs. If the choice is indeed conditioned by the verbs which develop the concept, then the *sun Christō* is conceived as the new form of existence of believers which is accomplished in the one process expressed by means of verbs, adjectives and nouns compounded with *sun-*. This form of existence is one of companionship with Christ into which man is grafted, and which outlasts his earthly death. The event whose accomplishment is expressed by these verbs, adjectives and nouns consists in man's being taken into companionship with Christ by the event which is Christ.

This is a process without parallel in the history of religions; it has shadowy analogies in the fidelity of the men of Qumran to the Teacher of Righteousness and in the similarity in Hellenism between the fate of the mystery God and that of his initiates; but it goes further than them all. This is clear from the way the man of antiquity answered the question of death. According to the view common in antiquity death is the entry into Hades, imagined as a kingdom of shadows; existence after death is seen as an unenviable shadow-life. Here Greeks and Israelites are in complete agreement (cf. Is 14 : 9; Ps 6 : 6). Greek philosophical religion develops the idea of the immortal soul, and on this basis arrives at the conviction of the worthlessness of earthly corporeal existence; seeing in the body only the prison of the soul. This perspective comes from Orphism : Plato has Socrates develop this most fully in the *Phaedo*, Socrates' farewell conversation with his disciples just before his death. Near Eastern vegetation-cults use natural generation and decay to arrive at the conception of dying and rising Gods, in whose fate their initiates share. Persian religion, made a historical religion by Zarathustra, speaks of a resurrection of the soldiers in the armies of light and of darkness for the final struggle between these two powers. In Israel, and especially in Pharisaic circles, the effect of this Persian notion was to centre faith upon the resurrection of the just or of the dead (Is 26 : 19—one of the earliest instances). Faith in the resurrection can be connected to an Old Testament notion which grew out of the pre-suppositions of the Old Testament faith in God itself : being taken up to Yahweh, as is recounted of Enoch (Gen 5 : 24) and Elijah (2 Kings 2 : 11), and as is transferred in older Jewish theology also to Abraham, Moses and others. This found its clearest expression in Ps 16, which is applied, in Acts 2 : 25-31 and 13 : 35, to the resurrection of Jesus. The author of this Psalm arrives at the conviction that the joy of his life, community of life with God, cannot be abolished by death. Expression is here given to the startling insight that God does not forsake in death those whom he has chosen for himself and joined to himself. It is found also in Ps 73 : 23-26. The New Testament links on to this point of view, not of course in the form of being snatched from death's grasp, but in the form of a passing through death and a resurrection from it, founded upon community with God. For Paul sin is a breaking away from God, and therefore leaves man on his own; sin destroys also the community of men with each other, for it is both 'ungodliness' and 'wickedness' (Rom 1 : 18); the cutting off of man is made final in death, as the choice of the concept 'to leave ones country *(ekdēmein)*' in 2 Cor 5 : 6-9 shows— being outside the community *(dēm-*, people) which is constituted by the body. Reconciliation with God through Christ creates a new community, and the love which springs from it in men's life with one another makes a new community also among men. Both elements, reconciliation to God and love for men, are affected in Christ and realized in company with him. The basis in Paul for the new existence of believers which outlasts death is not the immortal soul, or some resurrection based on a conception determined by natural categories, or some speculative apocalyptic of history; it is the community with Christ which God gives to men. Everything he says about resurrection is determined and directed by this central point, as is clear in 1 Cor 15. In Rom 8 : 29-30 we are told explicitly that justification is part of a complex of events which is completed by being made to resemble Jesus Christ.[42] A series of events is there put in order. They are based on God's providence and plan, which are directed towards the goal of being 'formed into the image of his son, so that he be the first-born among many brethren'. This plan of providence is realized in vocation and justification, which is justification by faith because it is the answer to the call of grace based on God's plan of providence. It is completed in glorification, which is identical with being formed in the image of God's son, while justification is only introduction into sonship (Rom 8 : 15).[43]

At this point, at which (as Rom 8 : 29-30 shows) justification by faith is completed, it is finally clear that the originality of this faith cannot be defined by concepts, a system or a history of the ideas; it is personal community with Jesus Christ, whom Paul sees as the initiator of a new eschatological race of men, as a second Adam. To explain it Paul can borrow themes both from Jewish theology and from Hellenistic mystery-religions. But the decisive point is this personal community. Faith justifies because it is the answer to God's call to Jesus Christ, who in his turn calls men to community with himself. It is this community with Christ which constitutes the justice of the believer.

In conclusion :   IV

1. Both the Teacher of Righteousness and Paul have a personal experience as their starting point. In both cases this experience is concerned with God's judgment and grace.

2. The Teacher of Righteousness describes, in phrases impregnated with Old Testament reminiscences, his experience of the guilt perceived through God's judgment-sentence, and becomes aware that God gives him a justification, springing from his own justice, which enables him to exist in God's sight. It binds him to faithful obedience

[42] J. Jervell. *Imago Dei. Gen 1: 26f. im Spätjudentum, in der Gnosis und in den paulinischen Briefen*, Göttingen, 1960, pp. 271-84.

[43] Cf. W. Grundmann, 'Der Geist der Sohnschaft. Eine Studie zu Römer 8 : 15 und Galater 4 : 6, zu ihrer Stellung in der paulinischen Theologie und ihren traditions-geschichtlichen Grundlagen', *Thüringer kirchliche Studien* 1 (1963), pp. 172-92.

to God's Torah. As the justice given to him is the renewal of the community of the alliance, shattered by guilt though it was, it leads him to keep the conditions of the alliance strictly and scrupulously.

3. The doctrine of the Teacher of Righteousness found little echo outside Qumran. It grows from roots in the Old Testament, and can be described as an 'extreme of serious Judaism'.[44]

4. Paul knows of a justice from faith even in the pre-Christian era, and illustrates it by Abraham; since the experience on the Damascus road he sees it as the only form of justice possible to man, and as given to man by community with Christ. Because he sinned against Christ and so against God in his zealous and blameless fulfilment of the Law, the connection made in Qumran between justice in grace and fulfilment of the law is not open to Paul. The place of the Law is taken by Christ. The place of the claims of the Law and their fulfilment is taken by existence in Christ and with Christ, in so far as justification is seen to be participation in the event which is Christ, a participation realized in love.

5. As sin is condemned and the Law superseded in the cross of Christ, so in his resurrection the new life is thrown open. Justification by faith is founded upon the situation by which Christ is for us and in our place. Faith is not human credulity but obedience to God's call to men in Christ. This call grafts men into Christ, and instals them in a life with Christ for God.

6. Paul's originality lies not in special concepts and thoughts, not in a new arrangement of them to make a new theological system, but in a strict connection with the Christ Jesus whom Paul encountered, and who henceforth determines his whole life for time and eternity. Paul acknowledges in the crucified and risen Jesus the promised messiah, whom Qumran awaited but failed to recognize.

[44] H. Braun, 'Römer 7: 7-25 und das Selbstverständnis der Qumran-Frommen', *ZTK* 56 (1959), p. 14

6

THE EPISTLE TO THE EPHESIANS IN THE LIGHT OF THE QUMRAN TEXTS*

Karl Georg Kuhn

IN order to do justice to our theme we must narrow down our selection of the problems to be dealt with. Thus we will limit ourselves to the Epistle to the Ephesians, leaving to one side the Epistle to the Colossians and the problem of the relationship between the two Epistles. The question as to whether or not the Epistle was composed by Paul and the problem regarding the address of the Epistle are not to be dealt with here either. We are concerned solely with discovering how far and in what way the Epistle to the Ephesians shows a particular relationship to the Qumran Texts as regards language, terminology, thought, and ideas—in fact with discovering whether it is likely that there is a connection in tradition between the special form of late Palestinian Judaism, which the Qumran Texts reveal to us, and the Epistle to the Ephesians. Our comparison, however does not need to limit itself solely to the Qumran Texts—indeed it must take into account further literature of Palestinian Judaism, in particular the *Book of Jubilees*, the *Testaments of the XII Patriarchs* and the Enoch literature, for not only were these last-named texts found in the library at Qumran, they are also most likely the work of the Essene community which we come across in Qumran.

Ernst Käsemann has recently laid stress on the fact that the

* Published in *NTS* 7 (1960-61) 334-46.

Epistle to the Ephesians shows a remarkable similarity to the terminology and motifs of the Qumran texts (*R.G.G.*, 3rd ed., 11, col. 517ff.). Heinrich Schlier too, in his commentary, points occasionally to parallels from the Qumran texts. These parallels are, however, much more numerous and much closer than they appear to be from Schlier's work and, moreover, the ideas and theological motifs which correspond in the two texts go much deeper. We shall attempt to illustrate this at various points in this work.

I

Let us first examine the language and style of the Epistle to the Ephesians. It has long since been observed that it is written in a Greek that shows Semitic influences, and the dissertation by Klaus Beyer (Heidelberg, 1960), which investigates the occurrence of specifically Semitic sentence-constructions in the Greek of the New Testament with special reference to conditional sentences, now shows just to what extent Semitisms appear in the Epistle to the Ephesians. From it we learn that such Semitic syntactical occurrences appear four times more frequently in the Epistle to the Ephesians than in all the remaining letters of the *corpus Paulinum*.

A major characteristic of the language and style of the Epistle to the Ephesians is the unusually long sentences without the clearly defined phrases one would expect from an author with a feeling for Greek, but made up of rather loosely joined phrases with rows of relative clauses, participle constructions, compound prepositional expressions, infinitive clauses, etc. Thus, as Schlier rightly says (p. 18),[1] the Epistle to the Ephesians is characterized by its preference for prepositional expressions, series of genitives, a wealth of synonyms and a general tendency towards plerophory as, for example, in the use of *pas* 'all'. All of these peculiarities which appear so often in the Epistle to the Ephesians are also characteristic of the Hebraic style of the Qumran Texts, of their 'liturgical', or rather hymnal, language. Thus, in the Hymns of

[1] Note especially E. Percy *Die Probleme der Kol.- und Eph.-briefe*, Lund, 1946, pp. 18f.

the Qumran Texts and in other places, we come across these long-drawn-out, loosely connected tape-worm sentences which cause difficulties to the translator as regards punctuation. Unfortunately we have not enough time at our disposal to quote examples of such sentences. However, whenever one reads through longer sections of the Qumran texts, paying particular attention to the sentence construction, one cannot fail to notice the striking similarity between a sentence such as the one we find in Eph 1 : 3-14 and the typical Hebrew sentence structure of the Qumran Texts (G. Schille, in his dissertation, *Liturgisches Gut im Epheserbrief*, Göttingen, 1953, was the first to point this out). Nowadays, as Schlier says rather vaguely on page 19, we can no longer speak of the language of the Epistle to the Ephesians as being influenced by a Jewish-Christian Gnosis. In the face of the extensive Qumran texts we must now say that the language of the Epistle to the Ephesians has been influenced specifically by *these* writings.

That this is true is shown also in detail.[2] Eph 1 : 19; 'the working of the power of his might'; Eph 3 : 7; 'the working of his power'; Eph 4 : 10; 'The power of his might', present us with an accumulation of expressions for 'the might of God' in synonymous genitive constructions. Exactly the same genitive constructions are to be found in various places in the Qumran texts. Thus we have in 1QH 4 : 32 *bkwḥ gbwrtw* 'in the might of his (i.e. God's) strength' and also in 1QH 18 : 8f.; 7 : 9f.; 15 : 4; 1QS 11 : 19f.; similarly but with other synonyms for 'might' we have 1QH 2 : 8; 1QM 11 : 5; and also Ethiopian *Henoch* 60 : 16; Greek *Henoch* 1 : 4.

This plerophory of synonymous genitive combinations is typical; it serves to express the colossal might of God which he bestows upon his community. Verbal combinations too, such as Eph 3 : 16 'to be strengthened in power' and 6 : 10 'be strengthened in the power', have exact parallels in 1QH 7 : 17

---

[2] The linguistic parallels mentioned here are dealt with in an article by a pupil of mine, Reinhard Deichgraber, which is due to be published shortly. I am indebted to him for various references and illustrations which enlarged the material I had gathered and which have been considered in this text.

and 19; 'to make strong in power' *(lhʿyz bkwḥ)*; 1QH 13 : 35 : *t]ḥzq bkwḥ* 'to become strong in might'; similarly 1QM 10 : 5. A parallel is also found between Eph 1 : 19 'the greatness of his power' and 1QH 14 : 23 'corresponding to the greatness of his power' *(kgdwl kwḥkh)*; see also 1QH 11 : 29. 1QH 3 : 34 and 1Q*19* 4 : 2 contain similar expressions.

To the plerophoric genitive combinations in Eph 1 : 5, 'the good pleasure *(eudokia)* of his will' and Eph 1 : 11; 'the decision *(boulē)* of his will', CD 3 : 15 offers the parallel *ḥpṣy rṣwnw* 'the will-expressions of his will'.

It has already been pointed out (cf. Schlier, *Kommentar*, pp. 60ff., and the literature there mentioned) that the New Testament expression *mystērion*, which is of such significance in the Epistle to the Ephesians, has a parallel in the frequent use of the word *rz* 'mystery' or of its synonym *swd* in the Qumran texts. Particularly significant, however, is the fact that phrases and idioms, which, especially in the Epistle to the Ephesians, contain the word *mystērion*, have corresponding phrases of idioms in the Qumran texts. Thus Eph 1 : 9 : 'the mystery of his will' corresponds to the phrase in 1QH 3 : 7f., *lrzy ḥpṣw* 'according to the mysteries of his (God's) will'. The expression 'to make known the mystery of his will', which in the N.T. appears *only* in Eph 1 : 9; 3 : 3; 6 : 19 and in the non-Pauline doxology Rom 16 : 26, is one that occurs frequently in the Qumran Texts: 1QpHab 7 : 4f. *hwdyʿw ʾl ʾt kwl rzy* 'to him (the Teacher of Righteousness) God has made known all secrets of. . . .'; 1QH 4 : 27f. *hwdʿtny brzy plʾkh* 'Thou (God) hast made known to me thy marvellous mysteries'; similarly 1QH 7 : 27; and the same phrase with the word *swd* 'mystery' in 1QH 10 : 4f.; 9 : 9, 16. Particularly interesting is Eph 3 : 4 : 'my insight into *(sunesis mou en)* the mystery'. Why do we have here the construction *synesis en* instead of a simple objective genitive? The reason may be one of style, for in the Greek, next to the subjective genitive *mou*, the objective genitive *tou mysteriou* would be very harsh. But we must also consider the fact that in Hebrew the verbs of revealing, including *hwdyʿ*, are usually constructed with *b* (= *en*). We find in the Qumran texts the substantive *dʿt*

'understanding, insight', which corresponds to the *synesis* of Eph
3 : 4 : 1QH 2 : 13 : *d't brzy pl'* 'understanding of the marvellous
mysteries' and 1QH 12 : 13 : *d't brzy sklkh* 'insight into the
mystery of his wisdom'.

In the Qumran texts the 'mysteries' are particularly those
of creation and God's eschatological time-table. That is why we
usually encounter the plural form, 'mysteries', whereas the Epistle
to the Ephesians speaks only of *'the* mystery'. It is *'the* mystery
of Christ', that is to say, Christology in all its fulness. Herein
lies the decisive theological difference : *what is new in Ephesians
with respect to the Qumran Texts is its Christology.*

Two further stylistic parallels should be mentioned. Whereas
the Old Testament refers to God with the adjectival phrase as being
rb ḥsd 'rich in grace' (Ps 103 : 8, etc.) the nominal expression 'the fullness, the richness of the grace (of God)' is used in
the Qumran Texts. Thus we find *rwb ḥsd* 1QS 4 : 4, 5; 1QH
11 : 28; 12 : 14; frag. 2 : 5; *hmwn ḥsdykh* 1QH 11 : 29f.;
similarly *gdwl ḥsdykh* 1QH 1 : 32; 16 : 12, and *rwb rḥmym*
1QS 4 : 3; 1QM 4 : 32; 7 : 27; 13 : 17; 18 : 14; *hmwn rḥmym*
1QH 4 : 36, 37; 6 : 9; 7 : 30, 35; 9 : 8, 34; 10 : 21; 15 : 16.
This expression so common in the Qumran texts, has its parallel
in Eph 1 : 7 : 'the richness *(to ploutos)* of his grace' and in
Eph 2 : 7 where it is strengthened by 'surpassing'. Here *to ploutos*,
corresponding to *rwb* and *hmwn* of the Qumran texts, is used
to strengthen the term 'grace', but in other passage an identical
function is fulfilled by *pas*. For example, Eph 1 : 3 : 'with all
(sorts of) blessings', 4 : 19 : 'every (type of) impurity'; and see
4 : 2, 31 (twice); 5 : 3; 6 : 18. This, too, corresponds to a similar
use of *kwl* in the Qumran Texts: e.g. 1QpHab 8 : 13 : *bkwl
ndt tm'h.*

In the Qumran texts it often happens that the enumeration
of two or more expressions that are similar, is effected by means
of *'m* 'with', e.g. 1QS 4 : 7, 8, 13; 11 : 2, 7, in order to achieve
variety of expression. In 10 : 2 we read of 'the completion of
my transformation *with* the uprightness of my heart' which is
the same as saying *'and* the uprightness'. Occasionally we also
find prepositional phrases with *b* 'in' which fulfil the purpose of

E

a final clause in this sense. Thus in 1QS 4 : 7 'and everlasting joy *in* eternal life' we could perhaps substitute '*and* eternal life'. The same would be true of 1QS 4 : 13; 1QpH 8 : 13 and CD 2 : 5. Eph 4 : 31 '*with* all malice' corresponds exactly to the first form of joining-up by means of 'with'. To this too belongs the series Eph 6 : 23 : 'peace . . . and love *with* faith', which Dibelius and Greeven also, and quite correctly, translate by '*and* faith'. Together with this we have the joining-on of the final clause by means of *en* in Eph 4 : 19 : 'unto the working of every sort of impurity *in* greed'. As the expression in Eph 5 : 3, 5 shows, this means the same as 'with greed'. The same connecting *en* would also be found in Eph 5 : 26 'the washing of water *in* word' *(tō loutrō tou hudatos* en *rēmati)* and in Eph 6 : 24 'grace *in* incorruptibility' (cf. Schlier, *Kommentar, in loc.).*

We see then that even as regards such stylistic peculiarities the Epistle to the Ephesians reveals many-sided and close connections with the language and style of the Qumran texts. At the same time it must be stressed that this close relationship cannot be explained merely by the fact that both texts, the Qumran texts on the one hand and the Epistle to the Ephesians on the other, reflect, each independently of the other, the style of the *Old Testament.* For all of the examples cited—and they are far from forming a complete list—deal with expressions and peculiarities of style which do not appear in the Old Testament in the same way and which are, however, characteristic of the Qumran texts. Thus it is difficult to avoid the conclusion that the relationship of the language and style of the Epistle to the Ephesians to that of the Qumran texts can hardly be explained except on the basis of a continuity of tradition.

II

Our second problem is that of the origin of the *paraenetic* tradition of the second main part of Ephesians (4 : 1-6 :20). Reliable investigation allows us to work on the assumption that as regards the admonitions and commandments in the paraenesis of the epistles of the N.T., we are dealing with pre-Christian traditions, partly Jewish, partly Hellenistic, which in the New Testament are more or less—indeed increasingly so—Christian-ized. The question is: where did this tradition, as found in Ephesians, originate? Here, too, I can only cite a few examples which, in my opinion, show that a part of these admonitions in the Epistle to the Ephesians comes *specifically* from the tradition of the *Essene* paraenesis as we find it in the Qumran Texts and the late-Jewish texts that are closely connected to them. I have limited myself to Eph 5 : 3-17.

Eph 5 : 3 names a group of three sins which are not to be mentioned in the Christian community: fornication, impurity, and greed (a similar group of three is also alluded to in 4 : 19 : gluttony, impurity and greed).[3] The formulation of Eph 5 : 5 shows that it is a question of three capital sins. The closest parallel to this is CD 4 : 15f., which speaks of 'the three nets of Belial' by means of which the Devil has led Israel astray: 'The first is fornication, the second gain, the third the defilement of the Holy Place'. These three appear again in *Test.Levi* 14 : 5-8. The fact that for the Essenes of the Qumran community these three sins were the worst of all makes it clear that we are dealing here specifically with an Essene tradition. For them the greatest obliga-tion was that of the preservation of priestly purity. That is why the summons to abstain from all impurity appears again and again, and why the inner circle of this order lived as celibates, while the wider circle, although they married, lived in the strictest monogamy. For the same reason fornication was for them the worst sin. And, finally, they feared defilement through dishonest possessions and gain so much that they—without any personal property—lived in a community where all possessions were the property of the community. That is why they are repeatedly warned of the dangers of riches and greed. In Eph 5 : 5 idolatry is named as the basic sin under which the three capital sins named above are subsumed. Compare *Test.Juda* 19 : 1,

[3] The expression in Eph 4 : 19, 'the working of every sort of impurity in greed', has a parallel in 1QS 4 : 10 where, in the enumeration of the effects of the 'spirit of wickedness' upon men of wickedness (or of darkness), we read, 'The paths of darkness *in the carrying out* (or in the doing) *of unclean things (b⁶bwdt tm'h)'.*

'Covetousness leads to idols'; *Test.Reuben* 4 : 6, 'fornication leads to idols'.

As regards the opposition in Eph 5 : 4 of wickedness *(aischrotēs)* and 'foolishness' *(mōrologia)* on the one hand and 'thanksgiving' *(eucharistia)* on the other hand, compare 1QS 10 : 2-4, 'foolishness *(= mōrologia*!) shall not be heard out of my mouth; malicious lies and deceit shall not be on my lips[4] . . . and atrociousness *(= aischrotēs*!) shall not be found in my mouth; rather for thanksgiving *(= eucharistia*!) will I open my mouth'. *Eutrapelia* is, in this context (i.e. Eph. 5 : 4), rather odd. For its actual meaning in Greek is, in the best sense of the word, a talent for witty speech. Yet its use *sensu malo* can here be explained by 1QS 7 : 9 where we read in the community's *Manual of Discipline* that 'anyone who says something foolish (or something silly)' will be punished[5] and, according to 1QS 7 : 14 anyone who 'indulges in raucous laughter at something silly (a joke)' shall also be punished.

In the commentaries it has already been pointed out that the phrase 'sons of disobedience *(apeitheias)*' of Eph 5 : 6 is a Semitism. Hebrew does not have a single word which corresponds exactly to *apeitheia*. In the Qumran texts the sinners are referred to as 'sons of perversity' or 'sons of darkness' or 'sons of destruction'. That one ought to have nothing to do with them, as Eph 5 : 7 tells us (cf. Eph 5 : 11), is also a constant demand in the Qumran texts; 1QS 5 : 1 : 'to keep apart from the company of the perverse', also 1QS 5 : 10f.; CD 6 : 14f : and various other passages.

The continuity of tradition between Eph 5 : 9f. and the Qumran texts is particularly clear : 'For ye were sometimes darkness but now (belonging to the community) are ye light in the Lord', (the 'in the Lord' is the Christianization of the tradition). And that means 'walk as children of light'. The antithesis 'light-darkness' is here something completely different from gnostic dualism. In the gnosis 'light-darkness' always means a substantial dualism : the substance of the divine world of light on the one side and of the earthly cosmos on the other. Here, however,

---

[4] Compare this with Eph 4 : 23.　　　[5] Compare this with Eph 4 : 29.

substance is not in question; it is rather an antithesis arising from two modes of existence, in, on the one hand, the doing of 'what is pleasing to God' and on the other hand, the anti-Christian existence of the performance of 'the works of darkness' (Eph 5 : 11). It is then an ethical dualism, a dualism of decision. This quality of decision is clearly evident in Eph 5 : 10 : 'discerning *(dokimazontes)* what is pleasing to the Lord'.

This is—not only terminologically but also in the whole thought-structure—exactly the same as the antithesis 'light-darkness' that we find in the Qumran texts. The members of the Essene community of salvation are 'sons of light', 'sons of righteousness' who 'walk in the ways of light' (1QS 3 : 20) who 'study and seek after God's will' (1QS 5 : 9) (= *dokimazontes*, Eph 5 : 10 !), who 'walk in (or : according to) his will'. And all those who do not enjoy the salvation of those received into this community, all those who are outside are 'sons of darkness, of malice', who 'walk in the ways of darkness' (1QS 3 : 21). 'All their works are in darkness' (1QM 15 : 9) and upon the blasphemer is put a curse that 'corresponds to the darkness of his works' (1QS 2 : 7).

The structure of Ephesians and that of the Qumran texts are thus similar in that in both texts the 'light-darkness' antithesis does not refer to the physical *nature* of the Heavens on the one hand and the Cosmos on the other, and thereby to the dual nature of man as body-matter on the one hand and light-soul on the other as it does throughout the gnosis, but rather to the fact that 'light' and 'darkness' are seen as the two opposing modes of *human* existence. The words refer to man's *relationship to God*, to his *personal* relationship to a *personal* God[6] who addresses himself to him; his doing of that which is pleasing to God, or his acting contrary to God's will, his sinning, his rebelliousness through the 'hardness of his heart' (Eph 4 : 18 and often in the Qumran texts).

Hence it is significant that Eph 5 : 9 refers to 'goodness and

[6] The God we encounter in the Gnosis is, on the other hand, quite different. Their God is the unattainable, the untouchable, the highest Light-being.

righteousness and truth' as 'fruit of light'[7] whereby these expressions are given an ethical content: 'to do good (towards one's neighbour)', 'to act justly', 'to practise true faithfulness'. For these demands appear—following Mi 6 : 8—again and again in the Qumran texts as the basic ethical imperatives: 1QS 1 : 5; 2 : 24-5; 4 : 5; 5 : 3-4; 5 : 25; 8 : 21 (the form of expression varies but the basic meaning intended is the same).

In Eph 5 : 11, we read: 'Have no fellowship with the works of darkness, *mallon de kai elenchete*'. What does *elenchein* mean? Let us look at the meaning of the corresponding Hebrew verb *hwkyḥ*. Both verbs mean 'to rebuke, to reprimand'. But *hwkyḥ* has, in the Qumran texts, a particularly significant meaning: it is the duty of each member of the Essene community who sees another member breaking God's commandment, in other words, committing a sin, to rebuke the person concerned, i.e. to say to him: What you have done or are doing is not just in the eyes of God. He must not express this reprimand angrily or with pride or with hatred, but rather 'with real faithfulness, humility and merciful love'. But he must make the other aware of his sin on the same day and may not postpone the matter until the next day, otherwise he is held responsible before God for any further sinning on the part of the other.[8] The main illustrations for this important Essene institution of mutual fraternal correction as regards the fulfilling of the Law are 1QS 5 : 25-6 : 1; 9 : 17; CD 7 : 2; 9 : 6-8. The purpose of this reprimand is that the other may regret his offence and not commit it again, that he be 'converted'. Yet if he continues to commit this sin he reveals himself as one who acts obstinately before God, who 'walks in the hardness of his heart' and who thereby earns eternal damnation from God.

I feel that the meaning of *elenchein* and the whole connection with Eph 5 : 11-15 only becomes completely clear when we

---

[7] This use of the expression 'fruit' and the distinction which Eph 5 : 9-11 (and Gal 5 : 19-23) makes between 'fruit' and 'works' are unknown in the Qumran Texts. *Test Nefth.* 2 : 10 speaks of 'works of light'.

[8] When, according to Mark 6 : 18, John the Baptist comes before Herod and tells him '. . . it is not lawful for thee to have thy brother's wife', we have an instance of the Essene practice of 'correction'.

consider it in the light of the continuity of tradition descended from this Essene practice : the proper way to act in the face of the works of darkness is to *rebuke* the person who commits the sin, i.e. to tell him that what he is doing is sinful. For, as we read in Eph 5 : 13, everything that is revealed as sinful in this manner ('everything that is reproved') is 'made manifest by the light'. *Phaneroun* (to manifest) here beside *elenchein* has a parallel in CD 20 : 3; *bhwpʿ mʿsyw* 'when his (the evil doer's) deeds *come to light*'. For here we have *hwpyʿ* 'to light up, to become bright' beside *hwkyh* (= *elenchein*) CD 20 : 4.

Eph 5 : 14 now quotes, as the basis *(dio legei!)* of the effect of the *elenchein* as *phaneroun*, a fragment of a Christian hymn whose origin is unknown :

> 'Awake thou that sleepest
> and arise from the dead
> and Christ shall give thee light.'

If this quotation is really intended to support what we have been discussing, then its meaning must be roughly this: Have done with sinning, let your transgressions be brought to light; thereby you will become a Son of Light or, as the song says, Christ will rise up in light before thee.

If this, in accord with the preceding, is the meaning of the quotation, then 5 : 15 as a continuation of the idea would be perfectly clear. 5 : 15 is then the *conclusion (oun!)* to be drawn from the quotation understood as above. If the 'giving of light by Christ', and thereby the 'being light' of the converted sinner in accordance with the quotation, has a connection with the 'coming to light' of his sins and with his conversion to one-who-no-longer-sins, then 5 : 15 holds good: 'See then that ye walk circumspectly, viz. not as foolish *(asophoi)* but as wise *(sophoi)*'. The 'foolish' walk improperly because they sin, the 'wise' walk properly because they do not sin, but rather do God's will. (In the similarly constructed v. 17, 'Know what is the will of the Lord' refers of course to the 'wise'.) The closest parallel to this meaning of *asophoi* and *sophoi* is 1QS 4 : 24 : *ythlkw bhkmh w'wlt* '(the two antithetical groups of people—the sons of light and of darkness) *walk in wisdom*[9] (on the one hand) *and in foolishness* (on the other hand)'.

The logical thought-sequence of Eph 5 : 8b-17, then, depends on the as yet hypothetically formulated interpretation of the hymn-quotation of v. 14. Is it possible to support this interpretation exegetically?

The current widely accepted interpretation of this Christian hymn or song fragment is different. It is pointed out that the 'giving of light by Christ' is best taken as a reference to baptism (cf. Heb 6 : 4 : 'Those who were once enlightened (in baptism)', and further illustrations in the commentaries *in loc.*). We are confronted, then, with what was originally a baptismal *hymn*. But this makes impossible the coherence of the quotation with the context v. 8b-14a, which speaks of *elenchein* as *phaneroun*, that is, the coming-to-light of the sins whereby light arises. That is why Dibelius-Greeven (*in loc.*), for example, prefer to refer the quotation to the conception in v. 8a, 'Now ye are light, for ye have also seen that whosoever awakes from sleep is given light by Christ'. They attempt the following paraphrase : 'Ye are now light, for ye also have been called at baptism; arise etc.'. But to refer the *dio legei* of v. 14b all the way back to v. 8a instead of to the actual context of the quotation (8b-14a) is very tricky and in so doing the logical connection of the quotation with v. 15-17, which we have mentioned above, is lost. That is why Dibelius-Greeven begin (incorrectly) a new part of the paraenesis with v. 15. More important is that the imperatives 'awake thou that sleepest and arise from the dead', which in the immediate context are evidently ethical imperatives, now directed factually at the believers who have already been baptized, become sacramental indicatives : 'Ye awoke at baptism and arose from the dead. Then Christ gave you light !'

Since Reitzenstein, the baptismal hymn so understood is often connected with the Gnostic 'awakening' of which there are so many illustrations in the Gnostic texts.[10] Thus, for example,

---

[9] The wording of Col 4 : 5 'walk in wisdom' corresponds more closely to this quotation.

[10] See the more recent commentaries *in loc.* and the literature they list.

Bultmann (*Theologie,* 3rd ed., p. 178) writes: 'The hymn (fragment) Eph 5 : 14 is expressed entirely in Gnostic language.' But the Gnostic 'awakening' is the call to the soul to awaken from sleep, to shake off the intoxication into which it—imprisoned in the darkness of the body—has sunk. Without the imagery, it means the call to proceed from the 'no-longer-knowing' about itself to the 'Gnosis' that the soul in reality is a spark from the world of light. It is, then, the call to knowledge about the origin of the soul, about what it always was, namely, a speck of light, and where it should again return, namely, to the heavenly world of light. In Ephesians, on the other hand, the thought does not move on the level of substance. Rather, as we have seen above from v. 8a and from the structure of the intelligibility of 'light-darkness', it is completely clear that it is not a question of knowledge about the nature of the actual self, but more a question of a decision of the will, *a change in one's walking,* away from sinful action towards action which is pleasing to God. That is something quite different from the Gnostic awakening.

I contend that the imperatives in this quotation, even though, or perhaps because, it is a fragment of a Christian baptismal hymn, are easily understandable as ethical imperatives and that only so understood is the quotation meaningful in the immediate context. In that case the meaning of *egeire ho katheudōn* must be: *awake from thy sinful sleep, turn about and sin no more.* Indeed this expression 'sinful sleep' is far from being unknown in late Judaism. I quote PsSal 16 : 1-4 :

1. 'When my soul slumbered (being afar) from the Lord, I had all but slipped down in the sleep of corruption when I was far from God.
2. 'My soul had been well nigh poured out unto death, when my soul departed from the God of Israel.
3. '(I had been) nigh unto the gates of Sheol with the sinner, had God not helped me with his everlasting mercy.
4. 'He pricked me, as the goad (of the driver) pricks a horse in order to stimulate it.
'My Saviour and Helper at all times kept me alive.'

The idea here is that by neglecting God (and thereby his commandments) one falls off into a sinful sleep which leads to destruction; and *parallel* to this is the contention that man, by being distant from God (as far as Jewish thought is concerned this is the same as neglecting God's commandments) comes close to *dying in sin*. This corresponds to the conception in line two of our quotation : 'arise from the dead'.

That *nekros* in Eph means 'dead in sin', is shown by Eph 2 : 1 : 'ye . . . who were dead in trespasses and sins, in which in time past ye *walked*. . . .' see also Eph 2 : 5 and Col 2 : 13 as well as Rom 6 : 11: 'Likewise reckon ye also yourselves to be *dead unto sin* but alive unto God. . . .' and Rom 6 : 13 : 'Neither yield ye your members as instruments of unrighteousness unto sin, but yield yourselves unto God *as those that are alive (risen) from the dead* and your members as instruments of righteousness unto God.' In this connection Paul interprets baptism as a *summons* to a new type of *conduct* (Rom 6 : 4); that is, he interprets the sacramental indicative of the dying and rising again with Christ in baptism as an *ethical imperative*; v. 13 quoted above is the development of this ethical imperative.

Eph 2 : 1, 5 points out, then, that the situation of the sinner who has neglected God's commandment, a situation in which Gentile Christians were formerly as pagans, is a 'being dead in sin', and that the new life that is given at baptism is the obligation to a new obedience of conduct in good works (Eph 2 : 10; 'created for good works in order that we may walk in them'. *Here* is where the ideas in Eph 2 : 1-10 are leading!).[11] Eph 5 : 14 'arise from the dead' must also be understood as a summons to rise up from being dead in sin.

But the passage quoted from PsSal 16 : 1-4 as a parallel to

---

[11] H. Schlier (*Christus und die Kirche in Eph.*, 1930, p. 74, n. 1), proceeds on the assumption 'that the author of Eph speaks the language of definite Gnostic groups', and for this reason he understands 'in your faults and sins' (Eph 2 : 1) and 'for good works' (Eph 2 : 10) as the author's clarification of 'you being dead' and 'created in Christ Jesus' respectively. This is an illustration of the pains which the author takes to represent the ideas of his mythological language in concrete terms. But the facts are exactly the reverse : 'created for good works' is a traditional Jewish idea, and 'in Christ Jesus' is its new Christian garb.

the first two lines of our baptismal hymn (fragment) is still not sufficient, for it contains no conception of a completely new beginning after the sleep of sin and the death in sin through acceptance into *an exclusive salvation-community*, as here in the Christian community through baptism. At this point an extract from the Qumran texts takes us a step further :

> 'I give thanks unto thee, O Lord,
> for thou hast freed my soul from the pit
> and drawn me up *from the slough of hell*
> *to the crest of the world.*
> So I walk on uplands unbounded
> and know that there is hope
> for him whom thou didst mould out of dust
> for the eternal community,
> and the perverse spirit thou hast cleansed from great sin
> and given it a place in the host of the holy ones.'

> (1QH 3 : 19f.)

This quotation shows that the poet is a member of the Qumran community, an exclusive salvation-community, and he thanks God for having purged him of great transgressions so that he can now take his place in the community *in the struggle against sin* (this latter fact is not stated here but is mentioned not infrequently in other texts). The poet tells us that this state of salvation, of membership of the community, is made possible by God's having drawn him up 'from the slough of hell to the crest of the world'. Here we really do have a parallel to the idea of 'rising from the dead' of Eph 5 : 14 : Once dead in sin, now— in the community—drawn up from the slough of hell.

As regards the third line of the quotation 'and Christ shall give thee light' attention must be drawn to the Hebrew verb *hwpy'* which means the same as *epiphauskein* in Eph 5 : 14. We have already come across the verb *hwpy'* in Eph 5 : 13 with *phaneroun*. In the Old Testament it is used in four places to describe the shining of Jahweh, his rising-up or his appearance to assist his people.[12] In CD 20 : 25f. it is also used to describe the

---

[12] Deut 33 : 2; Ps 50 : 2; 80 : 2; 94 : 1. That the LXX in none of these places translates with *epiphauskein* is of no consequence to our investigation for here we are concerned not with translation technique but with the reality that corresponds to the statement.

eschatological appearance of God in heavenly splendour to save Israel and to destroy the sinners: *bhwpʿ kbwd 'l* 'when the splendour of God will appear shining'. This appearance of God shedding his light is seen in 1QH as the salvation-event which is granted to the poet on his acceptance into the eschatological salvation-community.[13] 1QH 4 : 5-6 : 'I give thanks unto thee, O Lord, for thou hast *illumined* my face by thy covenant . . . on me you have risen radiant *(hwp'th ly)* as the perfect dawn for light.'[14] Similar is 1QH 4 : 23 : 'Thou in thy might hast shed upon me the perfect light.'[15] God has risen radiant on him, has illuminated him, the poet *has* salvation in the salvation-community. Here we have an exact parallel to our baptismal hymn; the only difference is that here, as so often in the New Testament (in contrast to the Old Testament and late Judaism), Christ takes the place of God as the agent of salvation: the Christian (on being baptized) has the light of Christ shed upon him.

The result of this interpretation in the light of the Qumran texts is as follows : in the hymn (fragment) of Eph 5 : 14 baptism, during which Christ sheds his light upon the person being baptized, is understood as the end of the sleep of sin in which he has been hitherto, as the end of his being dead in sin, as a *conversion* which from now onwards manifests itself in new conduct, in the doing of that which is pleasing to God. Thus understood is this quotation the *foundation* for *what was said earlier. The elenchein*, which takes place when the sinner is told : 'what you are doing is sinful', effects a revelation, a coming-to-light of the sin and is, as such, a *summons to the sinner to be*

[13] The Essene community of the Qumran texts certainly considered itself as such. More precisely stated; it sees its present as the last period before the end and regards itself as called—as in Is 40: 3—to prepare the way of the Lord.

[14] 'For light' is an attempted translation of the difficult word *l'wrtym* or *l'wrtwm*.

[15] IQH 9: 31 must be mentioned here: 'From my youth onwards *thou hast risen radiant on me through understanding of thy judgment.*' It must also be pointed out that *hwpy'* also occurs in another sense in the Qumran texts; it is used to denote the rising of the sun and the moon (or the stars) 1QS 10: 2; the rising up of enemies 1QH 5: 32; 7: 3; and, in 1QpHab 11: 7 it denotes the rising up of the Wicked Priest against the Teacher of Righteousness.

converted to new behaviour, that is, in effect, to *baptism* in which Christ sheds his light upon the person who up to now has been a sinner, a baptism through which a new life is given him among those who obey God's will in response to the ethical imperative. In this way, I suggest, the whole of this Christian hymn fragment becomes intelligible, both in itself and within its general context.

We have now examined one part of the paraenetic section of Ephesians as regards the origins of its tradition and, I feel, have been able to show that this tradition shows a clear relationship with the Essene community of the Qumran texts and the late-Jewish writings that are close to them. In conclusion it may be added that as regards the paraenetic tradition, other parts of the paraenesis, besides the extract Eph 5 : 3-15, which we have examined, clearly evidence the same Essene roots. For example, Eph 4 : 17f. and, above all, Eph 6 : 10-20, where the arming of the Christian in the struggle against the forces of the devil is described. In Kittel's *Theologisches Wörterbuch*, v. 297ff., I have already expressed my opinion on the importance of the Qumran texts for the understanding of that section.

The only paraenetic section which shows no trace of relationship to the Qumran texts is Eph 5 : 22-6 : 9. Here, as has been proved long ago, we are in the midst of a *Hellenistic-*Jewish tradition which in the final analysis goes back to the Stoics. Moreover, there is in the Qumran texts nothing whatsoever that approaches either the conception of the syzygy about Christ and the Church, or the head-body speculation. Indeed, in the Qumran texts we have no parallels at all as regards Christology, which of course in Ephesians also includes ecclesiology. Nor is that to be expected of a Jewish community such as that of the Qumran texts proves itself to be.

7

'MYSTERY' IN THE THEOLOGY OF SAINT PAUL AND ITS PARALLELS AT QUMRAN*

Joseph Coppens

THE presence and significance of the term 'mystery' in the theology of St Paul has been pondered over for a long time by exegetes and historians of comparative religion, not to mention theologians whose attention has been turned to the term and the concept by the brilliant studies on the question made by Dom O. Casel.[1]

Today excellent interpreters of the thought of the Apostle have come to the following conclusions in regard to the Pauline 'mystery':[2]

1. When St Paul introduced the terms 'revelation', 'mystery', 'knowledge', 'perfection', into his vocabulary, he linked them closely together. In so doing he elaborated a network of theological concepts which recalls that of the Qumran writers.

2. In its strict and religious sense, the term 'mystery' appears principally in the Captivity Epistles, but this

* Published in A. Descamps *et al.*, *Littérature et théologie pauliniennes* (Recherches Bibliques V), Bruges, 1960, pp. 142-65.

[1] The problem was posed, if not resolved, by W. Goossens, *Les origines de l'eucharistie sacrement et sacrifice*, Louvain-Paris, 1931.

[2] The most interesting studies from our point of view are: D. Deden, 'Le "mystère" paulinien', *ETL* 13 (1936), pp. 405-42; R. E. Brown, 'The Pre-Christian Concept of Mystery', *CBQ* 20 (1958), pp. 417-43; id., 'The Semitic Background of the New Testament Mysterion', *Biblica* 39 (1958), pp. 426-48; 40 (1959), pp. 70-87; B. Rigaux, 'Révélation des mystères et perfection à Qumran et dans le Nouveau Testament', *NTS* 4 (1957-58), pp. 237-62.

meaning is anticipated at least twice, namely in 1 Cor 2 : 7, and in Rom 16 : 25.

3. In its strict and religious sense, the term 'mystery' is generally used in the singular. The plural is rare. It is found in 1 Cor 4 : 1; 13 : 2; 14 : 2, and outside the Pauline epistles in Mt 13 : 11 and Lk 8 : 10.

4. In its strict and religious sense, the term 'mystery' designates the secret plan of universal salvation (*mystery at the level of divine being*), which was realized in Christ (*mystery at the concrete level of salvation history*), and which is offered to all humanity through the gospel and its reception in faith (*mystery at the level of human collaboration in the perfect realization of the divine mystery*).

5. The three levels at which the mystery is realized are translated by the expressions 'mystery of God', 'mystery of Christ', 'mystery of the Gospel, of faith, of religion'.

6. In the description of the mystery, the Apostle emphasizes the calling of the Gentiles. One gets the impression that in the early letters this aspect embodies the character of 'mystery' in a special way. Later, in the Captivity Epistles, the mystery becomes principally the mysterious being of Christ, the universal significance of this being, and the mystical participation in this being, the fullness of divine grace.

7. Through knowledge of the mystery, the Christian attains wisdom, and the power and glory of God. He thus in a way penetrates into the 'mystery of God'.

8. The knowledge of the mystery is reserved to perfect Christians.

9. The Christian becomes perfect from the time that he is capable of receiving the spiritual instruction in virtue of which he can experience the plenitude of the Christian life.

10. The believer realizes this plenitude of Christian experience and life through an efficacious participation in the plenitude of Christ.

11. Receptive attention to spiritual instruction, the Christian life fully realized, efficacious participation in Christ's plenitude : all of this can be obtained only through the gift of the Spirit.

12. Compared to the doctrine of the 'great' Pauline epistles, that of the Captivity Epistles is notably richer :

(a) The mysteries of the Christian economy are in some way concentrated in a single one : the mystery of Christ glimpsed in his being, his epiphany, in the riches this epiphany pours out and the paths it opens up to God.

(d) The mystery is no longer primarily the ultimate salvation of the Jews, nor the calling of the Gentiles, nor the miracle of the parousia, nor the glory of the final beatification in God; rather, all of that is recapitulated in Christ.

(c) The mystery is no longer reserved to a category of the faithful distinct from the mass or at least distinct from the initiated; all Christians are called to share in its revelation.

(b) The knowledge of the mystery becomes the ultimate end of the Christian life, whereas in 1 Cor 13 : 13 knowledge must give way to charity. Or, better still, at this point knowledge implies charity, or vice versa, charity has in a way absorbed knowledge. We are, so to speak, at the centre of the charismatic perichoresis.

What have the Qumran documents to offer us as against this Pauline synthesis? The Qumran texts were collected by E. Vogt, S.J. and then through the good offices of Fr Denis, O.P. who is collaborating with Professor Kuhn in the preparation of a Qumran concordance.[3]

---

[3] Cf. E. Vogt, in *Biblica* 37 (1956), pp. 247-57. Fr. Denis, O.P., a collaborator in the preparation of a Hebrew concordance of the Qumran texts, has been kind enough to furnish us with a complete list of the occurrences of *rz* 'mystery' in the texts so far published: 1QM 3: 9, 15; 14: 9, 14; 16: 11, 16; 17: 9; 4QMa 12; 1QS 3: 23; 4: 6, 18; 9: 18;

At Qumran the mystery, or rather the mysteries, have their centre in God. They constitute an ensemble of knowledge, of decrees, and of the riches of grace which are beyond human understanding. No one has access to them except through revelation and divine generosity. More than once the divine mysteries are termed marvellous.[4] But God in some way communicates some of his mysteries to the works he has accomplished, and to those he will accomplish in the course of time.

This leads us to a brief consideration of the *cosmic mysteries*. They include, among other things, the mysterious laws which direct the course of the stars and determine the calendar (1QH 1: 11, 13); the mysteries of the abyss (1Q27 f. 13: 3); the mysterious domain of a new Paradise (1QH 8: 6); the mystery of the measure and the harmony at the base of poetry and music (1QH 1: 29); and the mystery of human language (1QH 1: 28). Psalm 1 suggests the inclusion of many other realities in the cosmic mysteries, such as the destinies of the world (1QH 1: 24), even though the term 'mystery' is not used.

The mysteries of God penetrate the domain of history, too, insofar as history is entirely subject to the decrees of the divine will (1QH f. 3: 7; cf. for example 1QS 3: 15, 17, 23; 4: 18; 1QH 7: 14, 26). Some of the marvellous and mysterious interventions of Providence *(historical mysteries)* concern the fate of

11: 3, 5, 19; 1QH 1: 11, 13, 21, 29; 2: 13; 4: 27; 5: 25, 36; 7: 27; 8: 6, 11 (*bis*); 9: 23; 11: 10; 12: 13, 20; 13: 3, 13; f 3: 7; f 6: 5; f 17: 3; f 25: 1; f 50: 5; 1QpHab 7: 5, 8, 14; CD 3: 18; 1Q26 1: 4; 1Q27 1: 2, 3, 4, 7; 1Q30 4; 1Q36 f 99: 2; f 16: 2; 1Q40 f 1: 2. It may also be useful to have the references to terms close to *rz* in meaning: *hb'* 'to hide', *hbh* 'to conceal': 1QS 4: 6; 1QH 5: 11, 25; 8: 6, 18; 9: 24, *str*: 'hiding-place': 1QS 9: 22; 1QH 8: 18; 'to hide': 1QS 5: 11; 8: 11, 12; 9: 17; 10: 24; 11: 6; 1QH 1: 25; 3: 38; 5: 11, 26; 8: 10; 9: 19; 17: 9, 22; f 51: 1. *glh* 'to reveal': 1QM 10: 11; 1QS 1: 9; 5: 9, 12; 8: 1, 15, 16; 9: 13, 19; 1QH 1: 21; 5: 12; 6: 4; 11: 17; 12: 34; 13: 3; 14: 16; 17: 2; 18: 9, 24; f 2: 12; f 4: 7; f 5: 10; f 6: 5; f 55: 1; 1QpHab 11: 1; 1Q26 1: 4; 1Q27 1: 5 (*bis*), 6; f 2: 1.

[4] To designate the Qumran texts we employ the abbreviations proposed by the *Revue Biblique*. On Qumran and Christianity, cf. J. van der Ploeg *et. al.*, *La secte de Qumran et les origines du christianisme* (Recherches bibliques IV), Bruges-Paris, 1959. For a translation of the more important texts, cf. A. Dupont-Sommer, *The Essene Writings from Qumran*, trad. G. Vermes, Cleveland-New York, 1962. On the marvels accomplished by God, cf. 1QH 4: 28, 29; 5: 15; 6: 11; 7: 32; 9: 7; 10: 4, 14, 21; 11: 10, 17; 12: 12; 13: 2; 18: 22.

individuals. God grants man his pardon: mystery of mercy (CD 3 : 18);[5] and he raises him to himself in promising him an angelic state (1QH 1 : 21-22; 1QM 14 : 14; 1QS 11 : 5, 19); mystery of supernatural exaltation. Other interventions concern both individuals and the Israelite nation as a whole, for instance the trials which the mysterious wisdom of God inflicts on men (1QH 9 : 23; 1QM 14 : 11, 16; 17 : 9). Others, finally, concern the final end of the community of the elect: God will destroy iniquity (1QM 3 : 9; 14 : 11; 1QS 3 : 23; 4 : 18; 1Q27 1 : 6-7), he will save the elect (1QpHab 7 : 1-5, 8, 13-14), and assure them of the kingdom (1Q27 1 : 5). This would seem to be God's final victory, to which the *future mystery* is directed. This 'future mystery' is evoked in an important context which is, unfortunately, mutilated : 1Q26 f. 1 : 1, 4; 1Q27 1 : 3, 4; cf. 1QS 11 : 3-4, 9.

One of the mysteries realized by God in the course of history is that of the Teacher of Righteousness himself, because among his fellow citizens he appeared as the bearer of a great mystery, which he was charged by God to communicate to his disciples : 1QH 5 : 25; 8 : 11 (bis).

After the mysteries of the divine being and those of the divine works accomplished in the cosmos and in history, there occurs a single reference to a *scriptural mystery*, that is a mystery hidden in the Scriptures and destined to be unveiled in the last days : 1QpHab 7 : 5.

In opposition to the divine mysteries, Qumran recognizes also the *mysteries of sin or of iniquity* : 1QM 3 : 9; 14 : 9; 16 : 11; 1QS 3 : 23; 4 : 18; 1QH 5 : 36; f. 50 : 5; 1Q27 1 : 2. These mysteries, of course, depend ultimately on the providential order. Nevertheless, since God is not their direct agent, it is fitting to give them separate mention.

The nature and origin of the mysteries explain that God alone is, in the last instance, the one who reveals them (1QS 9 : 18; 11 : 19). It is through his 'spirit' that God communicates this knowledge : 1QS 4 : 3; 1QH 12 : 11; 13 : 19. In various places the Qumran psalmist chants the mystery of his marvellous

[5] Cf. 1QS 3 : 7-9; 5 : 5.

participation in the divine knowledge which has been accorded
him: 1QH 7: 26-33; 8: 4-40; 11: 9-10, 15-18; 12: 11-13;
19-20; 13: 14-15.[6]

Among those chosen by the Lord and his Spirit to communicate the knowledge of mysteries, we may mention, following
B. Rigaux: the prophet (1QpHab 7: 8), the sons of Sadoc
(1QS 5: 9; 1QSb 4: 27-28), the twelve men and the three priests
of the Council of the Community (1QS 8: 1), the *maskil* (1QS
3: 13; 9: 13-14; CD 12: 21), and finally the Teacher of
Righteousness, who, according to many authors, is the anonymous
author of the Hodayoth: 1QH 1: 21; 2: 13; 4: 27-28; 5:
11-15; 7: 27; 8: 11; 10: 4; 12: 13, 20; f. 6: 5; 1QpHab 7:
5; 1QS 11: 3, 5.

In the light of what we have gleaned from Qumran, we turn
again to the Pauline epistles. We will examine them in the chronological order generally given in the introductions to the New
Testament. Through a review of the entire Pauline corpus we
may attain a better understanding of the evolution of Pauline
thought and vocabulary, and, incidentally, throw some light on
the problem of the authenticity of the Captivity Epistles.

We will examine first the three passages where St Paul uses
the term 'mystery' in the plural, namely 1 Cor 14: 2; 13: 2;
and 4: 1.

The first passage need not detain us. The term seems to be
employed in a non-technical sense. It could be rendered freely
as 'mysteriously'. 'He who speaks in tongues speaks not to men,

---

[6] One may fairly ask if Qumran did not also know a *'liturgical mystery'*.
Reference is made to CD 3: 12-14, 18-20. Cf. the penetrating study of
O. Betz, 'Le ministère cultuel dans la secte de Qumran et dans le
christianisme primitif', in J. van der Ploeg *et al.*, *La secte de Qumran*,
pp. 165-202. No consensus has yet been reached on the *Sitz im Leben* of
the Qumran texts, or on their date of composition, or on the chronological
order of the principal texts. Three suggestions have been made with regard
to the *Sitz im Leben*: the persecution of Antiochus Epiphanes, the fall of
Jerusalem to Pompey, the destruction of Jerusalem by Titus and Vespasian.
The majority of authors date the texts in the first century B.C. Certain
among them have proposed the following chronological order: 1QM—
1QS and 1QH (period of the Teacher of the union)—1QpHab and CD
(period of the Teacher of Righteousness).

but to God. No one understands him. He speaks in spirit, mysteriously.'[7]

The second, more important, passage (13 : 2) presents some difficulties. E. Osty translates it as follows : 'If I should have the gift of prophecy, and should I know all mysteries and all knowledge. . . .' Is it question here of one or several charisms? It is possible that St Paul has in mind a single charism, namely prophecy. What follows, in this case, would simply be in apposition. We could read : 'Should I have the gift of prophecy, and should this charism give me complete knowledge of all mysteries. . . .' Paul would have in mind, then, the possession of the charism in a supreme degree. This is how Adolf Schlatter understands the text.[8]

Certain other authors distinguish a more subtle gradation in the text, and find in it allusions to three charisms : prophecy, the revelation designated by the 'knowledge of mysteries', and gnosis. The partisans of this distinction recognize, nevertheless, that further on in verse 12 the Apostle is content to oppose charity to gnosis alone, as if it resumed the three charisms.

In any case, the opinion that in Corinthians the term *gnosis* does not belong to the vocabulary of 'revelation and of mystery', and must be explained as peculiar to Corinthian language,[9] does not seem justified. It appears to be contradicted by such texts as 1 Cor 14 : 6 and 13 : 2 which link 'gnosis' and 'revelation', and by passages which establish a parallelism between the two charisms : 2 Cor 11 : 6; 12 : 1-7.[10] Moreover, the Qumran texts now give us further reason for questioning the validity of this opinion, since the expression 'the knowledge of mysteries' is common in them. The terms 'knowledge', 'to know' on the one

---

[7] In the *Bible de Jérusalem* E. Osty translates : 'Il dit en esprit des choses mystérieuses' (E.T. : 'he talks in the spirit about mysterious things'). On the other hand R. E. Brown (*art. cit.*, p. 443) is inclined to favour an exegesis which stresses the antithetical value of the particle *de* and understands 'mysteries' in the strict sense : glossolalia is not intelligible, but nevertheless on the level of the spirit it proffers 'mysteries'.

[8] A. Schlatter, *Die Korintherbriefe*, in *Schlatters' Erläuterungen zum Neuen Testament*, Stuttgart, 1950, fasc. 6, p. 158.

[9] J. Dupont, *Gnosis. La connaissance religieuse dans les Epitres de saint Paul*, Bruges-Paris, 1949, pp. 199-200.

[10] J. Dupont, *op. cit.*, p. 200.

hand, and 'mystery' on the other, are frequently associated (cf. 1QH 2·: 13; 12 : 13).

The third text, 1 Cor 4 : 1, is easy to translate, but the concrete object aimed at is not easily defined. Paul defines here the apostolic ministry in a formula which became classic, and which was taken up again by the Council of Trent. The Apostle, he affirms, must be considered as the servant of Christ and as the 'steward' of the mysteries of God. The context does not define these mysteries. Osty interprets them as 'treasures of doctrine and life revealed and given by God to men', and this commentary is no doubt substantially accurate. The Apostle does seem to have in mind all the truths relative to the economy of salvation and revealed by God, as well as—but only by way of consequence— the institutions and concrete structures which assure salvation and dispense it.

A Qumran text has been related to this last passage : 1Q36 f. 16. It refers to the 'nšy mšmrt lrzykh, that is, according to Barthélemy-Milik, 'the men (who mount) the guard of your mysteries'. The context of this curious expression is not intact. It is impossible to determine to what, exactly, it refers. The term mšmrt is frequent in the Old Testament and its meanings are numerous.[11] The Septuagint version translates it in various ways.[12] Here it is perhaps best translated, 'the men appointed to the service of divine mysteries'. This brings us quite close to the full significance of the Pauline passage.

A few conclusions can be drawn already from the three texts studied so far. First, it appears that St Paul is concerned with several mysteries, and that, consequently, his horizon is not limited to a single mystery, 'the great mystery', with which, some authors suggest, he was concerned from the beginning of his career. Secondly, it is evident that parallels in Qumran literature

[11] E. König, Hebräisches und Aramäisches Wörterbuch zum Alten Testament, 2nd and 3rd ed., Leipzig, 1922; F. Brown-S. R. Driver-C. A. Briggs, A Hebrew and English Lexicon of the Old Testament, Oxford, 1952; L. Koehler-W. Baumgartner, Lexicon in Veteris Testamenti Libros, Leiden, 1953.

[12] E. Hatch-H. A. Redpath, A Concordance to the Septuagint and the Other Greek Versions of the Old Testament including the Apocryphal Books, Oxford, 1897.

are not wanting. Leaving aside the obscure expression in 1Q36 f. 16, we can point to the relations between the terms 'gnosis' and 'mystery', the reference to the charism of prophecy as the primary source of the knowledge of the mysteries, and finally the expression 'mysteries of God', which has an exact parallel in the Qumran texts.

We must now take up the particular mysteries mentioned in the Pauline epistles.

The first in chronological order is found in the Second Epistle to the Thessalonians.[13] The context describes the second coming of Christ. The Apostle speaks of two precursory signs of the return: the first is the mystery of iniquity which St Paul sees already at work, and the second consists in the appearance of the 'man of sin', the 'son of iniquity', the Antichrist whose defeat will coincide with the parousia of the Saviour. St Paul speaks in the same context of a person and of an event or force which is holding back, as was commonly believed, the coming of Antichrist. This is why no one has thought of identifying the *katechon* (the restraining obstacle) with the mystery of iniquity or the great apostasy, nor the *katechōn* (the restraining personage) with Antichrist. Failing to make this identification, the exegetes get lost in conjecture as to the identity of the *katechon* and the *katechōn*.[14] This problem has little importance in relation to our aim here, however. It is sufficient for us to know that Paul glimpses, as preludes to the return of Christ and to the great eschatological victory of God, the appearance of a formidable apostasy and of a personage particularly hostile to God and to his Messiah.

Qumran offers us in striking terms a series of elements parallel to those running through this passage. We find, for instance, in

[13] 2 Thess 2: 1-12. Cf. B. Rigaux, *Saint Paul. Les épîtres aux Thessaloniciens*, Paris, 1956; C. Masson, *Les deux épîtres de saint Paul aux Thessaloniciens*, Paris-Genève, 1957. R. E. Brown (*art. cit.*, p. 435) rightly refuses Rigaux's interpretation: 'l'iniquité est mise en activité secrètement.'

[14] Among recent commentators R. Knox (*A New Testament Commentary for English Readers*, London, 1954, II, 312-313) suggests referring the two restrainers directly to the parousia of Christ and not to that of Antichrist. His identification of the two obstacles is no happier than those of his colleagues: the incredulity of the Jews and Satan provoking this lack of faith. Cf. infra, pp. 156-8.

the Qumran texts *bene* or *'anse haš-šahat* (CD 6 : 15; 13 : 14; 1QS 9 : 16; 10 : 19. Cf. Jubilees 10 : 3; 15 : 26; 17 : 12; Jn 17 : 12), an expression which corresponds to *huios tēs apōleias* (2 Thess 2 : 3). On the other hand the *bene 'awel* (1QS 3 : 21) are not too far removed from the *anthropos tēs anomias*.[15] Furthermore, the *mysterion tēs anomias* is found almost literally in the Qumran texts; cf. *rz pš'* in 1QH 5 : 36; f. 50 : 5. A text such as 1Q27 1 : 1 is particularly evocative,[16] and we must not forget that Qumran went through a period of great apostasy (CD 6 : 10; 1QpHab 5 : 7-8), and witnessed the final victory of God over iniquity.[17]

Some authors think they have found in 1Q27 1 : 7 an expression that is capable of throwing some light on the *katechōn*. It is difficult, however, to find in the term *tmk* the sense of 'hold back'. Furthermore, the meaning of the context is not clear. A. Dupont-Sommer, in fact, feels obliged to complete the text thus : 'And all of those who detain *(unjustly)* the marvellous mysteries. . . .'[18]

It remains that Qumran literature offers numerous partial parallels to our text, and what is more, places us in a situation closely resembling that described by the Apostle. God's final victory will be preceded by a time of iniquity during which men of sin and perdition will exercise wide-spread domination. But we must not lose sight of the differences; the texts do not speak, as does St Paul, of a personage who will be the ultimate incarnation of impiety, nor do they evoke the Messiah as the adversary and the conquerer of the man of sin.

The Epistle to the Romans furnishes two other passages where the term 'mystery' is used in the singular. As in the Second

[15] Cf. the figure of the 'impious priest', the expression 'impious humanity' (1QS 11 : 9), and the 'descendants of iniquity' (*mwldy 'wlh*: 1Q27 1 : 5). Is 57 : 4 reads *yalde pesa'*, which the LXX renders *tekna apōleias*.

[16] Cf. also the Aramaic *rz rš'* of 1QGenApoc 1 : 2, and note that according to 1QM 14 : 9 the mysteries of iniquity form part of the 'mysteries of adversity' of Belial: *rzy stmtw*.

[17] Cf. the texts already cited: 1QM 3 : 9; 14 : 11; 1QS 3 : 23; 4 : 18; 1Q27 1 : 7.

[18] A. Dupont-Sommer, *The Essene Writings from Qumran*, trad. G. Vermes, Cleveland-New York, 1962, p. 327.

Epistle to the Thessalonians, the mystery is considered in an historical perspective.

In Rom 11 : 25 Paul foresees an historical development of three phases in the diffusion of the gospel : the temporary rejection of Israel, the conversion of the Gentiles, and the final salvation of the Chosen People : 'Lest you be wise in your own conceits, I want you to understand this mystery, brethren : a hardening has come upon part of Israel, until the full number of the Gentiles come in, and so all Israel will be saved.' The mystery, then, is not the calling of the Gentiles. Cerfaux observes correctly, 'The conversion of the Gentiles is only accessory.'[19] Paul stops at the destiny of Israel, and his concern is to show the continuity of the divine work.

Qumran offers no parallel to this vision of the mystery of salvation : temporary rejection of a part of Israel and final salvation of the entire people. In fact, we find the opposite : salvation will belong immediately to Israel, but will be reserved finally to that portion of the elect represented by the community of the Desert of Judah. On the other hand, 4Esd 10 : 38-58 seems to describe an expectation similar to that of the Apostle to the Gentiles.

The construction of the second passage, Rom 16 : 26, is more complicated. It is not surprising that in the course of time copyists felt obliged to complete and clarify it. The 'mystery' is still on the historical plane, to be sure, but it takes on wider dimensions. 'The revelation of the mystery' appears to be identified with the kerygma of the 'gospel', of which Christ is the principal, central, and formal object. The 'mystery' is said to have been 'enveloped in silence' in the past, then 'foretold through the scriptures', and then announced to all the Gentiles. It should be noted that even in this text the mystery does not consist formally in the calling of the Gentiles. The mystery is rather the content of the gospels, and consequently, by way of induction, Christ appears for the first time in its perspective.

Qumran offers no parallel here, except to the degree that in both the Epistle to the Romans and the Qumran texts the new

[19] L. Cerfaux, *La théologie de l'Eglise suivant saint Paul*, Paris, 1948, p. 42.

revelation brought to the faithful is called a 'mystery', or includes 'mysteries'. Nevertheless, the properties of the mystery, its hidden character and its presence in scripture, are reflected quite faithfully in the Qumran writings. As we move forward in the interpretation of particular mysteries, the conclusion stated above is confirmed : the Apostle does not reserve the term 'mystery' to a single event or to a single reality which, by reason of its capital importance in the economy of salvation, appropriates the expression to itself.

In the First Epistle to the Corinthians a new 'mystery' emerges which once more has a particular fact in view, a fact different from all of those which up to this point have, in the eyes of the Apostle, merited the name mystery. In 1 Cor 15 : 51 Paul, writing of the end of time, terms 'mystery' the corporal metamorphosis willed by Providence for all men before their entrance into eternal life. Some will have to pass through the process of resurrection; others, on the contrary, 'the living', will suffer the eschatological transformation of their earthly bodies without passing through death.

Nothing at Qumran parallels this. Besides, it is well-known that the Dead Sea documents give us only a sketchy picture of individual eschatology as it will be worked out according to the eternal designs of God.

If 1 Cor 15 : 51 poses no problems, it is quite otherwise with 1 Cor 2 : 7. Here, for the first time, we begin to wonder whether Paul, seeing more and more deeply into the 'mystery', is not placing Christ himself at the centre of it. The text, unfortunately, is not easy to interpret.

The first question we must ask is to what the expression *en mysteriō* refers directly. The easiest answer would be that it refers to the participle following it. Paul, in this case, would be speaking of the 'divine wisdom hidden in (the) mystery'. Certain grammatical points, however, appear to militate against this interpretation.[20] Many authors suggest joining 'wisdom of God' and

[20] Cf. E. B. Allo, Saint Paul. *Première épître aux Corinthiens*, Paris, 1956, *in loc.*; According to Mitton (cited in R. E. Brown, *art. cit.*, p. 437) Paul's attention is concentrated on wisdom : 'The reference to mystery is secondary.'

'in (the) mystery', so that the expression would directly qualify the divine attribute.[21] Other equally competent exegetes prefer to link the term with the verb *laleō* 'to speak',[22] as if the character of mystery affected the manner of expression rather than the thing expressed.[23] This last interpretation seems to have dictated the translation, 'We preach the wisdom of God, in mystery',[24] whereas, arranging the Pauline text only slightly, another translator invites us to read a perfectly clear text: 'It is a divine wisdom, mysterious and hidden.'[25]

But what is the object of the mystery which, lest we forget, is not determined by the article? Some authors do not attempt to define it.[26] Others do specify, but the definitions given are sometimes vague. One author holds that the mystery concerns at once 'the divine plan of salvation', 'salvation, promised and realized', the 'concrete path chosen by God to realize this salvation', that is, Christ, and even the 'glory and the joys that God has in store for us'.[27] In brief, it would appear that a notable part of Pauline theology is included in the term, and, in particular, Christ would figure in the mystery.[28] Some find a confirmation of this Christological aspect in the fact that Paul has just called Christ 'the wisdom of God'. For these authors the term is extremely rich in meaning. They take little account of the absence of the article and relate the word to a wide context. They appear even to call upon the implied intention of the Apostle at the moment he was writing this text to support their thesis.

On the other hand, those who stay strictly within the limits

[21] Cf. P. Bachmann, *Der erste Brief des Paulus an die Korinther ausgelegt*, Leipzig, 1905, *in loc.*

[22] Cf. E. B. Allo, *loc. cit.*

[23] Cf. P. Bachmann, *loc. cit.*

[24] B. Botte. *Le Nouveau Testament. Traduction nouvelle d'après le texte grec*, Turnhout, 1944.

[25] E. Osty in the *Bible de Jérusalem*.

[26] B. Rigaux, *loc. cit.*, p. 254: 'In this passage Paul does not define precisely the object of the mystery.' Nevertheless he adds: 'It can be inferred, however, that it is a question of a more profound knowledge of the plan of God, and of a more intimate and complete entrance into new life.'

[27] L. Cerfaux, *La théologie de l'Eglise suivant saint Paul*, Paris, 1948, pp. 229-30.

[28] L. Cerfaux, *op. cit.*, p. 230.

of the context prefer to restrict the precise object of the mystery. Some hold (and verse 9 supports their view) that Paul had specially in mind the glorious state, the future glorification of the elect.[29] Others—and it is their viewpoint I am inclined to agree with—claim that the apostle gives us the key to the passage in verse 12 which resumes in a clear and concise formula the object of his spiritual instruction. The object of the mystery, according to this interpretation, is expressed in the phrase *ta charisthenta hēmin* 'the gifts that God has given us'. Paul, then, would not be referring directly to Christ, but rather to the totality of gifts given to Christians, those gifts by which they attain the spiritualized state evoked by the apostle in the entire passage, and which enable them to be permeated by divine wisdom.[30]

We should mention here the properties that Paul attributes to the mystery in this Epistle. We learn that it is 'hidden', that it is accessible only to those who have received the gift of the Spirit, that it gives the fortunate possessors of that gift the power to search the depths of God, and finally that it grants them, so to speak, a glimpse of the celestial glory reserved by God for his elect. Almost all of these characteristics—we will come back to this later in reference to certain texts of Colossians and Ephesians—are found in the Qumran passages treating of the mysteries. At Qumran, too, these mysteries are hidden truths or realities,[31] revealed to those who receive the gift of the Spirit.[32] These revelations enable those receiving them to know the

---

[29] R. Knox. *A New Testament Commentary for English Readers*: II *The Acts of the Apostles. St Paul's Letters to the Churches*, London, 1954, p. 132. Nevertheless the author adds: 'What precisely the Apostle had in mind, is not clear.'

[30] This is the opinion, for example, of A. Schlatter, *Die Korintherbriefe*, in *Schlatters' Erläuterungen zum NT*, Stuttgart, 1950, fasc. 6. He, however, includes final glorification, the benefits of individual eschatology, among the favours or graces conferred by God and envisaged by the apostle. For C. T. Craig (*The Interpreter's Bible*, New York, 1953), the mystery 'involves eschatological aspects of redemption, God's full plan of salvation'. Craig mentions, only to reject it, the opinion of those who identify the mystery with the 'word of the Cross' (1 Cor 1 : 18).

[31] Cf. the texts cited above, n. 3 *Swd* should be added to the terms there listed.

[32] Cf. J. Coppens, 'Le don de l'Esprit d'après les textes de Qumran et dans le quatrième évangile', in *L'évangile de Jean* (Recherches Bibliques III), Bruges-Paris, 1958, pp. 209-23.

immense riches of divine knowledge and power,[33] and to glimpse
the celestial glory awaiting the just in the world to come.[34]

The conclusion to be drawn from this study of the oldest
Pauline Epistles is the one already reached in two other contexts.
First, the Apostle does not restrict the term 'mystery' to a single
reality, or a single event in the economy of salvation. Second,
even among the particular mysteries mentioned by the Apostle,
the call of the Gentiles does not get special attention. It is
mentioned briefly, one might say in passing, principally perhaps
in so far as it is the object of what we have termed a 'scriptural
mystery'.

Before examining the Captivity Epistles and what has been
commonly called 'the great mystery', we must consider briefly
what has sometimes been judged to be the single indisputable
example of a 'scriptural mystery' in Pauline literature.

There are excellent authors who hesitate as to the precise
meaning of Eph 5 : 32.[35] To what exactly does the Pauline statement refer? Does the Apostle see the mystery in the biblical text,
or rather in the very act of conjugal union evoked in the citation?
It makes little difference for the meaning, but the distinction has
its importance in determining the category of mystery that is in
question here.

It would seem difficult here to separate the biblical text and
the fact it expresses. It would even appear that the author is
concerned especially with the fact and the law that it implies.
This law is the obligation of husbands to love their wives as their
own bodies. This norm is based on the corporal unity realized
in marriage, in conformity to the divine views expressed by the
word of the bible.

St Paul, however, adds to the fundamental idea of the bible

---

[33] For the theology of Qumran, cf. the fundamental study by F. Nötscher
Zur theologischen Terminologie der Qumran-Texte, Bonn, 1956.

[34] Should 1 Cor 2 : 1 be added to the dossier of Pauline texts? The reading
mystērion is not favoured by the critical editions. R. E. Brown (*art. cit.*,
444) rightly judges that there are serious reasons in its favour. The expression
'mystery of God' also occurs in 1 Cor 4 : 1; Apoc 10 : 7; Col 2 : 2.

[35] Note the hesitancy of L. Cerfaux, *La théologie de l'Eglise*, 235, n.l.;
Le Christ dans la théologie de saint Paul, Paris, 1951, p. 281, n.l.

and to the natural reality a new reason which confirms the scriptural statement: the mystical marriage of Christ with his Church. In the eyes of the sacred writer, this mystical union becomes the profound motif of the conjugal mystery. The antecedent of *anti toutou* 'for this reason' which is the same in meaning as *heneken toutou* is not to be found in verses 28-29a. It refers rather to 29b-30, with which it accords perfectly, that is to a new fact, a consequence of the Christian economy: the union of Christ with His Church. From now one, it is by reason of this union, *anti toutou*, that the law of marriage is verified, and it is perhaps this new reason which led St Paul to move away from the Septuagint reading *heneken toutou*. This is daring and original exegesis, to be sure, and the Apostle is aware of the fact, as is expressed by the particle *de*. This particle is neither superfluous nor purely explicative. It expresses an antithesis, but the opposition is not between Paul's opinion and the one circulating among those to whom the Epistle is addressed, but rather between his exegesis and the current interpretation of the cited passage. St Paul concludes: 'This mystery, that is the mystery of the conjugal union which unites two bodies in one, is great, that is certain; I, however, call it great in the light of the union of Christ with his Church.'[36] If this interpretation is correct, it becomes clear that Paul's statement is intimately related to the general doctrine of the Epistle. The expression 'great mystery' would be applied to marriage only in the light of what the Captivity Epistles have to say about the mystery *par excellence*, the only truly great mystery, Jesus Christ, the mystery of God.

Pauline thought has developed considerably. From now on, the Apostle will speak of a single mystery,[37] and this mystery will be in the foreground of his thought. From now on, too, the term and notion of mystery will serve as a framework for the speculations and the attempt at synthesis made by the Apostle in

---

[36] Botte's translation (*op. cit.*, p. 460), in my opinion, diverges from the literal sense: 'This is a great mystery, I speak of Christ and the Church.' The author of the epistle is still speaking of marriage, but in function of Christ and the Church—and he emphasizes the originality of this view.

[37] In the perspective of our explanation, Eph 5:32 no longer constitutes an exception.

order to present a general view of the Christian economy. And, finally, from now on Christ is in the foreground of the mystery, and on the verge of absorbing it completely.

St Paul does not forget, however, that the mystery of Christ has its source in God. Eph 1 : 9 affirms it categorically. Nevertheless, the mystery of the divine plan appears now as incarnated in Christ (v. 10), to the point of being identified with him.

To see Christ from this angle is to consider him in all his dimensions. There is first *the historical Christ*, as the concise formula of Col 2 : 2 indicates; but it is the historical Christ as glorified through his resurrection and heavenly exaltation, Col 2 : 3 sees mysteriously hidden in this glorified Christ, 'all the treasures of wisdom and knowledge', those treasures which New Testament Judaism (Qumran Judaism, for instance), and Paul himself in other passages, attribute to God.[38] The mystery, then, is concretely the divine pleroma incarnated in Christ.

The mystery is also *the mystical Christ*, that is the fullness of Christ communicated to the faithful who are united to him through faith and charity. In virtue of the glory received by Christ in his exaltation above all heavenly powers, he has become the chief of a *soma*, of a body which he 'fills' completely.[39] This aspect of the mystery, as has been pointed out, is explicitly developed in Eph 1 : 15-17, not however without an allusion to the mystery of the glorious Christ: Eph 1 : 19-23.

Finally, in the various exposés treating of the graces with which *the glorious Christ* fills the believers who are mystically united to him (mystery of the mystical Christ), the community aspect, or the ecclesial dimension (to use the term preferred today), and, consequently, the *ecclesial Christ*, is not lost from sight. Believers form a body. It is by reason of their incorporation in this body that they share in the graces distributed by Christ.

In general, the Captivity Epistles are more concerned with describing the riches of salvation than defining those who are called to participate in them. These latter, however, are evoked in a few passages, namely in Col 1 : 26-27; Col 4 : 3, and

[38] Cf. for example Rom 11 : 33-36.
[39] Cf. J. Dupont, *Gnosis. La connaissance religieuse dans les épîtres de saint Paul*, Bruges-Paris, 1949, p. 497.

especially in Eph 3 : 3, 4, 9. Here this new aspect of the mystery is fully developed, the aspect which Mgr Cerfaux calls *ecumenical*, and which one might also term *ecclesial*; the aspect, in short, of a Church embracing all of humanity, Jews and Gentiles.

Thus the divine *pleroma* (Col 2 : 9; Eph 3 : 19) incarnated in Christ and communicated through him to the faithful (Eph 4 : 10; 1 : 23) seeks universal salvation. Christ wishes to become all in all in order that at the end of time when he delivers his empire to the Father, God will be all in all.

Pauline theology thus issues in an oxymoron, a paradox : the pleroma of God and of Christ need a complement, the Church. This is the final affirmation of the prayer of Eph 1 : 15-23 : 'the Church is the body of Christ, the *pleroma* (complement) of the one who fills all in all'—unless we take the pleroma in a passive sense and translate : 'the body of Christ, that is, that which is filled by the One who fills all in all'.[40]

It is in this ecclesial and ecumenical aspect of the mystery of Christ that St Paul formally includes the calling of the Gentiles : Eph 3 : 3, 4, 9 (as compared with 6). It is only in the light of this aspect, which is, as we have seen, rather exceptional, that one can term the call of the Gentiles 'a central element of the mystery'.[41]

To recapitulate : in the Captivity Epistles the mystery is Christ in all his dimensions, in so far as in him the divine mystery is realized. Christ, then, is the mystery of God made visible, as the Church in its turn will render the mystery of Christ visible.

In his lengthy explanations of the mystery of Christ, *pleroma* of the divinity, and of the mystery of the Church, *pleroma* of Christ, St Paul underlines certain notions for the first time, or at least more forcefully than ever before. He links the notion of heritage, for instance, to the 'mystery' (Eph 3 : 6; 1QS 11 : 5-8); and the word 'glory' appears several times (Col 1 : 15-18, 19; Eph 1 : 12, 14; 1QH 13 : 13-14). Moreover, the knowledge of the mystery is expressed by *epignōsis* (Col 1 : 9; 2 : 2; 3 : 10)

---

[40] Cf. J. Dupont, *op. cit.*, p. 474.
[41] L. Cerfaux, *Le Christ dans la théologie de saint Paul*, p. 311.

and by *sunesis* (Eph 3 : 4), terms which are used for the first time in a 'mystery' context. Finally, the idea of totality, which is strongly emphasized, makes its first appearance in this connection. All, indeed, must be recapitulated in Christ.

It is precisely the notion of totality that leads St Paul to teach the subjection of angelic forces to the power of Christ (Eph 1 : 20-21; Col 1 : 16; 2 : 10, 15). Here, again, we have a new aspect thrown into sharp relief in the Captivity Epistles. We are tempted to conclude that the author wished to combat dangerously widespread errors concerning the angels (Col 1 : 16; 2 : 10, 15, 18; Eph 1 : 20-21); now, it is well known that at Qumran there was much speculation about the angels, as well as discussions about feasts and calendars (cf. Col 2 : 16).[42]

In considering the great mystery, we have relied on the Epistle to the Colossians and to the Ephesians without any reference to the objections raised against the authenticity of the latter. Certain renowned exegetes claim that the two documents do not agree.[43] In Colossians, they say, the mystery is said to be revealed to the saints (Col 1 : 26). It would seem to be question of an essentially religious experience, accessible only to the faithful and having as object the mystical union of believers which assures them of salvation. This same notion, according to these exegetes, is found in Eph 6 : 19, but elsewhere in that Epistle different ideas are expressed. In Eph 5 : 32 the mystery concerns the relations of Christ with the Church; in Eph 1 : 9; 3 : 3-4, 9 the mystery has to do with the access to salvation open to pagans, the entrance of pagans into the Church on the same basis as the Jews, and their union with the Jews in one and the same body. In the Epistle to the Ephesians, then, it is no longer question of a

---

[42] Other problems merit attention : the relationship of *logos* to *mystērion* (cf. R. E. Brown, *art. cit.*, p. 70, n. 2; p. 76, n. 1; B. Rigaux, *art. cit.*, pp. 252-7); the precise meaning of *teleios* (B. Rigaux, *art. cit.*, pp. 248-52). Rigaux distinguishes three concepts of *teleios*: that of 1 Cor 2 : 6 which enumerates two categories of Christians; that of Col 1 : 25-9 where every believer is considered to be perfect; and that of Eph 4 : 12-13 where all believers are on the way to perfection.

[43] M. Goguel, *Introduction au Nouveau Testament*, IV, 2ᵉ partie: *Les épitres pauliniennes*, 2ᵉ partie, Paris, 1926, p. 466.

personal religious experience, but rather of a collective phenomenon. Moreover, this fact is revealed, no longer to the saints as
in Col 1 : 26, but to the apostles and prophets (Eph 3 : 3, 5) for
future generations (Eph 2 : 7).

This sharp distinction between the two Epistles in their
doctrine of mystery appears unwarranted. The mystery of the
call of the Gentiles is certainly emphasized more in Ephesians,
but it is not absent from Col 1 : 26-27. And while it is true that
Colossians develops at length the mystical union of the faithful
with Christ, the mystery and riches of this union are also
contemplated in Ephesians, where the doctrine of the *pleroma*
has a very personal ring (cf. Eph 3 : 19; 4 : 13).

We are now in a position to appreciate what Qumran can
offer in the way of parallels in order to throw light on the 'great
mystery' spoken of in the Captivity Epistles. It is hardly necessary
to say that nothing, absolutely nothing, at Qumran evokes the
mystery of the glorious Christ, nor the mystery of Christ which
we have called mystical. On the other hand, we must not minimize the significance of the two passages where the psalmist of
Qumran, to be identified, possibly, with the Teacher of
Righteousness, is described as the bearer, the incarnation, so to
speak, of a mystery hidden and sealed in his person.[44] Attention
has been called to these two texts,[45] but in my opinion they have
not yet been sufficiently emphasized.

Qumran offers few or no points of comparison with the
Captivity Epistles' doctrine concerning the concentration of the
mystery in the person of Christ, the pleroma of the divinity, but
the passages wherein St Paul describes the content and un-
fathomable riches of the mystery evoke numerous Qumran
pericopes. Indeed, nowhere in Pauline literature do we find such
striking resemblances to the Qumran vocabulary as in the

[44] 1QH 5 : 25 'And they went among the sons of misfortune slandering
the Mystery which thou hast sealed within me'; 1QH 8 : 10-11 'And he who
causes the Shoot of holiness to grow into the planting of truth has remained
hidden with none to consider him, and his Mystery has been sealed with
none to know it' (translations by Dupont-Sommer). In 1QH 5 the 'mystery'
is paraphrased in v. 26 as 'the source of intelligence' and 'the secret of
truth'.

[45] R. E. Brown, *art. cit.*, p. 73, n. 2.

F

Captivity Epistles. Some of these resemblances, which have already been noted by others,[46] may be pointed out here: mysteries of the divine will: Eph 1: 9; 1QH f. 3: 7; wisdom and knowledge present in the mystery: Col 2: 3; 1QH 12: 13; 13: 13-14; knowledge and wisdom present in the mystery: Col 1: 6; 1QH 2: 9-10; divine glory present in the mystery: Eph 1: 2, 14; 1QS 11: 5-8; 1QH 13: 13-14; marvels of the mysteries: Col 2: 2; 1QH 2: 13; 4: 27-28; 7: 26-27; 11: 9-10; 12: 12; knowledge of the mysteries: Col 2: 2; 1QH 2: 13; 4: 27-28; 7: 27; 11: 10; 12: 12; penetration of the meaning of the mysteries: Eph 3: 4; 1QH 12: 20; 11: 9-10; 1QS 11: 18; between knowledge and penetration set in parallel: 1QH 4: 27-28; 7: 27; 11: 9; 2: 13; 12: 13; 13: 13-14; 2: 9-10; 1QS 4: 6; 11: 5-8 (Eph speaks of *synesis*, Col prefers *epignosis* cf. 1QH 11: 9-10); heritage as fruit of the possession of the mystery: Eph 3: 6; 1QS 11: 5-8; opposition between light and darkness: Col 1: 12-13; Eph 5: 8; 1QS 3: 18; opposition to evil spirits: Col 1: 16; 2: 10; Eph 2: 2-3; 4: 27; 1QS 4: 1; the final eschatological victory Eph 1: 19-21; 1QS 4: 17-20; 1QM 14: 14-15; the saints and the perfect called to be the beneficiaries of the knowledge of the mystery: Eph 2: 19; Col 1: 26, cf. *La secte de Qumran* p. 165, and 1QS 5: 13; 4: 5. We could multiply these comparisons, but those we have given suffice to illustrate the point.

It should not be forgotten, though, that there is a fundamental difference, namely the place of charity among the virtues. In 1 Cor Paul placed charity above all, even above all knowledge. In Col and Eph charity concerns this primacy. It enhances science in the measure that it penetrates it, or that it becomes the proper and formal object of the only true knowledge, that derived from grace and union with Christ.

It must be added that at Qumran the mysteries do not attain to the divine being itself,[47] while in Pauline theology, the 'spirit'

[46] R. E. Brown, *art. cit.*, pp. 70-84.

[47] The statement is true as a generalization. There are, however, a few rare passages where the mystique of Qumran appears to reach the very being of God: 1QS 11: 5-6. On this point, cf. F. Gerltrain, 'Contemplation à Qumran et chez les Thérapeutes', *Semitica* 9 (1959), pp. 49-57.

communicated to believers searches the divine depths (1 Cor 2 : 10). The *pleroma* of God descends upon Christ, and from Christ descends upon the Church.

The similarities in the texts cited above raise the question of the origin of the Pauline doctrine of mystery. Contrary to the opinion of historians of religion who were anxious to underscore the influence of Hellenism, quite a few authors today judge that Paul could have elaborated the theology of mystery solely from Jewish antecedents, drawing now from apocalyptic sources, now from the sapiential traditions.

It would be difficult to trace out the exact limits of the influence exercised by these two sources which are, certainly, distinct, but which had already joined hands in the Book of Daniel.[48] Eschatological elements are clearly present. We have only to recall the 'mystery of iniquity', 'the mystery of the final victory', 'the mystery of the struggle against the evil angelic spirits', the mysteries of the parousia and of the final glorification.[49] But, on the other hand, wisdom themes are equally numerous. Paul draws on a vocabulary comprising two registers here : an apocalyptic register and a sapiential one.[50]

It seems safe to say that the sapiential register tends to dominate. Paul is inclined to keep the revelations of an apocalyptic nature within certain definite categories; the category, for instance, of the prophets and the 'glossolalists',[51] though the mysteries babbled by these latter remain unintelligible. For the ordinary faithful, even the saints, the perfect, the spirituals, the charism of wisdom tends to dominate, and we are told that in the last instance it must yield to charity.

[48] This is recognized by R. E. Brown (*art. cit.*, pp. 438-9). Cf. for example Dan 2 : 27-28.

[49] The number of contacts with the apocalyptic literature mounts if the other apocryphal works are taken into account: cf. R. E. Brown, *art. cit.*, p. 438 (4 Esd 12 : 36-37), p. 439 (Hen 48: 6; 62 : 7), p. 441 (Hen 38 : 3; 51 : 3), p. 442 (Hen 41 : 1; 52 : 2; 61 : 5; 63 : 3; 68 : 5; 71 : 4; 42 : 9; 51 : 3), p. 444 (Hen 103 : 2), p. 448 (Hen 104 : 10-12; 4 Esd 12 : 36-37; 14 : 5), p. 73 (Hen 51 : 3), p. 81 (Hen 61 : 8-10), p. 86 (Hen 63 : 3).

[50] Cf. R. E. Brown, *art. cit.*, p. 438 (Wis 6 : 22; 7 : 21; Sir 4 : 18), p. 439 (Wis 8 : 4; Sir 4 : 18; 14 : 20-21; 48 : 24-25; 3 : 21-23), p. 444 (Wis 2 : 22).

[51] Eph 2 : 20; 3 : 5.

If there can no longer be any doubt that the Pauline mystery is rooted in Jewish tradition, is the Hellenistic influence for that reason excluded? A priori, this would be unlikely in a bilingual author who frequented various milieux and had close connections with two distinct cultures. A posteriori, the improbability grows as authentic Hellenistic expressions are found amidst the avalanche of Jewish terms and concepts, at least in the Captivity Epistles. One such instance is *pleroma*.[52] Another, no doubt, according to L. Cerfaux, is *embateuein*.[53] We can, then, count the author of the Captivity Epistles among the Jews tinged with Hellenism,[54] a wide category in which the Apostle of the Gentiles includes himself quite naturally.

It remains to be determined whether the evolution in the usage of the term 'mystery' is such that we must distinguish between the author of the Captivity Epistles and the author of the first Pauline epistles. A recent study by Mgr Cerfaux provides an answer to this problem.[55] We invite our readers to consult the conclusions of this study by an expert commentator of St Paul.

To conclude: contrary to the opinion generally accepted, the call of the Gentiles does not constitute the primary object of the Pauline 'mystery'.[56] The Epistle to the Ephesians is the only one in which this call figures as an important element of the 'mystery'. Furthermore, the very notion of 'mystery' underwent a noticeable evolution.[57] In the pre-Captivity Epistles, the Apostle men-

[52] On *pleroma* and its antecedents, cf. J. Dupont, *op. cit.*, pp. 396, 419-27, 438, 453-76, 486, 491-2.

[53] On this term, cf. L. Cerfaux, 'L'influence des "mystères" sur les épîtres de S. Paul aux Colossiens et aux Ephesiens', in *Sacra Pagina*, Gembloux, 1959, vol. II, pp. 374-5, who opts for influence of the vocabulary of the Hellenistic mysteries. M. Goguel (*op. cit.*, p. 406) is of the same opinion. He refuses to accept the textual correction proposed by Westcott-Hort and taken up by A. More, Courcelle, C. Taylor, who propose to read: *aera kenembateuōn*.

[54] J. Dupont, *op. cit.*, p. 492.

[55] Cf. L. Cerfaux, 'En faveur de l'anthenticité des épîtres de la captivité', in A. Descamps *et al.*, *Littérature et theologie pauliniennes* (Rech. Bibl. V), Bruges, 1960, pp. 60-71.

[56] R. E. Brown recognizes this in part (*art. cit.*, p. 446), at least as far as Rom 11 : 25 is concerned.

[57] R. E. Brown, *art. cit.*, p. 440: 'At the beginning of his literary career (Paul) had not yet fixed his usage'.

tions various mysteries, almost all of which are on the historical plane. The great mystery whose object is the glorified Christ, the mystical Christ, and the ecclesial Christ, is elaborated only in Colossians and Ephesians. The former develops above all the riches of the mystical union of the faithful with the glorious Lord; the latter dwells at length on the doctrine of the ecumenical Christ, the Christ enveloping in his mystical and ecclesial extension both Jews and Gentiles, uniting them in a single body: the Church, his pleroma.[58]

As for the beneficiaries of the 'mystery', Pauline literature identifies them three times with the 'perfect': 1 Cor 2: 6; Col 2: 25-29; Eph 4: 12-13.[59] Nowhere does the term signify the 'initiated'. It is true, of course, that in 1 Cor 2: 6, the pericope seems to allude to a special class of Christians, those, namely, who have progressed in the realization of the ideal Christian life, but there is nothing astonishing about that. The fact is that Paul speaks of several paths of perfection. Sometimes he lavishes his advice with an eye to the states of perfection (1 Cor 7: 8-9); sometimes he suggests the possibility of acquiring a more profound Christian life (1 Cor 3: 1ff.); and sometimes he insists on the development of a Christian life considered in its entirety (cf. Phil 3: 12ff., as well as the metaphor of the 'edification').

In the Captivity Epistles, or at least in Col 1: 28, the perspective changes. Though Paul continues to distinguish between Christians in regard to charisms, he nevertheless pro-

---

[58] Mitton (cited by R. E. Brown, *art. cit.*, 76, n. 1) finds a slight difference in the conceptions of these two epistles of the Christ-mystery. The term 'mystery' is found in two texts of the Pastoral Epistles (1 Tim 3: 9, 16) whose Pauline authenticity is much disputed. The mystery is described in 1 Tim 3: 16 in such a way as to resume the principal aspects that the Pauline literature has revealed to us. Twice the expression employed evokes Eph 6: 19. In Eph 6: 19 we read: 'the mystery of the gospel'. In the Pastorals the term 'gospel' is replaced by 'faith' in the first text and by 'religion' in the second. In all three cases there is a shift of meaning from the content to the container. Paul has no objection to using metonymy. The term 'faith' poses no problems, and *eusebeia* is well attested in the Pastorals and the *Secunda Petri*. Via an appeal to Hen 63: 3, R. E. Brown (*art. cit.*, p. 86) links it with *ṣedeq, dikaiosunē*. Note that the LXX adds *eusebeia* to the six gifts of the spirit listed in the Hebrew text of Is 11: 2.

[59] In the Pauline letters *teleios* also appears in Rom 12: 2; 1 Cor 13: 10; 14: 20; Phil 3: 15; Col 4: 12; Heb 5: 14; 9: 11.

claims that all men—note the triple repetition of 'every man'—
are called to acquire the wisdom of the perfect. Eph 4 : 12-13
appears to suggest, however, that the fullness of wisdom is
reserved to a collectivity, the Church. It is together that the
faithful grow till together they realize the 'perfect man' who is
Christ.[60] Here, then, is a nuance to be added to the differences
already indicated above by a commentator of St Paul.

This is not the place to enter greater detail concerning the
notion of *teleios*.[61] It is enough to have shown its affinities with
the concept of mystery, and thus to have pointed out once more
a certain parallel, at the very least verbal, with the Qumran
documents.

APPENDICES

Note on the 'obstacles' of 2 Thess 2 : 7

In his commentary on Thessalonians, B. Rigaux admits that
he has not found the solution to the enigma. In fact, no recent
author has succeeded in making any progress toward the interpretation of the text. Shall I be so naïve as to hope to succeed
where so many more competent exegetes have failed? I shall, at
any rate, and at the risk of being corrected by my colleagues,
submit to them a few reflections which might possibly indicate
a way out of the impasse.

The major difficulty which up till now has made any new
solution difficult, if not impossible, is the fact that verse 7b is
interpreted as referring to the coming of the Antichrist. Conse-

[60] Cf. F. W. Beare, *The Epistle to the Ephesians*, in *The Interpreter's
Bible*, New York, 1953, X, 639. P. Benoit, *Les Épîtres de S. Paul aux
Philippiens, à Philémon, aux Colossiens, aux Éphésiens*, Paris, 1949, pp. 94-5
adopts the same point of view. He considers (p. 94, n. *d*) that the 'saints'
of v. 12 has in mind missionaries and other teachers. If this is correct it
would constitute a fourth difference by comparison with Col in what concerns the 'mystery'. In my opinion—and Father Benoit would not refuse
this exegesis—the saints can be identified with the faithful. The charismatics
(v. 11) organize the collectivity of the saints or faithful (v. 12) in view of the
growth of the body of Christ.
[61] For a complete study of *teleios*, cf. B. Rigaux, *art. cit.*, pp. 248-52. On
pleroma, cf. A. Feuillet, 'L'Eglise plérôme du Christ d'après Eph 1 : 23',
NRT 78 (1956), pp. 449-72, 593-610; P. Benoit, 'Corps, tête et plérôme dans
les épîtres de la captivité', *RB* 63 (1956), pp. 5-44.

quently, the *katechōn* and the *katechon* must be understood as obstacles in the way of this coming, and therefore distinct from the man of iniquity and the great apostasy which delay the coming of Christ. If verse 7b could be understood as referring to this latter coming, that of the Saviour, all would be clear : the *katechōn* would be identical with the man of iniquity, and the *katechon* would consist in the great apostasy, both obstacles being opposed to the parousia of Christ.

But verse 7b can in no way, we are told, refer to the coming of Christ, since :

1. the term *apokaluptein* is used in the context of the apparition of the Antichrist (v. 3).
2. the verse 7b is too far removed from verses 2-3, where it is question of Christ's return, for the pronoun *autos* of verse 7b to refer to the Saviour.
3. the time, or *kairos*, referred to is that of the Antichrist.

The last reason can easily be questioned. *Kairos* can just as well refer to the time reserved by Providence to the parousia as to that of the man of sin. As for the use of *apokaluptein*, why should we suppose that Paul is perfectly consistent in his use of this term, when in the same context the term parousia designates both the return of Christ (v. 1) and the appearance of his adversary (v. 8-9)? Finally, verse 7b may seem far removed from verses 2-3, but we must not forget that in verse 6 Paul seems to return to the beginning of the entire pericope. He in effect says : *and now*, i.e. after all the explanations, you know what is preventing the return, namely that of Christ, the only one he was intent on explaining.

Once verse 7b has been understood as referring to the coming of Christ, the *katechōn* and the *katechon* recall quite naturally the two obstacles, one personal, the other impersonal, already mentioned as being opposed to this parousia. What is more, the sentence, though elliptical, and rather awkward in its construction, is perfectly understandable according to one of my students who is Greek by birth and culture. A free translation which might bring out better the meaning of the text would be : 'And now (after these explanations) you know what it is that holds him back (Christ . . . the *autos* refers to Christ, for Paul is going back here to verse 6 and the problem of the day of the Lord introduced in verses 1-2), in order that he manifest himself in his time. True, the mystery of iniquity has already begun its work. Only at this moment *(arti)* (there remains) the *katechōn*, until he is put down. And then (here Paul passes brusquely to the description of this suppression, a stylistic mannerism of his) the man of sin will reveal himself, but the Lord Jesus will cut him off with the breath of his mouth.'

Notes on the views of Monsignor Cerfaux

In this same issue[62] Mgr Cerfaux also touches on the problem of the 'mystery'. He repeats that in writing his letter to the Corinthians from Ephesus, Paul already expressed himself in terms of 'mystery' (p. 70), that this epistle contains the seeds of a 'theology of mystery' that goes beyond simple faith in the gospel (p. 70); that Rom 2 : 33-36 and 1 Cor 2 : 6-16 distinguish 'mystery' as from 'gospel' as an object of a superior initiation (p. 64); that in Colossians and Ephesians the conception of 'mystery' is identical (p. 68, n. 1); that in Col and Eph 'mystery' becomes a key word (p. 68); and that the apostles appear in these latter Epistles as preachers of the 'mystery', rather than of the 'gospel'. (p. 68.)

These views are substantially those of earlier studies of this author. On the other hand, it seems to me that in the description of the content of the mystery his views have evolved. According to him, Paul is thinking of the *celestial Church* which manifests the mystery of Christ to the Powers (p. 66, 69), or, using another formula, of the *ideal Church* realized by God in the mystery of Christ (p. 70). As to origins, Cerfaux admits that a 'syncretist mystery' existed at Ephesus, and that an external pressure coming from Asian milieux influenced the thought of the apostle (p. 70, 69).

---

[62] Cf. the study referred to in n. 55.

8

CONTRIBUTIONS MADE BY QUMRAN TO THE UNDERSTANDING OF THE EPISTLE TO THE EPHESIANS*

Franz Mussner

K. G. KUHN has already drawn attention to certain parallels in language and style between the paraenetical section of Eph and the Scrolls.[1] The present essay aims at extending this investigation into various important recurring themes, concepts and patterns of thought in the Epistle.

I. 'MYSTERY'[2]

The term *mystērion* appears six times in Eph (1 : 9; 3 : 3, 4, 9; 5 : 32; 6 : 19). The same word recurs frequently in the Scrolls, and indeed in a pattern of thought that in part overlaps that of the Epistle.

* Originally published in *Neutestamentliche Aufsätze* (Festschrift J. Schmid), ed. J. Blinzler *et al.*, Regensburg, pp. 185-98.

[1] 'The Epistle to the Ephesians in the light of the Qumran Texts' (chapter 6 in this volume).

[2] Cf. also F. Nötscher, *Zur theologischen Terminologie der Qumrantexte*, Bonn, 1956, pp. 71-7; E. Vogt, ' "Mysteria" in textibus Qumran', *Biblica* 36 (1956), pp. 247-57; H. Schlier, *Der Brief an die Epheser*, Düsseldorf, 1957, p. 60, n. 3; R. Follet-K. Prümm, 'Mystères', *DBS*, vol. VI, pp. 178f.; M. Mansoor, *The Thanksgiving Hymns*, Leiden, 1961, pp. 65-74; O. Betz, *Offenbarung und Schriftforschung in der Qumransekte*, Tübingen, 1960, pp. 82-8; J. Coppens, ' "Mystery" in Pauline Theology and its parallels at Qumran' (chapter 7 in this volume).

1. THE SCROLLS :[3]

(a) 1QS 4: 18-19

'And God in the mysteries *(brzy)* of his understanding and in his glorious wisdom has set a time *(qs)* for the duration of perversity, and at the time of the visitation he will destroy it for ever, and then will arise for ever the truth of the world (for the world).'

The community is convinced that all time is determined by God, especially the hour of his action at the end of time. Time lies 'in the mysteries' of his wise providence.

(b) 1QS11: 5-6

'From the fount of his righteousness flow (flows) the laws (my [his?] righteousness)[4] as light in my heart. From the mysteries of his wonder (from his wonderful mysteries), (which are hidden) in the eternal Being.[5] My eye has beheld knowledge,[6] which is hidden from men; insight and prudence (are hidden) from the sons of men.'

The psalmist, as the representative of the community, has, by God's grace, been granted insight into the 'mysteries' of heaven which are known only to God and withheld from the children of men (cf. 1QS 11 : 3; 1QM 14 : 14 '. . . and the mysteries of thy wonderful deeds are in the heights of the heavens'). Noteworthy too is the close association of the synonyms 'insight', 'knowledge', and 'prudence' (in Greek probably *gnōsis, epignōsis, dianoia*).

(c) 1QpHab 7:13

'For all God's times *(qysy)*[7] will arrive at their goal *(ybw'w ltkwnm)*, as he has ordained it for them in the mysteries of his wisdom.'

[3] In all instances only particularly important and illuminating passages from the Scrolls are quoted.

[4] *Msphty* is either plural (cf. S. Rin, '*y* as an Absolute Plural Ending', *BZ* 5 [1961], pp. 255-258) or a noun with the suff. of the 1st per. sing. Others read *msptw* (suff. of 3rd per. sing. masc.).

[5] *(B)hwwh:* part. act. *Qal* masc. sing; possible the same Aramaic root *(hwh)* as in the divine name *Yhwh* (I owe this suggestion to H. Gross).

[6] H. Bardtke translates: 'through him who is eternity hath mine eye espied knowledge'.

[7] The Greek would be *kairoi*.

The translation and interpretation of this passage are much disputed, especially with regard to the meaning of *ybw'w ltkwnm*. I. Rabinowitz maintains that the periods of time ordained by God reach 'their full measure'.[8] R. Elliger is of the opinion that the periods of time reach their goal, in the sense that they attain the objective set by God.[9] J. Maier interprets it as the 'ordained sequence' of times,[10] supporting his argument by reference to syr Bar 81 : 4.[11] *Tkn* means 'ordained measure or quantity',[12] and the meaning of 1QpHab 7 : 13 is therefore probably that all (periods of) time attain(s) that measure which God in the mysteries of his wisdom has ordained. As the context shows, the problem is the duration of the final period of time ('the last time will endure for ages' 7 : 7!).[13] It is important to note that in the perspective of Eph (cf. 1 : 10!) there are also 'times', 'the last time', and the 'completion of time' (7 : 2) determined by the will of God. Their *oikonomia* is determined by God's mysterious plan, of which partial knowledge has been granted to the Teacher of Righteousness.[14]

(d) 1QH 1: 21

'This I perceived from thy insight, for thou hast opened my ear to wonderful mysteries.'

The context makes it clear that the 'insight' gained by the psalmist refers to the 'wonderful mysteries of creation' (cf. 1 : 6-20). In this way the psalmist (the Teacher of Righteousness) has become for the chosen ones of righteousness the 'bearer of knowledge in wonderful mysteries' (2 : 3), which are now made to refer to the salvation of the community, their wonderful deliver-

---

[8] *JBL* 72 (1952), p. 27 ('full measure').

[9] *Studien zum Habakuk-Kommentar vom Toten Meer*, Tübingen, 1953, p. 194.

[10] *Die Texte vom Toten Meer*, II (Anmerkungen), München-Basel, 1960, p. 146.

[11] 'And he hath declared unto me the mysteries of the times and the passing of the periods did he show unto me' (Kautzsch, vol. II, p. 443). Cf. also 4 Esd 14 : 5.

[12] Cf. L. Koehler, *Lexicon in VT Libros*, s.v.

[13] Cf. esp. A. Strobel, *Untersuchungen zum eschatologischen Verzögerungsproblem*, Leiden, 1961, pp. 7-14.

[14] Cf. O. Betz, *Offenbarung* . . . , pp. 75-82.

ance from the hosts of Belial. Cf. also 1QH 4 : 27f. ('and through me thou hast illuminated the face of many, . . . for thou didst reveal to me the mysteries of thy wonder . . . to make known thy mighty works to all the living'); 7 : 26f.; 11 : 4, 8, 9, 27, 28; 12 : 11f. The psalmist's congregation has become a community of those who understand God's salvific plan!

2. COMPARISON WITH EPHESIANS :

In essence the teaching concerning 'mystery' in the Epistle is as follows :[15]

(i) God has made known to the Christian community an eschatological 'mystery', whose execution will lead to the fullness of time : the subjection of the universe to the unifying sovereignty of the Risen Christ (1 : 10).

(ii) God manifests to the Apostle a hitherto unrevealed 'mystery' : the inclusion of the Gentiles among the eschatological people of God. The apostle, together with the (other) apostles and Christian prophets, proclaim this mystery to the community (3 : 3f.).

(iii) The apostle lays bare the execution of a 'mystery', hitherto known only to God, but now made known to the heavenly powers through the Church as the manifold wisdom of God (3 : 9f.). This is probably a reference to the universal reign of Christ that is already beginning.

(iv) In Gen 2 : 24 a 'mystery' is cloaked. The apostle recognizes its 'real' meaning by making it refer to Christ's relationship to his Church. Hence the scriptures have their own special mysteries (5 : 32).

(v) The 'mystery of the Gospel' is to be proclaimed 'boldly' by the Apostle. Hence Christians are exhorted to pray for him (6 : 19). By the 'mystery of the Gospel' is probably meant Christ himself.[16]

---

[15] Cf. also R. E. Brown, 'The Semitic Background of the New Testament *Mysterion* (II)', *Biblica* 40 (1959), pp. 74-84; W. Bieder, 'Das Geheimnis des Christus nach dem Epheserbrief', *TZ* 11 (1955), pp. 329-43; R. Follet-K. Prümm, *DBS*, vol. VI, 203-18.

[16] Cf. H. Schlier, *Der Brief an die Epheser, in loc.*; Col 4 : 3.

This teaching exhibits many contacts with the 'mystery-doctrine' of the Scrolls :

(i) A pattern of common, interconnected ideas ('mystery', 'insight', 'wisdom', 'intelligence', 'knowledge', 'revelation', etc.).

(ii) The mysteries of salvation were hitherto hidden in God.[17]

(iii) They have special reference to the events of the last days.

(iv) They were revealed to the Teacher of Righteousness, and through him to the community, so that its members, too, now possess this 'knowledge'.

(v) The Scriptures have their own mysteries, which stand in need of interpretation (cf. 1QpHab 7 : 4f. 'All the secrets of the words of his servants, the prophets').[18]

However, there are also notable differences :

(i) It is striking that Eph speaks of 'mystery' only in the singular.

(ii) The mystery is unequivocally Christ's eschatological reign, and the incorporation of the Gentiles into the Body of the Church.

These differences, especially (ii), are conditioned by the historic Christ-event, of which the sect naturally knew nothing.[19]

It is not possible to affirm *direct* dependence of Eph on the Scrolls on the basis of the term 'mystery'. The Jewish apocalyptic writers, like the Essenes, spoke of supernatural 'mysteries of God', which are to be revealed at the end of time.[20] Nonetheless there are many points of similarity between the two in their conception of the mystery of God, especially in their formal presentation. Both the Qumran community and the Christian Church are the 'chosen ones', who know the eschatological mysteries of God, though neither knows when the end is to be (cf. 1QpHab 7 : 2 'But the consummation of time he did not make known to him').

---

[17] Cf. J. Trinidad, 'The Mystery hidden in God. A study of Eph 1 : 3-14', *Biblica* 31 (1950), pp. 1-26.

[18] Cf. esp. O. Betz, *Offenbarung* . . . , pp. 86f.

[19] 'What is new with respect to Qumran is the Christology' (K. G. Kuhn, above p. 119). Cf. also W. Bieder, *TZ* 11 (1955), p. 330.

[20] Cf. *TWNT*, vol. IV, pp. 821f. (G. Bornkamm).

II.   The Bond between the Community and Heaven

1. THE SCROLLS :

(a) 1QS 11: 7f.

'To those whom God hath chosen has he given as an eternal possession (= righteousness, power, and the dwelling-place of glory),[21] and hath given them an inheritance in the lot of the saints, and hath united their community *(swdm)*[22] with the sons of heaven to be a congregation of unitedness and an assembly of the sacred building.'

In all probability the 'saints' are heavenly beings, and not the central nucleus of the faithful on earth; cf. 1QH 3 : 22 ('host of the saints'); CD 20 : 8 ('all the saints of the Most High');[23] 1QM 12 : 1 ('For the legion of saints is [with thee] in heaven, and the hosts of angels [are] in thy eternal dwelling-place'); 1QM 12 : 4 ('Together with thy saints [and with] thy angels'); 1QM 12 : 7 ('And the congregation of thy saints is in the midst of us to be our eternal succour').[24] It is not possible to ascertain who exactly are meant by the 'saints' in heaven. It may be that they are angels. They could also be the souls of the just (of the Old Testament or of the community?) taken up to heaven after their death.

(b) 1QH 3: 21-23

'And thou hast cleansed the perverse spirit from many sins that he might enter into station with the army of the saints and enter into communion with the sons of heaven. And thou hast cast an

---

[21] Cf. 11 : 6f. For the translation cf. P. Wernberg-Møller, *The Manual of Discipline*, Leiden, 1957.

[22] For the term *swd* in the Scrolls, cf. esp. O. Betz, 'Felsenmann und Felsengemeinde', *ZNW* 48 (1957), pp. 57f.

[23] Cf. Dan 7 : 18, 22, 27.

[24] Cf. also Wis 5 : 5 ('How was he numbered among the sons of God, and how is his lot among the sains?'; Ps 89 : 6, 8, on which cf. M. Noth, 'Die Heiligen des Höchsten', in *Gesammelte Studien zum AT*, München, 1957, pp. 274-90 ('the saints of the Most High' = heavenly beings); similarly L. Dequecker, *Le Fils de l'homme et les Saints du Très-Haut en Daniel VII, dans les Apocryphes et dans le NT*, Paris-Bruges, 1961, pp. 51-54; Bousset-Gressmann, *Die Religion des Judentums im späthellenischen Zeitalter*, Tübingen, 1926, 321; F. Nötscher, 'Heiligkeit in den Qumranschriften', *RdeQ* 2 (1959-60), pp. 163-81, 315-44 (esp. 321-6).

everlasting destiny for man in the company of the spirits of knowledge, that he might praise thy name in concord, and recount thy marvels before all thy works.'

The purpose of purifying the perverse spirit in man, presumably through a radical conversion to the Law of Moses and through sacred rites, is 'entry into station with the army of the saints', and 'communion with the sons of heaven'. The expression 'to enter into station' means 'to take one's place', 'to appear'.[25] This has been understood as a reference to life after death and the hope of immortality.[26] In actual fact, however, behind this concept in 1QH 3 : 21-23 lies a priestly tradition,[27] which had a decisive influence on the self-understanding of the Qumran community :[28] the elect on earth already form a liturgical community with the inhabitants of heaven. Hence the Essenes could say in 1QH 6 : 13 '. . . and they (the members of the community) stand in a common lot with the angels of the face';[29] (cf. also 1QSa 2 : 8f. 'For holy angels are in their community').[30] The Qumran community felt itself constituted as the true sanctuary of Aaron, in which perfect worship is offered, in place of the Temple in Jerusalem,[31] which in their eyes had been defiled. J. Maier rightly points out that this belief in the already existent union between the community and heaven worked against a futurist eschatology and in favour of an eschatology of the

[25] Cf. L. Koehler, *Lexicon*, s.v. *ysb*; also 1QH 11 : 5, 13; 13 : 16.

[26] Cf. esp. R. B. Laurin, 'The Question of Immortality in the Qumran *Hodayot*', *JSS* 3 (1958), pp. 344-55; M. Mansoor, *The Thanksgiving Hymns*, pp. 84-9 (further bibliography).

[27] Cf. J. Maier, *Die Texte vom Toten Meer*, vol. II, pp. 77-9.

[28] Cf. K. G. Kuhn, *RGG³*, vol. V, pp. 746f.; L. Rost, 'Gruppenbildung im AT', *TLZ* 80 (1955), pp. 1-8; O. Betz, 'Le ministère cultuel dans la secte de Qumran et dans le christianisme primitif', *La Secte de Qumran* (Rech. Bibl. 4), Paris-Bruges, 1959, pp. 163-202; J. Gnilka, 'Das Gemeinschaftsmahl der Essener', *BZ* 5 (1961), pp. 39-55.

[29] Instinctively we think of the Cherubim above the mercy seat (cf. Ex 20 : 18-20; 37 : 7; Num 7 : 89; 3 Kg 6 : 23-28; 1 Ch 21 : 18; 2 Ch 3 : 10-13). The idea of a link between the Holy City and heaven was prevalent in later Judaism, especially in 2 Macc where we read 'the boundaries of heaven and earth melt away in Jerusalem' (D. Arnhoevel, 'Die Eschatologie der Makkabäerbücher', *TrierTZ* 72 (1963), p. 266.

[30] Cf. 1QH 11 : 9-14; 1QSb 4 : 25f.; Tob 12 : 23.

[31] On the desecration of the sanctuary, cf. CD 4 : 18; 5 : 6; 11 : 22; 12 : 1f; 20 : 23.

present, and that this came to intensify the problem of the duration of the final age.

The ultimate purpose of the union between the community and the inhabitants of heaven is, according to 1QH 3: 23, the praise of God and his wonderful works. It is, therefore, essentially liturgical (cf. 1QH 6: 10-14!). Because of its communion with the heavenly world, the community shares in the knowledge of heavenly mysteries.[32]

2. COMPARISON WITH EPHESIANS :

According to the Epistle both Jews and Gentiles have 'access to the Father' (2: 18) in the community of the Church. The context makes it clear that the writer is here thinking of an idea, which he will deal with explicitly later, viz. that the community of the Church is the eschatological temple-sanctuary.[33] Whereas the Gentiles were previously *(pote)* 'strangers and foreigners', they are now 'fellow-citizens with the saints, and members of the household of God'.[34] As such Christians have already become citizens of the heavenly world,[35] and thus at all times have 'access to the Father'.

This perspective greatly clarifies the statement: 'he made us sit with him in the heavenly places in Christ Jesus' (Eph 2: 6). Just as the members of the Qumran community 'enter into station with the army of the saints', through their reception into the 'community of unitedness' (1QH 3: 21), so God permits those who have been brought to life through baptism with Christ to join him in the heavenly region in Jesus Christ. This should not be taken to mean that the baptized have already ascended into heaven. The meaning is that in the Risen Christ in the Church and as the Church they have been admitted into the existent heavenly region, which is identical with the eschatological temple-sanctuary.

[32] Cf. 1QSb 1 : 5.

[33] For greater detail, cf. F. Mussner, *Christus, Das All und die Kirche. Studien zur Theologie des Epheserbriefes*, Trier, 1955, pp. 107-18.

[34] In my book (previous note) I interpreted the 'saints' in Eph 2:19 as an allusion to Judaeo-Christians. This I no longer consider tenable.

[35] Cf. also Acts 26: 18; Col 1: 12f.; Heb 12: 22f; R. Schnackenburg, *Die Kirche im Neuen Testament*, Freiburg, 1961, pp. 130f.

The verbal statements of Eph 2 : 5f. *(sun)ezōopoiēsen,* *(sun)ēgeiren, (sun)ekathisen,* have their counterparts in 1QH 11 : 10-12 ('Thou hast purified man from sin . . . to raise from the dust the worm of the dead . . . that he may enter into station before you together with the eternal host'), and 1QH 3 : 19-22 ('Thou hast redeemed my soul from the pit, and from the Sheol of the abyss thou hast made me rise to everlasting heights . . . in order that he might enter into station with the army of the saints'). Salvation through grace from (spiritual) death is here understood as an elevation into the company of the inhabitants of heaven. Similarly, behind the *(sun)ekathisen* of Eph 2 : 6 lies the idea of being raised into the presence of the Risen Christ (compare 2 : 6 with 1 : 20). The tradition that underlies Eph 2 : 6, therefore, is not Gnostic,[36] but closely akin to the theology of the Scrolls.

Indubitably such a doctrine, as with the *Hodayoth* from Qumran, leads away from a futurist eschatology towards an intense awareness of the eschatological character of the present, but the former is by no means rejected in the Epistle (cf. note 56). This is not to be looked on as a deviation, or as a 'gnosticizing' tendency, but as a necessary consequence of the Christological and soteriological kerygma of the primitive Church, as is given classical formulation in Col 3 : 1 'If you then be risen with Christ, seek *those things which are above*, where Christ sits at the right hand of God.' Because the Church located the central point of its eschatological expectation in the Risen Lord, it had necessarily to adapt its futurist eschatology to one of the present.[37] The heavenly and the terrestrial communities already form a unity and a communion, whose main purpose is 'the praise of his glory', both according to Eph (1 : 6, 12, 14) and the Essenes (1QH 3 : 23; 9 : 14).[38]

---

[36] Cf. F. Mussner, *Christus, Das All und die Kirche,* 91-94.

[37] Cf. J. Körner, 'Endgeschichtliche Parusieerwartung und Heilsgegenwart im NT in ihrer Bedeutung für eine christliche Eschatologie', *EvTh* 14 (1954), pp. 177-192; F. H. Kettler, 'Enderwartung und himmlischer Stufenbau im Kirchenbegriff des nachapostolischen Zeitalters', *TLZ* 79 (1954), pp. 385-392.

[38] Cf. F. Mussner, 'Kirche als Kultgemeinde', *LitJahrbuch* 6 (1956) 50-67. For the OT, cf. esp. G. von Rad, *Theologie des AT,* I, München, 1957, pp. 353-67.

III THE COMMUNITY AS TEMPLE AND CITY[39]

1. THE SCROLLS :

(a) 1QS 8: 4-10

'When these things come to pass in Israel the community of
unitedness shall be established in truth as an everlasting planting :
a house of holiness for Israel and a company *(swd)* of infinite
holiness for Aaron. . . . It is the tried wall, the precious corner-
stone (cf. Is 28 : 16); its foundations shall not tremble nor flee
from their place. It is the dwelling of infinite holiness for Aaron,
in total *(kwlm)*[40] knowledge unto the covenant of justice in order
to make offerings of sweet odour. It is the house of perfection
and truth in Israel to establish a covenant (according to) everlasting precepts.'

In this passage, best described as a hymn,[41] the community is
seen both as the true, i.e. spiritual, temple, and as a divine planting (cf. 1QS 11: 8; 1QH 6 : 15; 8 : 5, etc.), whose eternal
duration has been promised. The distinction implied in the terms
'a holy house for Israel' and 'an assembly of infinite holiness for
Aaron' is clearly aimed at the Temple in Jerusalem. Priests and
laity together form a spiritual temple-sanctuary, which feels so
secure as to consider Is 28 : 16 ('Behold, I lay in Sion for a
foundation a stone, a tried stone, a precious corner-stone, a sure
foundation') as referring to itself. The change from 'stone' to
'wall' was probably influenced by Is 30 : 13.[42] Whereas, according to the image there used, the 'high wall' suddenly crashes

---

[39] Cf. also J. Pfammatter, *Die Kirche als Bau*, Rome, 1960 (with bibliography), pp. 155-63; O. Betz, *ZNW* 48 (1957), pp. 49-77; H. Kosmala,
Hebräer-Essener-Christen, Leiden, 1959, pp. 363-78; J. Maier, *op. cit.*,
vol. II, pp. 93f.; F. Mussner, *Christus, Das All und die Kirche*, pp. 107-18;
O. Michel, *TWNT*, vol. V, pp. 122-51; Th. Schneider, *RAC*, vol. I, pp. 1265-
78; G. W. MacRae, 'Building the House of the Lord', *AER* 140 (1959),
pp. 361-76; G. Wagner, 'Le tabernacle et la "vie en Christ". Exégèse de
2 Cor 5 : 1-10', *RHPR* 41 (1961), pp. 379-393.
[40] Bardtke and others read *'wlm* ('everlasting knowledge').
[41] Cf. P. Wernberg-Møller, *The Manual of Discipline*, p. 124.
[42] Cf. J. Maier, vol. II, p. 95 (on 1QH 7 : 9).

down, the community is conscious of itself as a wall tried by many storms, and whose foundations are immoveable.

Lines 9f. appear to present an eschatological view. The already existent congregation of 'the chosen of God's grace' (line 6) is the guarantee of 'knowledge' for the totality *(kwlm)* in the salvific future. Then once again will pleasing sacrifices be offered to God, and a house of perfection and truth will be set in Israel, a covenant for laws that will abide for ever. Here, then, the esoteric self-awareness of the community is at the same time the expression of the hope of salvation for all Israel. Just as once this hope had been bound up with the Temple in Jerusalem, now the spiritual temple of the community is the bearer and guarantor of salvation for all Israel.[43]

(b) 1QS 9: 5b f.

'In those days they shall choose (separate) from among the members of the community a holy house for Aaron that infinite holiness may be assembled together *(lhyhd*, Nifal),[44] and a house of unitedness for Israel, all those who walk in perfection.'

In the preceding passage (9 : 3f.) we read of the 'founding' of holy thought ('Holy Spirit') and eternal truth. This is seen as a means of expiating degeneration and of achieving 'good-will for the land' through the sacrifice of the lips (= prayers) and perfect walking (= spiritual sacrifices). The 'time' of foundation is the time when the 'members of the community' at Qumran will build 'a sacred house for Aaron' consisting of a 'holy of holiness' (for the priesthood) and 'a house of unitedness for Israel' (for the laity). This statement is likewise obviously aimed at the Temple; the community looking on itself as the true temple of Israel, wherein 'the perfect' are already assembled.

[43] Is the Qumran community to be regarded as a sect? J. Maier believes that the answer is yes : 'as the only possible means of conversion, as the only place where the covenant is preserved, and finally as the symbolic, sole-atoning temple-sanctuary' *(ZAW* 72 (1960), p. 163 n. 82).

[44] So Maier. Wernberg-Møller and others look upon it as a noun *(hyhd)* combined with the preposition *l* and interpolated into the original (cf. Wernberg-Møller, *The Manual of Discipline, in loc.*).

(c) 1QH 6: 25-27

'And I was like a man who entered a fortified city and unshakable (*n'wz*, Nifal of '*zz* with an active meaning)[45] through a high wall for deliverance . . .'[46] O my God. For thou set the foundation *(swd)*[47] on a rock, and a supporting beam *(kpys)*[48] according to the measuring-cord of righteousness, and the level [in order to test (them)],[49] *bochan*-stones in order to build a strong [wall],[50] unshakable. And none who enter there shall stagger.'

Although the text is partially damaged and there are difficulties in interpretation, it is nonetheless clear that the community is to be seen as the fortified city that affords to him that enters a sure defence against the assaults of enemies (cf. the wider context of the passage).

(d) 1QH 7: 8f.

'Thou hast set me up as a strong tower, as a high wall, and hast established my building,[51] and everlasting foundations for my community *(lswdy)*, and all my walls are a *bochan*-rampart[52] which nothing can shake.'

Here the psalmist himself is the edifice built upon a rock and immoveable. The 'I' of the psalmist, however, at the same time represents the community,[53] which is again seen as a city built

---

[45] Cf. M. Mansoor, *The Thanksgiving Hymns, in loc.*

[46] Damaged text.

[47] Maier comments: ' "Foundation" : *swd* (counsel, council, intimate circle) but occasionally interchangable with *yswd*, hence, "foundation". Also used metaphorically for the community. . . .'; cf. 1QH 7 : 9.

[48] For the meaning of *kpys*, cf. Gesenius-Buhl, *Handwörterbuch*, and M. Jastrow, *Dictionary*, s.v.; O. Betz, *ZNW* 48 (1957), pp. 62f.

[49] Damaged text, conjectural restitution.

[50] Maier comments: 'These *bochan*-stones = members of the community build the wall. This restitution is suggested by 1QS 8 : 7'; Bardtke supplies 'city', and Mansoor 'tower'.

[51] = my community; cf. also K. G. Kuhn, 'Der Spruch von Petrus und dem Felsen: Mt 16: 17-19', *Evangeslisch Autorität-Katholische Freiheit*, Bad Boll, 1959, p. 6f. (pro manuscripto).

[52] Is 28: 16 '*bn bhn* = a tried, i.e. proven (corner-)stone (cf. Gesenius-Buhl, s.v. *bhn*; 1QH 6 : 27).

[53] Cf. H. Bardtke, 'Das "Ich" des Meisters in den Hodajoth von Qumran', *Wiss. Zeitschrift der Karl-Marx-Univ. zu Leipzig* 6 (1956-57), vol. I, pp. 93-104.

on firm ground. The idea of the 'rock' on which the 'edifice' of the community is built was probably inspired by the holy rock on which the Holy of Holies (or the altar of sacrifice) of the Temple in Jerusalem was built, and which played such an important role in rabbinic speculation.[54] In the Scrolls the rock-foundation is spiritualized: it is eternal truth, knowledge of which has been achieved in the community (cf. 1QH 6: 25; 1QS 9: 3). In fact, the community has been posed by God as a 'foundation for Israel, for the Community of the eternal Covenant, to redeem all those who will it, to be a sanctuary in Aaron and a house of truth in Israel' (1QS 5: 5f.; translation of J. Maier). The Qumran community, as emphasized before, fulfils a representative function for the whole of Israel, and lives in the hope that, through it, the nation may once more become a sanctuary for God.

The highly flexible use of the building metaphor in the above quoted passage is worthy of note. The community is variously described as the 'foundation', 'wall', 'city', 'sanctuary' and 'proven stone'. It is pointless to try to explain the different terms on the basis of constitutional changes within the community. The building metaphor can also be applied to individuals.

2. COMPARISON WITH EPHESIANS:

Eph 2: 20-22:

'. . . built upon the foundation of the apostles and prophets, Christ Jesus himself being the corner stone, in whom the whole structure is joined together and grows into a holy temple in the Lord; in whom you also are built into it for a dwelling-place of God in the Spirit.'[55]

The profusion of building metaphors in this short passage (*epoikodomēthentes, oikodomē, naos hagios, katoikētērion tou theou*) are to be interpreted spiritually (*en pneumati*, v. 22). The Christian Church, composed of Jews and Gentiles, is a 'building'

---

[54] Cf. O. Betz, *ZNW* 48 (1957) 59; J. Jeremias, *Golgotha*, Leipzig, 1926, pp. 51-68.

[55] For a more detailed analysis of this passage, cf. F. Mussner, *Christus, Das All und die Kirche*, pp. 107-111.

and a 'holy temple in the Lord'. Its self-understanding is, therefore, similar to that of the community at Qumran.[56] The idea admittedly appears in the New Testament outside Eph,[57] but here it is closely related to the concept, already discussed, of the Church as being in communion with the heavenly world (compare Eph 2 : 20f. with 2 : 18f.), just as in the Scrolls.

The differences, however, should not be overlooked. They are due to the new dimension of salvation effected by Christ :

(a) The 'foundation' in the Christian Church is constituted by the apostles and the prophets.

(b) The 'corner-stone' is not to be taken ecclesiologically as in the Scrolls,[58] but Christologically, as always in the New Testament.[59]

(c) In the majority of instances the 'growth' of the spiritual temple is an allusion to the inclusion of the Gentiles in the community. At Qumran, on the contrary, the hope was for the incorporation of all Israel into the holy community.

(d) In Eph 2 : 20-22 there is no reference to the Church as a 'city'.

[56] It has to be borne in mind that in the question of the heavenly and earthly dwelling of God it is not simply a case of a terrestrial copy of a heavenly original. They form one indissoluble unity. This conviction should not lead us to any false ethical conclusion, e.g. libertinism. The eschatological perspective is not altogether lost in this basic conviction. In Eph it comes most clearly to light in 2 : 21 where Paul speaks of the house 'growing' into a holy temple in the Lord. This points to the future, and indicates that there is room for a maturing process.

[57] Cf. F. Mussner, *Christus, Das All und die Kirche*, pp. 112f.; M. Fraeyman, 'La spiritualisation de l'idée du temple dans les épîtres pauliniennes', *ETL* 23 (1947), pp. 378-412; J. Pfammatter, *Die Kirche als Bau*, *passim*.

[58] The Qumran community took the notion of the 'proven stone' (= rock of Sion) from Is 28 : 16, but 'put it into the plural, and so democratized it' (O. Betz, *ZNW* 48 (1957), p. 62).

[59] The close association in the Scrolls between 'corner-stone' and 'foundation' is an indication that in Eph 2 : 20 Christ is not to be taken as the 'lintel', as J. Jeremias has done; cf. also F. Mussner, *Christus, Das All und die Kirche*, pp. 108-10; J. Pfammatter, *Die Kirche als Bau*, pp. 140-51; S. Virgulin, 'Il significato della pietra di fondazione in Is 28 : 16', *Rivista Biblica* 7 (1959), pp. 208-20; R. J. McKelvey, 'Christ the Cornerstone', *NTS* 8 (1961-62), pp. 352-9; K. T. Schäfer, 'Zur Deutung akrogōniaios Eph 2 : 20', *Neutestamentliche Aufsätze* (Festschrift J. Schmid), Regensburg, 1963, pp. 218-24.

However, the fact remains that, just as in Eph, we find in the Scrolls an 'ecclesiological' spiritualization of the building metaphor. For this reason it is highly unlikely that the vision of the author of the Epistle was inspired by any kind of Gnosticism. But, on the other hand, there is no imperative reason to postulate his direct dependence on the Scrolls, especially since the symbolic use of building terminology is to be found elsewhere in the New Testament. A Christian tradition along these lines was already in existence when the epistle was written.

The matter dealt with in sections II and III are intrinsically connected, as both the Scrolls and the Epistle witness. The idea of the temple and the concept of union with the heavenly world belong together. This, too, is in keeping with a traditional line of thought. J. Jeremias, in his detailed study of late Jewish speculation concerning the holy rock in Jerusalem, came to the following conclusion : 'The holy rock is the entrance to heaven';[60] 'The ascent to the holy rock is Jacob's ladder, for it is the gate of heaven, the connecting link between heaven and earth. Indeed, it is part of the heavenly world, whose support it is. It is, thus, the place of the presence of God . . . and of the inhabitants of the heavenly world.'[61] In this perspective it is readily understandable that both in the Scrolls and in Eph the idea of the temple should be indissolubly and organically linked with the concept of the union obtaining between the community and the heavenly world. . . . Here we have 'access to the Father', and are already 'fellow-citizens with the saints'. Both the Qumran community and the Church had broken with the terrestrial Temple in Jerusalem,[62] and this particularly provided a basis for common ideas.

[60] Golgotha, p. 54.

[61] Golgotha, p. 67. According to Jubilees 4 : 26 Mount Sion will 'be sanctified in the new creation for the salvation of the earth'. At Qumran heaven was also obviously looked upon as a 'temple' and a 'holy city' (as in Apoc. and in the later Jewish writings); cf. J. Strugnell, 'The Angelic Liturgy at Qumran—4QSerek sirot olat hassabbat', Suppl. VT 7 (1960), pp. 318-45 (esp. 335); H. Bietenhard, Die himmlische Welt im Urchristentum und im Spätjudentum, Tübingen, 1951, pp. 53f., 123f., 192.

[62] Cf. O. Cullmann, 'L'opposition contre le Temple de Jérusalem', NTS 5 (1958-59), pp. 157-73.

IV. RE-CREATION[63]

1. THE SCROLLS:

(a) 1QH 11: 8b-14

'Through thy wrath (come) all the judgments of chastisement, and through thy goodness the abundance of pardon, and thy mercy is obtained by all the sons of thy loving-kindness. Thou hast given them knowledge in the assembly *(bswd)* of thy truth, and they were instructed in thy wonderful mysteries. And thou hast cleansed man from sin because of thy glory that he may be made holy for thee from all unclean abomination and from (every) transgression of unfaithfulness, that he may be joined [with] the sons of thy truth and the lot of thy saints;[64] to raise from the dust the worm of the dead to (an) [eternal] community *(swd)*, and from the spirit of perversity to insight . . .[65] that he may enter into station before thee with the everlasting host and with the spirits of [knowledge][66] that he may be renewed *(lhthds)* with all that shall be, and with them that know[67] in a common rejoicing.'

This passage describes the change from sinful man (= 'the worm of the dead')[68] into a new creature[69] as a three-stage process: (i) 'purification' from sin; (ii) 'elevation' from the dust; (iii) 'entrance' into the heavenly community.

[63] Cf. E. Sjöberg, 'Neuschöpfung in den Toten-Meer-Rollen', *ST* 9 (1955), pp. 131-136; F. Mussner, *Christus, Das All und die Kirche*, pp. 94-7; W. D. Davies, *Paul and Rabbinic Judaism*, London, 1955, pp. 86-146; G. Schneider, *Die Idee der Neuschöpfung beim Apostel Paulus und ihr religionsgeschichtl. Hintergrund* (Diss. Teildruck, Trier, 1959); id., *TrierTZ* 68 (1959), pp. 257-70; K. H. Kosmala, *Hebräer-Essener-Christen*, pp. 208-39; N. A. Dahl, 'Christ, Creation, and the Church', in *The Background of the NT and its Eschatology* (Festschrift C. H. Dodd), Cambridge, 1956, pp. 436-8; K. Prümm, *Diakonia Pneumatos*, vol. II/1, Rome, 1960, pp. 348-55; O. Betz, 'Die Geburt der Gemeinde durch den Lehrer', *NTS* 3 (1956-57), pp. 314-26.

[64] Alternatively (if we read *'am* instead of *'im*): 'In the lot of the nation of thy saints' (so Bardtke, Dequecker).

[65] Damaged text. Mansoor supplies *'l* 'of God'.

[66] Damaged text. Habermann supplies *smym*, and Mansoor *'mt*. In the light of 3 : 23 *d'ct* seems more probable.

[67] Angels? Cf. 1QSb 1 : 5 'knowledge of the saints' = angels.

[68] Cf. 1QH 6 : 34; 'predicate of humility as in 1QM 11 : 13 "to kneel in the dust" ' (J. Maier on 1QH 11 : 12).

[69] Cf. E. Sjöberg, 'Neuschöpfung in den Toten-Meer-Rollen', *ST* 9 (1955), pp. 131-6.

(b) 1QH 3: 19-23 (already quoted in part in II, 1):

'I give thee thanks, O Lord, because thou hast redeemed my soul from the pit (corruption, *sht*),[70] and from the Sheol of the abyss thou hast made me rise to everlasting heights. And I walk in a level plain without bounds, and I know that there is hope for him whom thou hast shaped *(ysrth)* from the dust for the everlasting assembly. And thou hast cleansed the perverse spirit from many sins, that he might enter into station with the army of the saints, and enter into communion with the sons of heaven. And thou hast cast an everlasting destiny for man in the company of the spirits of knowledge, that he might praise thy name in concord and recount thy marvels before all thy works.'

The pattern is similar to the previous passage : (i) deliverance from corruption; (ii) (re-)creation from the dust; (iii) entry into the army of heaven. Delivery, re-creation, and entry are achieved through acceptance into the company of the chosen on earth, which gives knowledge of the wondrous mysteries of God, his holy spirit, and his righteousness.[71] In 1QH 11 : 13f. this re-creation of the member of the community is associated with the universal renewal of all creation, of which it is the inauguration here and now.[72]

2. COMPARISON WITH EPHESIANS :

The pattern of salvation outlined above from the *Hodayoth* also underlies the argument in ch. 2 of Eph :

(i) Deliverance through grace from a state of death caused by sin, and elevation into the heavenly region (2 : 1-11).

(ii) The transformation of 'both' (Jews and Gentiles) into one new man (2 : 13-17).

(iii) Entry into the heavenly community in the spiritual temple of the Church (2 : 18-22).

We further find certain parallels in the presentation of individual themes :

[70] Cf. Ps 16 : 10.
[71] Cf. E. Sjöberg, *op. cit.*, pp. 134f.
[72] Cf. James 1 : 18.

(a) 1QH 11 : 8b-14 compared with Eph 2

'Anger'	*orgē* (2 : 3)
'Goodness'	*chrēstotēs* (2 : 7)
'Mercy'	*eleos* (2 : 4)
'Sin'	*paraptōma, hamartia* (2 : 1, 5)
'With thy saints'	*tōn hagiōn* (2 : 19)
'To raise'	*(sun)kathizein en tois epouraniois* (2 : 6)
'Worm of the dead'	*nekroi* (2 : 1, 5)
'Perverse spirit'	The spirit, who is at work in the sons of disobedience; 'the lusts of the *sarx*' (2 : 3)
'Entry into station'	*echomen prosagōgēn pros ton patera* (2 : 18)
'Together with the eternal host'	*sumpolitai tōn hagiōn* (2 : 19)
'To make new'	To create one new man (2 : 15)

(b) 1QH 3 : 19-23 compared with Eph 2

'To lead up from Sheol to everlasting heights'	*(sun)egeirein, (sun)kathizein en tois epouraniois* (2 : 6)
'Thou hast created'	'Created' (a new man) (2 : 15)
'To (eternal) community'	cf. *en heni sōmati* (2 : 16)[73]
'Thou hast cleansed the perverse spirit from many sins'	cf. 2 : 5
'To enter into station'	*echomen tēn prosagogēn* (2 : 18)
'Together with the eternal host'	*sumpolitai tōn hagiōn* (2 : 19)
'To come into the'	cf. *en (heni) sōmati* (2 : 16)[73]
'With the company of the sons of heaven'	*sumpolitai tōn hagiōn* (2 : 19)

In addition are all the other parallel concepts that have already been mentioned. If we were to adopt the reverse process and take concepts from Eph and look for counterparts in the Scrolls we would find an even greater degree of correspondence. This correspondence would be not only in the ideas themselves, but in the 'atmosphere' of the text, and in the unanimity of the basic conception. The need for brevity precludes a more detailed analysis here, and a comparison of two further ideas from the Scrolls with Eph must suffice.

[73] More details below.

V. Two Further Comparable Concepts

1. 'TO MAKE NIGH' (to enter, come into):

In the first place full membership is described in terms of 'bringing near', 'permitting to near', 'addition' to the community (1QS 6 : 16, 22; 9 : 15f.; 8 : 19).[74] Above all, however, it is said of God that he 'brings his chosen ones near'; e.g. 1QS 11 : 13 ('in thy mercy dost thou permit me to draw near', i.e. to thee); 1QH 14 : 13f. ('. . . and thou bringest me near thy understanding, and I come ever nearer'); 1QH 16 : 12 ('to purify me through thy holy spirit, and in thy loving-kindness to make me draw near, in accordance with thy great mercy').[75] Presumably both the idea and the terminology are rooted in a liturgical milieu (the Temple).[76]

A related concept appears in Eph. Those afar off become near (2 : 13; cf. 2 : 17; Is 57 : 19),[77] and both Jews and Gentiles have access to the Father in the community of the Church. God grants them, the members of his 'household' (2 : 19), nearness!

The differences between the Scrolls and the epistle are great, but easily explainable in virtue of the diverse *Heilssituation* of the two communities. Those afar off are the Gentiles, who have become 'near' through the sacrificial blood of Christ. 'Access' to the Father is effected in the spiritual temple of the Church. It is noteworthy, however, that the concept of belonging to a community should remain complementary to the idea of 'drawing near' to God, both in the epistle and in the Scrolls. This is closely bound up with their shared view of the community as the true temple of God.

2. 'UNITEDNESS' *(yhd)* :

Again it is not possible here to attempt a detailed treatment of this significant concept, which is unique and of supreme

[74] Terms : *ngs, qrb, ysp.*   [75] Terms : *ngs, qrb.*
[76] Cf. J. Maier, II, 27, 107; M. Delcor, 'Le vocabulaire juridique, cultuel et mystique de l' "initiation" dans la secte de Qumran', *Qumran-Probleme*, ed. H. Bardtke, Berlin, 1963, pp. 109-34; also the privilege enjoyed by priests in the O.T. of 'approaching' Yahweh (Ex 19 : 22; Ezek 45 : 4); also G. von Rad, *Theologie des AT*, vol. II, pp. 231f.
[77] Cf. F. Mussner, *Christus, Das All und die Kirche*, pp. 106f.

importance for the self-understanding of the Qumran community.[78] Mention of two important passages must suffice:
1QH 3 : 21f. ('That he enter into station with the army of the
saints, and enter into unitedness with the company of the sons
of heaven'), and 1QH 11 : 7f. ('to those whom God choose . . .
he gave a share in the lot of the saints, and has joined their
assembly with the sons of heaven to become the community of
unitedness *('st hyhd)*, and the community of the holy building').
J. Maier suspects with good reason that the notion *yhd* 'is used
exclusively in the service of the symbolism of the temple, and
consequently signifies the practical representation of the true
temple-sanctuary through the community'.[79] This term inevitably
reminds one of the 'one body' in Eph. Jews and Gentiles are
reconciled 'in one body' (2 : 16) with God. It is hardly necessary
to point out that the comparison instituted between *yhd* and
'one body' does no more than draw our attention to a *material*
parallel, which in both the Scrolls and the epistle is closely
related to certain ideas that the two have in common.[80]

For the rest, the outlook of Eph is very different from that
of Qumran, for everything is seen in an entirely new perspective,
conditioned by the Christ-event, and the Christian mission.

It should now be evident that the Scrolls throw much light
on Eph, not only with respect to various individual themes, but
also to a whole series of connected concepts, especially in the
central section formed by Eph 2. We find here a thematic
association of ideas, which is also in evidence in the Scrolls. This
intensifies the belief that the thematic material of Eph has its
roots in a tradition that is also represented at Qumran, and which
is far removed from later Gnosticism.

---

[78] Cf. esp. J. Maier, 'Zum Begriff *yhd* in den Texten von Qumran', *ZAW*
72 (1960), pp. 148-66; E. Koffmahn, 'Rechtsstellung und hierarchische
Struktur des *jhd* von Qumran', *Biblica* 42 (1961), pp. 433-42.
[79] *Art. cit.*, p. 166.
[80] I still maintain that *en heni sōmati* is a reference to the Christian
community (in the sense of the classical concept of an organism) and not
to the body of Christ; otherwise Eph 2 : 16 should read *en tō sōmati autou*
(cf. F. Mussner, *Christus, Das All und die Kirche*, pp. 99f.).

9
TRUTH: PAUL AND QUMRAN*

Jerome Murphy-O'Connor, O.P.

THAT there are traces of Essene influence in the Pauline corpus
is now generally admitted, for there are points of contact which
cannot be explained simply in terms of the Old Testament background shared by both. The precise extent and form of this
influence, however, are still far from being accurately determined,
and many detailed comparative studies, such as that of W. D.
Davies on 'Flesh and Spirit',[1] will be needed before the final
answers can be recorded. The choice of 'truth' as the point of
comparison studied in this essay was made for two reasons.
Firstly, the intrinsic interest of the theme in the Pauline epistles
—the noun *alētheia* occurs forty-four times and for the most part
in contexts that are theologically very significant—which does
not appear to have been given the attention it deserves.[2] Secondly,
F. Nötscher's summary classification of the 120 odd occurrences
of the theme in the Qumran literature[3] suggested that certain

---

* Published in *RB* 72 (1965), pp. 29-76.
[1] In *The Scrolls and the New Testament*, ed. K. Stendahl, New York,
1957, pp. 157-82.
[2] Apart from Bultmann's study in the *TWNT*, vol. I, pp. 242-5, the only
formal treatment, as far as I am aware, is that of D. J. Theron, '*Alētheia*
in the Pauline Corpus', *EvQuart* 26 (1954), pp. 3-18, which was not available to me.
[3] ' "Wahrheit" als theologischer Terminus in den Qumran-texten' in
Festschrift Viktor Christian, ed. K. Schubert, Wien, 1956, pp. 83-92. This
study is reprinted in F. Nötscher, *Vom Alten zum Neuen Testament*, Bonn,
1962, pp. 112-25.

aspects of the concept of truth current among the Essenes might clarify a number of Pauline expressions.[4]

I. TRUTH

The difficulties inherent in every effort to determine the influence of thought upon thought are not diminished in the present instance by the fact that the concept of truth shared by the Essenes and by Paul differs radically from that to which we are accustomed. From our point of view, 'truth' evokes correspondence or conformity. A thing is true if it exists and acts in perfect conformity with the exigencies of its own nature. A statement is true if it is an accurate representation of the facts. In this we show ourselves to be the heirs of a tradition whose origins lie in Greece.

Alētheia, according to Bultmann, 'originally signified a fact or a state of affairs, in so far as it is seen, indicated or expressed, and is fully revealed in such seeing, indication or expression, with special reference to the fact that it might be concealed, falsified or diminished'.[5] To grasp the truth of a thing is to see it as it really is, that is, to penetrate it so fully that nothing is hidden to the mind.[6] To know truth is to exclude the possibility of having to reverse one's judgement, a danger that is only too real if one is satisfied with the phenomena. The opposite of *alētheia* in this sense is *doxa*. According to Diogenes (IX, 22) Parmenides divided philosophy into *tēn men kata alētheian, tēn de kata doxan*.

If this truth, the genuine reality of things, can be perceived by man, it can also be spoken of by him. Hence, from Homer

---

[4] Except for slight modifications in detail the following translations have been used. For 1QS: P. Wernberg-Møller, *The Manual of Discipline*, Leiden, 1957. For 1QH: S. Holm-Nielsen, *Hodayot-Psalms from Qumran*, Aarhus, 1960. For CD, 1QM, and 1QpHab: A.-Dupont-Sommer, *The Essene Writings from Qumran*, trans. G. Vermes, Cleveland, 1962.

[5] *TWNT*, vol. I, p. 239. This section is but a brief resumé of Bultmann's fundamental study, 'Untersuchungen zum Johannesevangelium: A. II *Alētheia* in der griechischen und hellenistichen Literatur', *ZNW* 27 (1928), pp. 134-63. The essential elements are condensed in *TWNT*, vol. I, pp. 239-41.

[6] *Alētheia* is commonly derived from *a* (privative) = 'not' and *lath* (the root of *lanthanein*) = 'to be hidden'. Hence 'not-hidden'.

on, 'truth' appears as the object of verbs of saying. 'To speak truth' however is not so much to make an accurate statement, but rather so to frame one's expression that the thing may be seen as it really is. 'Truth' as a quality of speech may be verified only by someone who has immediate experience of the situation of reality described. If, lacking this experience, he forms a judgment purely on the basis of another's report it is because he recognizes *alētheia* as a quality of the witness. Hence the meaning of *alētheia* as 'truthfulness' or more basically 'reliability, trustworthiness'. Mediate awareness of the truth of things is conditioned by the truth both of the statements about them and of him who makes them. Above all therefore, 'truth' is an intellectual category. 'Truth' is reality, seen as it actually is. It is also genuine knowledge of reality as expressed by the mind.[7]

This conception received its greatest impetus from Plato, whose influence on his successors and in the West has been incalculable. He refused to consider as real anything subject to change. Consequently, for him 'truth' is fully realized only in the realm of the universal, the eternal, the divine. *Alētheia* is found only in the realm of Ideas because it alone *is* (*Phaed.* 248b). *Alētheia* formally is 'reality as such'; materially it is 'the eternal, the divine'. It is opposed to *eidōlon*, which characterizes the realm of phenomena, shadows or symbols of the real.

The same point of view is to be found in the Hermetic writings, particularly the *Peri Alētheias*, according to which 'truth' is only in things eternal, whereas on earth (and then not everywhere) are found only imitations of truth.[8] In the Corpus Hermeticum *alētheia* also appears as the designation of revelation. It is the teaching in which the divinity makes itself known, and as such it is not mere doctrine but a divine power (*C.H.* XII, XIII, 9). In this perspective *alētheia* is closely bound up with gnosis. To accept revealed truth, to know in this way, is to be

---

[7] *Alētheia* hovers between these two meanings in Philo. Dodd, however, notes that it is hard to find passages where the word clearly has the sense of 'reality' as distinct from the apprehension of reality. He does point to *De Migr. Abr.*, 190, where the mind is said to gaze upon *alētheia* as in a mirror, abandoning all *phantasiai* of the senses, cf. *The Interpretation of the Fourth Gospel*, Cambridge, 1960, p. 173.

[8] Cf. Bultmann, *art. cit.*, p. 153.

already divine (*C.H.* IV, 4-5, X, 9), to be an inhabitant of the
sphere of truth.

These are the ideas which unconsciously have conditioned our
minds and from which we must endeavour to abstract if we are
to do justice to the concept of truth elaborated in the Old
Testament. Far from being atemporal and suprahistorical, 'truth'
in the O.T. can be fully appreciated only within the framework
of an historical event, the Covenant. *'mt* which is most frequently
translated by *alētheia* (but also by *pistis*, *dikaiosunē*, etc.) is not
an intellectual category but a moral one.

'Truth' characterizes not only the written form of the Covenant
(the Law) but also, and especially, the fidelity of both its con-
tracting parties. It bears a reference to activity, not to speculation. It is to be done and not merely to be contemplated. If
Yahweh is said to be a 'God of truth' (Ps 31(30): 6; Jer 10: 10;
2 Chron 15 : 3) the sacred writer's intention is not to designate
him as the Supreme Reality, but to qualify him as fully committed to realizing the promises embodied in the covenant (Mi 7 :
20). Having power thus to *do* something for his people
immediately distinguishes Yahweh from all other so-called gods,
who, compared to him, are 'nothings' (Jer 10: 8). 'Truth',
therefore, evokes the reality of God, just as it does in certain
Greek writings, but whereas the Greek conception is static, the
Hebrew is intensely dynamic, so much so that the idea of reality
is embedded in the notion of reliability. Yahweh is the real,
genuine, authentic God because he has exhibited himself as
entirely worthy of man's confidence (Is 10 : 20). *'mt* primarily
connotes the quality of steadfastness. Applied to God's word
(2 Sam 7 : 28, Ps 19(18): 10; 111(110): 7; 132(131): 11) it
means that it is completely trustworthy. On it man can base
himself without any fear of deception (Ps 119(118) *passim*). This
is one point where the meanings of *'mt* and *alētheia* overlap, but
with a slight difference in emphasis. For a Semite the truth of
a statement is an extension of the truth of its maker. For a Greek
the reference is primarily to the truth of the object about which
the statement is made.

In the sapiential and apocalyptic tradition this aspect of truth (as a designation of revelation) undergoes a new development. In Proverbs it appears as *sophia*. Wisdom says, 'my mouth proclaims truth' (8 : 6), and man is exhorted 'to lay hold of truth and do not sell it, wisdom, discipline, intelligence' (23 : 23). Elsewhere it has more explicitly the character of *revealed* doctrine, especially in Wis (3 : 9; 6 : 22) and in Dan (10 : 21; 11 : 2). Anticipating a point that will be raised later, it should be noted that in this tradition 'truth' as a term of revelation does not mean the Law. In Wis it means God's salvific design in general, and in Dan it designates the revelations accorded to Daniel by an angel.

'Truth' can also be a human quality. 'Men of truth' (Ex 18 : 21, Neh 7 : 2) are those whose dependability merits the trust of others, a confidence extended also to their words (Gen 42 : 16; 1 Kings 22 : 16; 17 : 24). In the O.T., however, 'truth' appears most frequently as a generic description of the virtues of the genuinely religious man (Jos 24 : 14; 1 Sam 12 : 24). Loving truth (Zech 8 : 19), he does truth (Gen 32 : 11; 2 Sam 2 : 6; 2 Chron 31 : 20) and walks in the ways of truth (Tob 1 : 3; Wis 5 : 6). His prayer is of value only if it is 'in truth' (Ps 145 (144) : 18; cf. Jer 29 : 13). 'Truth' is in effect a synonym of 'righteousness', which explains the varying translations of the LXX.

In the concept of truth manifested in the Qumran literature we find the same three strands noted in both the Greek writings and the O.T. : it is applied to God, to revelation, and to man.

As we might expect, the truth of God plays a major role in the teaching of those whose way of life was founded on complete confidence in God's fidelity to his promises. Despite the fact that the formula 'truth of God' occurs only three times (1QS 3 : 6; 11 : 4; 1QM 4 : 6; 'God of truth' 1QH 15 : 25), the theme permeates the writings of the Essenes, particularly the *Hymns*. 'Truth' as a designation of revealed doctrine (embodying both the Law and its interpretation) is also frequently met with, as we shall have occasion to see in some detail. The principal emphasis of the Qumran literature lies on 'truth' as a quality of moral behaviour. Each and every aspect of the Essenes' activity is viewed under the optic of 'truth'.

Candidates for membership in the community are termed 'volunteers for thy (God's) truth' (1QS 1 : 11; 5 : 10). Their entrance is a conversion to truth (1QS 6 : 15) because they bind themselves by oath to the precepts of truth (1QS 1 : 15). This radical change in their lives, which contrasts sharply with those of their predecessors (1QS 1 : 26), has been made possible only because God has chosen them 'unto truth' (CD 13 : 10). It is through his gracious providence that they are 'in the lot of truth' (CD 13 : 12), that is, within the sphere of influence of the spirit of truth (1QS 3 : 24). This is the crucial point, for it is in proportion as a man is dominated by this spirit that he loves truth (1QS 4 : 17, 24). His mind purified by contact with truth (1QS 1 : 12), the sectary grows in the knowledge of truth (1QS 9 : 17) through instruction in the marvellous mysteries of truth (1QS 9 : 18). And just as truth plays a part in cleansing him of sin (1QS 3 : 7), so too at the end of time will it be poured out on the world and all lying abominations will come to an end (1QS 4 : 20-21). But until the moment of final victory the Essene must see that his hands do not slacken in the service of truth (1QpHab 7 : 10). Consequently, in the catalogues of the virtues which should adorn the perfect member 'to practise truth' always holds pride of place (1QS 1 : 5; 5 : 4, 25; 8 : 2). God is mindful of the effort this entails and he himself directs man's steps in truth (1QH 7 : 14), thus enabling him to walk 'in the ways of righteousness of truth' (1QS 4 : 2). To follow one's own will is tantamount to a betrayal of truth (1QS 7 : 18), but the man who is docile to the divine guidance serves God in truth and with an undivided heart (1QH 16 : 7). His situation is very different from that of those who seek God with a double heart, because they are not established in his truth (1QH 4 : 14). These are the 'sons of deceit' (1QS 3 : 20, etc.) whom he as a 'son of truth' (1QS 4 : 5, etc.) is obliged to detest (1QS 1 : 10, etc.). Only another 'son of truth' can be the object of his loving affection (1QS 4 : 5; 5 : 4, 25). His behaviour towards all is governed by 'the measure of truth' (1QS 8 : 4) and this particularly in the matter of speech (1QS 10 : 23). Thus he can claim that all his deeds are in God's truth (1QH 6 : 9). The community, whose members faithfully show forth revealed truth to the extent of being 'witnesses of truth' (1QS 8 : 6), thereby lays a foundation of truth (1QS 5 : 5) and in fact constitutes a community (1QS 2 : 26) or house (1QS 5 : 6; 8 : 9) of truth. In sum, to quote the striking expression of the *Hymns*: 'Thou art righteous and all thy elect are truth' (1QH 14 : 15).

As this brief summary shows, the Essene concept of truth is homogeneous with that of the O.T. and exhibits no traces of Greek influence. Many new and more vivid phrases have been coined to express it, and the theme occupies a much more central place in the teaching of the sect than it does in the O.T. A marked evolution is perceptible in the idea of 'truth' as revelation, and one is immediately struck by the emphasis on 'truth' as a quality, or rather *the* quality, of the community and its members. Both of these developments are most probably to be explained in function of the historical circumstances which gave birth to the community. The cause of the separation of the sect from the main stream of Judaism is seen by Cross to lie in the transference of the high-priesthood from the Zadokites to the Hasmoneans.[9] This was resisted by the Teacher of Righteousness who, though he won a following among the Hasîdîm, was eventually forced to flee to exile in the desert of Qumran, where he established the community of the New Covenant. 'In short', to quote Cross, 'the Essenes are a counter-Israel organized by a counter-priesthood, the "true" Israel led by the "legitimate" priesthood'.[10] This suggests that every mention of 'truth' has polemic overtones.[11] It was inevitable in these circumstances that at every hands turn it should be emphasized that the interpretation of the Law current in the community was 'truth', and that the pattern of behaviour based on this teaching was also 'truth'—the implication being

[9] *The Ancient Library of Qumran and Modern Biblical Studies*, New York, 1958, Ch. 3, esp. pp. 116-7.

[10] *Op. cit.*, p. 96.

[11] Cf. O. Betz, *Offenbarung und Schriftforschung in der Qumransekte*, Tübingen, 1960, p. 59.

that neither the 'official' teaching nor the conduct it inspired could be anything other than 'deceit'.

A priori we should expect to find marked similarities both of thought-content and terminology between Paul's concept of 'truth' and that of the Essenes, because, whatever the influence of Hellenistic thought on the Apostle, it is certain that the roots of his mind go deep into the O.T., the soil in which 'the everlasting plant' (1QS 8 : 5) at Qumran flourished. Contacts are significant, therefore, only in the measure that they are on points peculiar to Paul and Qumran. This study does not pretend to be an exhaustive examination of either the Pauline or the Essene concept of 'truth'. Its much more modest object, as stated already, is to attempt to fill in the background of certain aspects of the use of *alētheia* in the epistles by reference to the Qumran literature. It strives to answer questions to which Greek and O.T. sources do not provide fully satisfactory replies. What, for example, is the origin of Paul's description of the Law as the form of knowledge and truth? Under what influences did the concept of the Gospel as 'truth' evolve? Why is the characterization of the Christian life as 'truth' restricted to one Epistle? Do parallels exist for the expressions 'knowledge of truth' and 'foundation of truth'?

II. REVELATION

The Law

Despite the ironical flavour of the context, commentators are agreed that Paul was representing a genuine view of the Law in describing it as 'the form *(morphōsis)* of knowledge and truth' (Rom 2 : 20). Principally because he elsewhere describes it as good (1 Tim 1 : 8), holy (Rom 7 : 12) and spiritual (Rom 7 : 14) and certainly includes it under the *logia tou theou* of Rom 3 : 2.[12] A slight difficulty against this interpretation is raised by the only other instance in the New Testament of *morphōsis*. It appears in 2 Tim as governing *eusebeia* in the catalogue of corruption

---

[12] Cf. P. Bläser, *Das Gesetz bei Paulus*, Münster, 1941, pp. 44-5.

predicted for the 'last times' (3 : 1-9) and means 'the outward form of piety' in the most pejorative sense possible, because the context insists that the reality is entirely lacking (v. 5). *Morphōsis* does not occur in the LXX, but its use in *Test. Benj.*, 10 : 1 to designate the 'form of the countenance' of Joseph indicates that the connotation of falsity in 2 Tim 3 : 5 belongs to it purely by reason of the context. Consequently, we must see in Rom 2 : 20 a description of the Law as the visible and concrete embodiment of knowledge and truth.

None of the commentators attempts to clarify the reality designated by 'truth'. Lagrange insists that it is not to be taken as a qualification of 'knowledge', but his distinction between the two is rather cryptic : 'Law as the incarnation of religious and moral *knowledge* and of *truth* which is even better.'[13] The context makes it easy to establish the content of 'knowledge'. It is the 'knowledge of the will of God' mentioned in v. 18, that is, the terms of the Covenant as committed to writing in the Law. It is noteworthy that knowledge is here associated with the Law in a teaching context,[14] for this is the context in which the two are associated in the synoptic and prophetic traditions. In Lk 11 : 52 Christ berates the lawyers who have hidden the key of knowledge from those who thirsted to know, an accusation that echoes Hosea's indictment of the priests : 'My people perish through lack of the Knowledge *(dʿt)*.[15] Because you have rejected the Knowledge I will expel you from my priesthood. You have forgotten the Law of thy God. I will in turn forget you' (4 : 6). This passage well suggests the resonance that Paul's characterization of the Law as the embodiment of knowledge could have in well-informed Jewish ears. The theme is taken up again by Malachi in a form that at first sight presents us with a closer analogy in that it associates truth with knowledge and Law. He institutes an unfavourable comparison between the priests of his time and their father Levi : 'The law of truth *(nomos alētheias)*

---

[13] *S. Paul: Épitre aux Romains*, Paris, 1950, p. 52.

[14] Through the Jews the light of the Law was to be mediated to the nations; cf. Is 2 : 3, 5; Wis 18 : 4; Josephus, *Contra Apion*, 2, 41.

[15] On the objective value of *dʿt* here cf. H. W. Wolff, *Dodekapropheton I: Hosea*, Neukirchen, 1961, p. 97.

was in his mouth and no wrong was on his lips. . . . For the lips of a priest should preserve knowledge *(gnōsis)*, and law *(nomos)* should they seek at his mouth. For he is the messenger of the Lord of hosts. But you have turned aside from the way, and many you have made to stumble through the law' (2 : 6-8). This translation is based on the LXX, since it is this version or a rescension thereof that Paul knew and used. *Nomos* here renders *torah*. It is not always a felicitous translation,[16] because *torah* basically means 'instruction' and can be applied to the directives given by a father to his son or by a sage to his pupil. *Nomos* in the centuries immediately preceding the Christian era meant 'law' in the sense we understand it today, that is, a single statuary enactment, or the legal corpus of a given community.[17] Malachi, however, gives *torah* a similarly legalistic value,[18] employing it of the precepts governing offerings elaborated in Lev 22 : 18-25. It is because the priests bring 'the mangled, the lame, and the sick' (1 : 13) to sacrifice that they do not have the *nomos alētheias*. This makes it clear that the genitive 'of truth' has only the force of an adjective, distinguishing genuine instruction from the corrupt, diluted version proposed by the priests.

Thus, despite the fact that it unites the three terms Law, knowledge and truth, it is evident that this passage provides a very inadequate background for the Pauline expression. The prophet's conception of *nomos* (at least in this passage) is narrower than the Apostle's, who evidently is using *nomos* to designate the entirety of divine revelation, certainly that conserved in the books of the O.T., and very probably also the interpretation associated with these writings.[19] This is very close to the Deuteronomic con-

---

[16] On the nuances separating the two, cf. C. H. Dodd, *The Bible and the Greeks*, London, 1935, pp. 25-34, who concludes that 'over a wide range of meanings the rendering of *torah* by *nomos* is thoroughly misleading'.

[17] Cf. Dodd, *op. cit.*, p. 26.

[18] Cf. A. Robert, 'Le sens du mot "Loi" dans le Ps CXIX', *RB* 46 (1937), pp. 194-5.

[19] In NT times *torah* in its widest meaning was used as a collective designation for the whole of the authoritative tradition, not merely that codified in sacred scripture, but that also which was carried forward orally. The whole of the oral tradition did not originate as scripture interpretation, but that did not prevent the rabbis from seeing (in principle) the oral *torah* as the interpretation of the written *torah*. Cf. B. Gerhardsson, *Memory and Manu-*

ception of *torah* as the totality of divine revelation, understood
as a rule of life, which we find reflected in Ps 119(118).[20] This
has its importance, for in this psalm we find the only other O.T.
association of the Law with truth. A simple affirmation : 'thy
Law is truth' (v. 142), which is reiterated in synonymous phrases :
'the word of truth' (v. 43), 'all thy commands are truth' (v. 151),
'the essence *(r'š)* of thy word is truth' (v. 160). Many commentators[21] take the *r'š* of v. 160 as 'sum'. It is undeniable that
r'š can bear this sense (cf. Ps 139(138): 17), but it is difficult to
see what meaning it can have when coupled with a noun in the
singular. Dhorme, followed by Tournay *(BJ)*, because of the
parallelism with 'forever' in the next line, prefers the sense of
'principle'.[22] If we understand this 'principle' not as extrinsic
but as intrinsic, the well-spring from which the word derives its
very being, we arrive at something very close to the rendering
'essence' proposed by Kissane[23] and Deissler.[24] Their main
argument in favour of this translation is the context as established
by vv. 142 and 151.

What does the psalmist mean by 'truth' here? The whole
psalm is a hymn in praise of the divine Law. The centre of his
universe, it polarizes his entire existence. He prays for greater
knowledge (vv. 27, 29, 33, etc.) that he may ever conform himself
more perfectly to it (v. 44). In a world where evil ever attempts
to suck him down into its mire (vv. 61, 78, 85, 95, etc.) it is the
one thing on which he can rely with absolute confidence (v. 133).
Opposed to unreality (v. 37), it is the supremely real. To sum up
in one word all that the Law meant to him he could hardly
have chosen better than *'mt*, whose basic idea is solidity, firmness;

*script. Oral Tradition and Written Transmission in Rabbinic Judaism and
Early Christianity*, Uppsala, 1961, pp. 19-21, 82; also G. F. Moore, *Judaism
in the First Centuries of the Christian Era*, vol. I, Cambridge, 1927,
pp. 253-5.

[20] Cf. A. Robert, *art. cit.*, p. 206; A. Deissler, *Psalm 119(118) und seine
Theologie*, München, 1955, pp. 78, 294-7.

[21] E.g. Zorell, Cales, Bird, Boylan.

[22] *L'emploi métaphorique des noms de parties du corps en hébreu et en
accadien*, Paris 1923, p. 33.

[23] *The Book of Psalms*, Dublin, 1954, vol. II, p.160.

[24] *Op. cit.*, p. 252.

it is the quality that makes a being dependable, deserving of confidence.

In the light of all this, it is undeniable that the O.T. does provide a background for the description of the Law as the embodiment of knowledge and truth, in the sense that all the terms have an O.T. history. It is not, however, entirely satisfactory, as Schlier has obviously felt, for he develops Lietzmann's hint that the phrase 'form of knowledge and truth' may be drawn from a work destined for Jewish proselytes, by suggesting that it may even be the title of such a work.[25] As a background the O.T. is defective principally on two counts. Firstly, the association of truth *as a term of revelation* with the Law.[26] (The context of Rom 2 : 20 excludes the two O.T. meanings 'fidelity' and 'reality'. The former would square badly with *morphōsis*, and the latter is out of place because the nations are not conceived as enemies but almost as suppliants.) Secondly, the link between truth *and* knowledge and the Law. The Qumran literature throws a certain amount of light on both these points.

At the beginning of the *Manual of Discipline* we read: 'All those who devote themselves to his truth, all their discernment and their strength and their property shall come into God's community, so that they can clarify their discernment by the truth of the ordinances of God *(b'mt ḥwqy 'l)*' (1QS 1 : 12). The parallel with 1 : 7 : 'those who devote themselves to do the ordinances of God', and the prescription of 1 : 15 : 'they must not turn aside from the ordinances of his truth', make it quite

---

[25] *Die Zeit der Kirche*, Freiburg, 1958, p. 44.

[26] It is not denied that the *torah* was considered by the O.T. as an enlightenment—cf. G. Vermes, 'The Torah is a Light,' *VT* 8 (1958), pp. 436-8 and the references there given—but conceived as such it was never characterized as 'truth'; cf. C. H. Dodd, *The Interpretation of the Fourth Gospel*, Cambridge, 1960, p. 176. That Hebrew thought was evolving in this direction is possibly suggested by the expression 'to walk in thy truth' which occurs in a number of psalms (25(24): 3; 26(25): 3; 86(85): 11). I de la Potterie ('Vérité', *Vocabulaire de théologie biblique*, ed. X. Léon-Dufour, Paris, 1962, p. 1092) holds that in these passages, 'truth' is not moral behaviour but the Law. It is, however, equally possible that 'thy truth' should mean the fidelity due to Yahweh, the pronominal suffix thus corresponding to the 'before Yahweh', which is invariably found elsewhere as the determinative of 'to walk in truth' (1 Kg 2 : 4, 3 : 6, 2 Kg 20 : 3 = Is 38 : 3, Tob 3 : 5).

clear that it is the Law that is in question here. Conceived as an interior illumination, it is described as 'truth'.[27] 'The Law' at Qumran meant not only the Law of Moses (CD 15 : 9; 16 : 2) but the whole of the O.T., since it seems only reasonable to associate the immense exegetical labour manifested in the *pešerim* with the emphasis laid on the study of the Law (1QS 5 : 2; 6 : 6).[28]

'Truth', however, as a term of revelation, could also designate a reality even wider than the Law thus understood. The candidate on being admitted to the community was obliged to take two oaths : (i) 'to return to the *Law of Moses*, according to everything which he has commanded with all heart and soul, according to *everything which has been revealed from it. . . ,* and according to the multitude of the men of their covenant who devote themselves to the truth' (1QS 5 : 8-10); (ii) 'to separate himself from the men of deceit . . . for they cannot be reckoned as being in his covenant since they have not sought nor inquired after him in his statutes in order to know *the hidden things*' (1QS 5 : 10-11). These 'hidden things', as CD 3 : 13-15 makes clear, consisted of his holy sabbaths, his glorious feasts, his testimony of righteousness, his ways of truth, the desires of his will. They constitute 'the wondrous mysteries of truth' (1QS 9 : 18-19) in which full members must be perfectly instructed, and which may perhaps be identified with the revelation effected by the prophets under the guidance of the holy spirit (1QS 8 : 16). Entrance into the Covenant, which involves the acceptance of all this as normative, is 'to turn to the truth' (1QS 6 : 15; cf. 1QH 10 : 30). Hence, 'truth' when not obviously restricted in meaning, should be understood as designating the entire revelation accepted by the Essenes as authoritative because divinely guaranteed.[29] It

---

[27] This understanding of the Law as 'truth-revelation' existed side by side with the O.T. concept of the Law as 'truth-reality', cf. 1QH 9 : 31-2. Compare 1QH 7 : 20; 10 : 17 and Ps 119(118): 115, 160.

[28] Apropos of the use of the O.T. in the *Hymns* Holm-Nielsen points out that much greater use is made of the prophets and the psalms than of the Pentateuch, *Hodayot-Psalms from Qumran*, Aarhus, 1960, p. 287, n. 23.

[29] The doctrine of the Teacher of Righteousness is considered to come 'from the mouth of God' (1QpHab 2 : 2, cf. 2 : 8-9). Cf. O. Betz, *Offenbarung und Schriftforschung in der Qumransekte*, Tübingen, 1960, pp. 55.

is, therefore, co-extensive with the contemporary rabbinic notion of *torah*.[30]

This 'truth' was naturally the source of the special knowledge on which the Essenes prided themselves: 'Thy truth thou causest to shine forth unto endless glory and eternal peace. Praised be thou, O Lord, for thou [unto the children of men] hast given the insight of knowledge to understand thy wonders' (1QH 11 : 27-28; cf. CD 15 : 3). And again: 'I [thank thee, O Lord,] for thou hast given me insight into thy truth, and the mysteries of wonder thou hast made known to me' (1QH 7 : 26-27). Consequently, truth and knowledge are frequently associated,[31] and in view of the nature of the community there is always an underlying reference to the Law. Two passages are particularly impressive. 'Thou hast made me . . . a foundation of truth and knowledge for the righteous of way' (1QH 2 : 9-10). 'Because of their guilt thou hast hidden the fountain of knowledge and the foundation of truth' (1QH 5 : 26). The precise meaning of both these passages will be discussed in detail further on, but even as mere formulae they provide a closer analogy to Paul's expression than anything discoverable in the O.T.

The Gospel

Unconsciously influenced by St John, perhaps, commentators seem inclined to assume that Paul used 'the truth' as a synonym for 'the gospel' right from the beginning. As a preliminary corrective to this assumption it is instructive to note that while both Paul and John make use of the phrase 'to speak the truth' they never employ it in the same sense. In the Fourth Gospel it always means the proclamation of the genuine revelation.[32] But while in the Epistles *lalein* occurs more than once with the meaning 'to preach'[33] the entire phrase is never more than an

[30] Cf. note 12 above.

[31] Compare 'All his sons of truth shall be glad in everlasting knowledge' (1QM 17 : 8) and 'The men of truth (are those) who observe the Law, whose hands do not slacken in the service of truth' (1QpHab 7 : 11).

[32] Jn 8 : 40, cf. R. Bultmann, *Alētheia*, *TWNT*, vol. I, p. 246.

[33] Rom 15 : 18; 1 Cor 2 : 6; 2 Cor 2 : 17; 4 : 13; 12 : 19; Eph 6 : 20; Col 4 : 3; Tit 2 : 1, 15. In this Paul conforms to the use of *lalein* in the LXX version of the prophetic books, cf. J. Dupont, *Gnosis*, Paris, 1949, pp. 220-30.

affirmation of veracity.[34] In fact, a close examination of the texts would seem to indicate that the identification of the Gospel with 'the truth' was first made in Galatians and did not win full acceptance until the Pastorals.

The phrase 'God choose you from the beginning for salvation in sanctification of spirit and faith of truth' which occurs in one of Paul's earliest letters (2 Thess 2 : 13) is understood by Rigaux as an evocation of the two complementary processes in the salvation of the individual: the divine action through the Holy Spirit and man's response which is faith.[35] For him both 'of [the] Spirit' and 'of [the] truth' are genitives of origin. Sanctification is that given by the Spirit and faith is that given by the truth. This truth, then, can be nothing other than the Gospel. But this conception of the Gospel as an almost autonomous salvific power is found for the first time only in later Epistles (1 Cor 1 : 18; Rom 1 : 16). The same is true of the parallel to which he alludes: 'faith of the Gospel' (Phil 1 : 27). Furthermore, nothing in the context demands that 'of truth' be understood as a genitive of origin. Frame,[36] and the majority, take it as denoting direction: 'faith in the truth', but they too identify this truth with the Gospel. It would be unrealistic to deny—given the context of Christian salvation—that 'truth' here has some reference to the Gospel, but it seems to me that it is only an allusion and not a formal designation.

Paul's reference to 'faith in the truth' in v. 13 must be understood in the light of references in previous verses to 'belief in the truth' (v. 12), and 'love of truth' (v. 10), and to 'belief in the lie' (v. 11). Here we find 'truth' opposed to 'falsehood' (v. 11) and to 'injustice' (v. 12). To one acquainted with the O.T. concept of truth this sounds a very familiar note. 'Truth' is the genuine, the real, the trustworthy. 'Faith' is to give one's confidence to, to put one's trust in. It is a question of the eschatological judgment. Those who reject the 'love of truth', which

---

[34] Rom 9: 1; 2 Cor 7: 14; 12: 6; Eph 4: 25; 1 Tim 2: 7.
[35] *S. Paul: Épitres aux Thessaloniciens*, Paris, 1956, p. 685.
[36] *A Critical and Exegetical Commentary on the Epistles to the Thessalonians*, Edinburgh, 1912, p. 281.

with Spicq[37] we understand as an openness to truth as such, i.e.
to all that is genuine, are borne on to give their entire confidence
to that which is only appearance, and which will fail them at the
crucial moment. Then Paul's attention swings to the Thessalonians : 'Through God's grace, you have put your trust in what
is really worthy of it; you have chosen the genuine, the real.'
This 'reality' is wider than the Gospel, for it certainly includes
God and his power and will to save. The atmosphere is very
much that of the O.T. 'Truth' englobes the Gospel as a part
within the whole, and it is easy to see how the name once given
the whole could eventually become the property of the part. But
as yet 'truth' is not a term of revelation.

The same vague sense seems also to be one most consonant
with the context of Rom 2 : 8. Addressing himself to the Jews,
Paul warns them of the judgment of God and its consequences.
For those who do good—eternal life. But for those 'who do not
acquiesce in the truth but give their allegiance to iniquity'—
wrath. This is a delicate invitation to the Jew to cling to what
is real and, in view of the judgment, to put his trust in what is
lasting.[38] It is hardly necessary to stress the contacts with 2 Thess
2 : 10-13. But what is real ? Given the tenor of the passage, which
is essentially a suggestion that the Jew is not even availing himself of the light given him, it is hard to escape the conclusion
that 'truth' here is the Law. Paul could not mention it explicitly
for fear of giving a wrong impression to some of his readers, and
'truth' contained an area of ambiguity which he could later
exploit by showing that what was once the substance is now
only shadow. Obviously this would be easier to achieve with
someone who was making a genuine effort to know God's will
than with someone whose moral judgment was clouded by his
commitment to evil. If the deliberate ambiguity of the term be
admitted, and the perspective of ch. 9-11 kept in mind, it can
hardly be doubted that the idea of the Gospel was close to the
surface of Paul's mind when he wrote this verse.

---

[37] *Agapé dans le NT*, Paris, 1959, vol. II, p. 32.
[38] There is another instance of this theme in a specifically Christian context in Phil 4 : 8.

It is in Galatians that 'truth' is first explicitly associated with
the word of God. Paul's reason for refusing to circumcise Titus
is 'in order that the truth of the Gospel may remain among you'
(2 : 5), and he records with some pride his reprimand to Peter
and those with him for 'not walking according to the truth of
the Gospel' (2 : 14). The value of *alētheia* here is much more
Greek than Hebrew, for it refers to the correspondence between
revelation and its interpretation. Peter's interpretation was
incorrect and misleading, as Paul's would have been had he
consented to circumcision. This use of 'truth' to signify the
genuine content of the Gospel was obviously a big step on the
way to terming the Gospel as such 'the truth'. 'You were running
well. Who has hindered you in your submission to truth?' (5 : 7).
Despite the absence of the article, 'truth' here can hardly be
anything other than the apostolic teaching from which the
Galatians were tempted to deviate. But why call it 'truth'? It
was almost certainly dictated by the nature of the error menacing
the Galatians. No single term could better mark the contrast
between the reality of the Gospel and the ineffectiveness of the
Law. In itself it holds in embryo the idea that will find expression
in Rom 1 : 16 : 'the Gospel is a divine power for the salvation
of all who believe'.

To us 'the truth' is so perfect a description of the word of God
that we find it difficult to imagine it not passing into current use
once discovered. The situation as presented by 2 Cor suggests,
however, that its value was not at first fully realized. In this
Epistle we find four expressions—'the truth' (4 : 2), 'word of
truth' (6 : 6), 'the truth of Christ' (11 : 10), and once again 'the
truth' (13 : 8)—all apparently synonyms for the Gospel but in
point of fact endowed with very different meanings :

a) 'Word of truth' occurs in a catalogue of the virtues of a true
'servant of God' (6 : 4). In view of the fact that this title is the
equivalent of 'minister of the Gospel' (cf. 1 Cor 3 : 5; 2 Cor 4 :
2) it is virtually certain that *en logō alētheias* (6 : 6) is not to be
understood as a reference to the message with which he is
entrusted, for that would be tautological, but to the manner in
which it is transmitted, that is, 'veraciously'. Furthermore, 'word

of truth' is always preceded by the article when it indisputably designates the Gospel.

b) 'I kept myself from being a burden to you and will continue to do so. As the truth of Christ is in me, this boast shall not be checked in my case in the regions of Achaia' (11 : 10). Just as elsewhere Paul claims to possess the mind of Christ (1 Cor 2 : 10) and the Spirit of Christ (Rom 8 : 9), so here, the truthfulness of Christ (13 : 3). 'Truth' here denotes the indwelling of Christ as the guarantee of moral integrity.[39] But there may also be overtones of the solidity and reliability associated with the Hebrew 'mt, particularly in view of the accusations of levity and instability levelled at the apostle (1 : 17 sq).

c) The assumption that Paul is referring to the Gospel when he says, 'we can do nothing against the truth, but (only) for the truth' (13 : 8), encounters three main difficulties : (i) the apostle's consciousness of his liability to fail to conserve the deposit entrusted to him (2 Tim 1 : 12), (ii) his explicit assertion that the word of God can be adulterated (4 : 2), and (iii) the fact that the statement is made to support a claim to *pray* for what is best for his readers. Héring may be correct in seeing the phrase as a maxim of general value and not forged *ad hoc*.[40] The meaning would seem to be that it would be utterly at variance with the character of a minister of God to wish ill to anyone.

d) Only in 4 : 2 does 'the truth' mean the revelation entrusted to the ministers of the New Covenant (3 : 6). 'We have renounced the concealment prompted by shamefacedness, not acting deceitfully nor adulterating the word of God, but by the manifestation of the truth commending ourselves to everyman's conscience before God. But if our Gospel is veiled. . . .' The force of the expression is unique and none better could be found to characterize the function of one charged with the administration of the mysteries of God (1 Cor 4 : 1).

By comparison with 2 Cor 4 : 2 the Captivity Epistles represent a regression that is difficult to explain. The word of God is never

[39] Cf. G. Henrici, *Der zweite Brief an die Korinther*, Göttingen, 1900, pp. 358-9.

[40] *La seconde épitre de S. Paul aux Corinthiens*, Neuchâtel-Paris, 1958, p. 102.

simply 'the truth'. It is 'the word of the truth of the Gospel' (Col 1 : 5), and 'the word of the truth, the Gospel of your salvation' (Eph 1 : 13). It is difficult to see the utility of the explanatory phrase, unless 'the word of the truth' were not in current use as a designation of revelation. The same is true if all the genitives are understood as explanatory. This would give a rather clumsy linking of synonyms : 'the word' (as in 2 Thess 3 : 1) = 'the truth' (as in 2 Cor 4 : 2) = 'the Gospel' (as in Rom 1 : 16).

With the Pastorals we reach the final stage of this rather stumbling evolution. With the exception of one allusion to the Gospel as 'the word of the truth' (2 Tim 2 : 15), it is regularly designated 'the truth'. Apart from the expressions 'knowledge of truth' and 'foundation of the truth', which will be considered in detail a little further on, we can point to 2 Tim 2 : 18 : 'those who have erred with regard to the truth, teaching the resurrection to have already taken place'. The parallel with 1 Tim 6 : 21 shows 'truth' here to be the equivalent of 'the Faith'. These opponents are later compared to Jannes and Jambres, 'As they resisted Moses so do these resist the truth' (2 Tim 3 : 8). The mention of Moses indicates that 'the truth' is that preached by the authorized representatives of God. 2 Tim 4 : 3-4 warns Timothy that 'there will come a time when people will not endure sound doctrine . . . and will turn away their ears from the truth'. 'Sound doctrine' is a technical term in the Pastorals for revelation in its pristine purity[41]—and its correlative is a healthy religious life. Paul is aware that Titus' subjects may be upset by Judaizers and, in consequence, warns him to rebuke them sharply 'that they may be sound in the faith and not give credence to Jewish fables and ordinances of men who turn their backs on the truth' (Tim 1 : 14). The atmosphere of opposition evoked by these passages is very noticeable, and the prevalence of heterodox teaching (1 Tim 1 : 3; 6 : 3) may have been a factor, if not the chief one, motivating the characterization of the Gospel as 'truth'.

Does the Qumran literature shed any light on this evolution? A categorical affirmation or negation is impossible. It has been

[41] Cf. 1 Tim 1 : 10-11; 6 : 3; Tit 1 : 9; 2 : 1, 8; 2 Tim 2 : 13.

suggested more than once that it was at Ephesus that Paul came into contact with influences emanating from Qumran.[42] It may be pure coincidence that it was in a letter written at Ephesus (Gal) that 'truth' first appears as the synonym of revelation, the meaning it commonly has among the Essenes.

The term occurs with the same value in 2 Cor 4 : 2 : 'the manifestation of truth'. We remarked on the unique character of this expression. Thus to find a parallel in the Qumran literature would be very strong evidence for literary dependence. In Burrows' translation of the *Damascus Document* there is one. 'He caused them to know by his anointed his Holy Spirit and *a revelation of truth*' (CD 2 : 12-13).[43] This passage, however, demands closer examination.

The Hebrew text as found in Rabin's transcription reads : *wywdyʻm byd mšyḥw rwḥ qdšw wḥwh* [or *wḥwt*] *ʼmt wbprwš šmw*.[44] He translates : 'And he made known to them by the hand of his anointed ones his Holy Spirit and showed *them* (or : demonstration of) truth, and with exactitude he set out their names'. The key-word, read by Rabin as *wḥwh*, is far from clear in the text. Rost, for example, reads *whwʼ*.[45] And even where the letters are clear the sentence is sown with problems. These have been most lucidly discussed by Wernberg-Møller.[46] He argues convincingly that the first part of the phrase should be translated : 'He caused them to know by the hand of those anointed with the Holy Spirit'; he refers to Is 61 : 1 for 'anointing' with the Spirit as a figure of speech for prophetic inspiration. This interpretation was independently suggested by Yadin in an article which appeared about the same time.[47]

Wernberg-Møller's treatment of the phrase which interests us is less felicitous. Convinced that there is a close similarity between

[42] Cf. R. Brown, 'The Semitic Background of the NT Mysterion', *Biblica* 40 (1959), p. 81, n. 1; P. Benoit, 'Qumran and the New Testament' (see above, pp. 17ff.).

[43] *The Dead Sea Scrolls*, New York, 1955, p. 350.

[44] *The Zadokite Documents*, Oxford, 1954, p. 9.

[45] *Die Damaskusschrift*, Berlin, 1933, p. 9.

[46] First of all in 'Some Passages in the "Zadokite" Fragments and their Parallels in the *Manual of Discipline*', *JSS* 1 (1956), pp. 115-8, and again in *The Manual of Discipline*, Leiden, 1957, pp. 62-3.

[47] 'Three Notes on the Dead Sea Scrolls', *IEJ* 6 (1956), p. 158.

CD 2 : 12-13 and 1QS 3 : 7, he suggests that the word read as *wḥwh* by Rabin 'may be transcribed as *wḥwd = yḥyd'*.[48] Having already asserted that *yḥd* 'community' is found in the CD in the form *yḥyd*, he thus renders the whole phrase : 'He made known to them, through those who were anointed with the holy spirit of his true community. . . .' However, the enlarged photograph of the key-word published by Yadin[49] shows conclusively that what Rabin takes as the left vertical stroke of a *He* cannot be a smudge on the manuscript as Wernberg-Møller thought. Yadin himself, after an examination of the original, is convinced that the *He* read by Rabin is in fact a *Zain* plus a *Yod* : *wḥwzy* 'the seers'.[50] He translates : 'He made them known—through the hand of his anointed (ones) with the Holy Spirit and (through) his seers of truth—their exact names'. It is undeniable that this makes perfect sense, but to reach it he has to remove the *waw* from the beginning of *bprwš* and attach it to *'mt* as a personal suffix. There is no justification for this in the facsimile of the text published by Zeitlin,[51] and without this emendation the meaning is not quite so satisfactory. The absence of article or suffix would not be so marked were the reading in fact *wḥwh*. In view of this uncertainty it would be temerarious to draw any conclusions from a possible relationship between CD 2 : 12-13 and 2 Cor 4 : 2.

The phrase 'word of truth', rare in the O.T.,[52] is not found at all in the Qumran literature.

The sharp rise in the frequency of usage of 'truth' unqualified in the Pastorals may be due to Essene influence, but this hinges on the validity of our conclusions with regard to the expressions 'knowledge of truth' and 'foundation of the truth'. But once again, is it a pure coincidence that, although Timothy and Titus were in almost identical circumstances in having to contend with

[48] *Art. cit.*, p. 118; *op. cit.*, p. 63.
[49] *Art cit.*, plate 28A, facing p. 201.
[50] This is the reading adopted by the editors of the *Konkordanz zu den Qumrantexten*, Göttingen, 1960, p. 19, and by J. Maier, *Die Texte vom Toten Meer*, Basel, 1960, vol. II, p. 45, who cites the 2nd ed. of Rabin's study in the same sense.
[51] *The Zadokite Fragments*, Philadelphia, 1952, plate II.
[52] In Ps 119(118): 43 it is one of the synonyms for the Law. The plural is found in Prov 22: 21 and Eccl 12: 10 with the rather wide meaning of 'wisdom'. *Dbr 'mt* in Ps 45(44): 5 must be rendered 'for the cause of truth'.

opposition, 'truth' appears far more frequently in the Epistles addressed to the former—in Ephesus?

Revelation frustrated

One final instance of 'truth' as a term of revelation remains to be considered. And from one point of view it is inappropriate that it should be considered last, since it concerns a revelation that antedates the Mosaic and, *a fortiori*, the Christian revelation. Addressing himself to the pagan world, Paul says: 'For the wrath of God is revealed from heaven against all impiety and wickedness of men, of such as in wickedness are repressing the truth *(tōn tēn alētheian en adikia katechontōn)*, because what can be known about God is clear to them for God himself had made it manifest' (Rom 1 : 18-19). Though it has absolutely no support in the Greek MSS, it is easy to see why the Vulgate should render v. 18 : 'qui veritatem *Dei* in iniustitia detinent', because it is clear from the context (v. 20) that 'truth' here is truth about God, and in particular, his eternal power and his divinity as revealed through his material creation.[53] Cornely explains *en adikia katechein* as a refusal to receive truth when it is presented, injustice creating an obstacle.[54] This concords neither with the meaning of *katechein*,[55] nor with the context which implies that the pagans possess a certain knowledge of the truth (v. 19). Consequently, the majority of commentators prefer to interpret the phrase as a holding captive of the truth, not precisely by injustice (as if it were an instrument), but rather in a situation permeated by injustice.[56] What this 'holding truth captive' means in effect is that 'having known God they have not rendered him glory or gratitude' (v. 22). Knowledge of this sort is a monstrosity

[53] ' "Truth" here is neither correct knowledge of God nor the true religion, but the genuine reality of things in which God simultaneously both hides and reveals himself.' H. Schlier, *Die Zeit der Kirche*, Freiburg, 1956, p. 30.

[54] *Epistola ad Romanos*, Paris, 1896, pp. 79-80.

[55] 'To hold back, hinder; to hold down, suppress; to hold fast; to confine (in a prison).' W. F. Arndt-F. W. Gingrich, *A Greek-English Lexicon of the New Testament*, Chicago, 1959, pp. 423-4.

[56] 'Truth and injustice are contrary forces. Since the pagans are in a state of injustice, truth is chained, whereas if it were free it should blossom forth into justice.' M. J. Lagrange, *L'Épître aux Romains*, Paris, 1950, p. 22.

because it coexists with injustice. In the tradition of the O.T. 'knowledge of God' implies the positive exclusion of injustice.

J. Schmitt considers that this phrase is paralleled by 1QS 4 : 19. To use his own words : 'Rom (1 : 18) répond à ce point au texte 1QS 4 : 19 sur *"la vérité* qui était *retenue dans* les voies de *l'iniquité"* que l'expression paulinienne *katechein* éclaire—pensons nous—son parallel qumrânien *gll* d'une attestation rare et d'un sens imprécis dans la littérature palestinienne contemporaine'.[57] A full translation of the passage in question shows that there is no analogy either in thought or vocabulary. 'At the time fixed for visitation he will destroy it [deceit] forever, then the truth of the earth *('mt tbl)* will appear for ever, for it has polluted itself in the ways of ungodliness during the ascendency of deceit.' The meaning of 'the truth of the earth' is controverted. Davies, disagreeing with Brownlee and Yadin who understand it to be a personification of the Messiah as truth, thinks it probably best to take the phrase as a kind of synonym for the spirit of truth which will appear at the End and will be sprinkled upon man (line 21).[58] In either case, the conception differs radically from that of Paul, concerning as it does the final triumph of truth, which moreover is not a revelation but a moral power.

The one passage that could be even considered as a parallel to Rom 1 : 18 is 1Q27 1 : 7 : 'those who hold fast the mysteries of . . . will be no more'. But unfortunately here again the text is uncertain. Milik supplies *pl'* 'wonder' with a confidence that the photograph (plate XXI) does not seem to justify.[59] In view of the fact that 'mysteries of wonder' in the Qumran literature means either the sect's interpretation of the Law (1QpHab 7 : 1; 1QS 9 : 18; 11 : 5; 1QH 2 : 13; 4 : 27; 7 : 27; 11 : 10) or the cosmic mysteries in a good sense (1QH 1 : 21), this means that *tmk* 'to hold fast' must be given a pejorative nuance, for otherwise the punishment would be unmotivated. Hence he translates 'tous ceux qui détiennent les mystères'. Dupont-Sommer makes

[57] 'Les écrits du NT et les textes de Qumrân. Bilan de 5 années de recherches', *RevScRel* 30 (1956), p. 281—his italics.
[58] 'Paul and the Dead Sea Scrolls: Flesh and Spirit,' in *The Scrolls and the New Testament*, ed. K. Stendahl, New York, 1957, p. 173.
[59] *Discoveries in the Judean Desert: Qumran Cave I*, Oxford, 1955, p. 103.

the same point more emphatically by inserting a word: 'tous ceux qui détiennent (injustement) les mystères merveilleux'. Unfortunately this meaning of *tmk* in entirely without parallel either in the O.T. or in the scrolls themselves where, when used with a religious or intellectual object, it means simply 'adhesion to' (1QH 2 : 21; 4 : 22; 7 : 20). *Tmk* can be given its full value and the phrase becomes limpidly clear if, as Vogt suggests,[60] we read not *pl'* but *pš'* 'iniquity', the formula 'mysteries of iniquity' being found in 1QH 5 : 36 and frag. 50 : 5. (Cf. 2 Thess 2 : 6-7). Were the reading *pl'* certain, however, it could be convincingly argued that the allusion is to the same type of aborted knowledge based on divine revelation that is in question in Rom 1 : 18.

III. The Life of Faith

When we turn to the passages of the Epistles in which the Christian life is characterized as 'truth', we immediately become aware of a phenomenon analogous to that noted apropos of the truth of God. The idea plays a much smaller role than it does in the Qumran literature or in the O.T. In the Epistles 'truth' yields pride of place to love, which in Paul's eyes is God's chief attribute (Eph 2 : 4) and the one which above all he desires to see mirrored in his children (Eph 5 : 1-2). Nonetheless the theme of truth is not entirely absent. It appears once in 1 Cor and five times in Eph.

In his reproof addressed to the Corinthians because of their toleration of the incestuous man (1 Cor 5 : 1-13) Paul draws a parallel between incorporation into the Church and the Jewish paschal ritual. Just as the Jewish household, the Church should not contain any leaven, since through the death of Christ, the Paschal Lamb, all its members are unleavened bread. 'Wherefore let us hold festival, not with old leaven, not with leaven of malice and iniquity, but with the unleavened bread of sincerity

---

[60] ' "Mysteria" in textibus Qumran', *Biblica* 37 (1956), p. 251, n. 7. Cf. also R. Brown. 'The Pre-Christian Semitic Concept of "Mystery" ', *CBQ* 20 (1958), p. 442, n. 93. In a recent study O. Betz claims to be able to read a *lamed* in the photograph, which would support Milik's interpretation ("Der *Katechon*', *NTS* 9 (1962-63), p. 281).

(eilikrineia) and truth' (v. 8). The genitives are all genitives of apposition. The leaven *is* malice and iniquity. The unleavened bread *is* sincerity and truth. Paul's mind is evidently dwelling on the symbolic value of the approaching paschal feast. The 'passing over' from one state to another radically different should result in a manifest change in the mode of life (Eph 2 : 10, Tit 2 : 14). This was just the point made by Joshua at the moment of the renewal of the Covenant at Shechem, and it is his phraseology that Paul adopts to fill out the positive aspect of his thought. Having evoked the marvels that made possible the Exodus, Joshua says : 'Fear Yahweh and serve him in integrity *(tmym)* and truth' (Josh 24 : 14). Basically *tmym* means 'without defect' (it is used to describe the condition of the paschal lamb, cf. Ex 12 : 5) and on the human level is very close in meaning to *eilikrineia*, which when applied to a person connotes probity of character, hence 'sincerity' (2 Cor 1 : 12; 2 : 17).[61] In this perspective 'truth' is seen to have the meaning 'fidelity', loyalty. A very remote analogy, which may also be influenced by Jos 24 : 14, is to be found in 1QH 16 : 7.

With this one exception, whose importance is somewhat diminished by the secondary place the theme of truth occupies in it, all the other references to the Christian life as 'truth' are concentrated in Eph. One is merely a verbal quotation from Zech 8 : 16 : 'Let each one speak truth to his neighbour' (4 : 25).[62] Of the four other instances two (5 : 9; 6 : 14) occur in contexts which for other reasons are held to manifest the influence of Qumran.[63]

[61] Cf. W. Barclay, *A New Testament Word Book*, London, 1955, pp. 32-3.

[62] The corresponding passage in Col reads 'Do not lie to one another' (3 : 9). The writer of Ephesians, in adding the citation from Zech, has deliberately grafted the theme of truth on to an idea from Col. This assumes new significance when we recollect that for the Essenes veracity was one of the most essential virtues. Commenting on 1QS 10 : 22, Dupont-Sommer cites Josephus, *Jewish War*, II, §135 : 'Every word they speak is stronger than an oath', and §141 : 'He swears always to love truth and persecute liars' (*The Essene Writings from Qumran*, tr. G. Vermes, Cleveland, 1962, p. 100, n. 4).

[63] Cf. P. Benoit, *'Qumran and the New Testament'*, above, p. 17. For details of the authors who see the influence of Qumran in these passages, cf. H. Braun, 'Qumran und das Neue Testament. Ein Bericht über 10 Jahre Forschung (1950-1959)', *TRu* 29 (1963), pp. 239, 242.

We turn first to Eph 5 : 9 : 'For the fruit of light consists in all goodness *(agathōsunē)*, and righteousness *(dikaiosunē)* and truth.' Without going as far as Molin, who considers that Eph 5 : 3-11 could be inserted in 1QS or CD without causing any surprise to the Essenes,[64] there can be little doubt that this passage manifests the influence of the ideas proper to the sect. It is structured on the opposition of Light and Darkness, the image used at Qumran to express precisely the same form of ethical or functional dualism, that is, man's personal commitment for or against a personal God. But apart from this basic correspondence many parallels on particular points have been noted, especially by K. G. Kuhn in his contribution to this volume.[65]

The number and character of these contacts can hardly be explained except on the hypothesis that the author of Eph[66] had a rather detailed acquaintance with the Qumran literature. Hence the characterization of the Christian life as 'truth' draws its inspiration from the Essenes.[67] The association of righteousness and truth is frequently met with at Qumran, most often as divine attributes (1QS 4 : 40; 11 : 4, 7; CD 3 : 15; 1QH 1 : 26-7; 9 : 31-2) but also as human virtues (1QS 4 : 24; 5 : 4; 8 : 2). The same can be said of the link between goodness and truth, but together these are particularly associated with God (1QH 10 : 16-7; 11 : 9). Apart from the mention of goodness, righteousness and truth in close proximity among the effects of the spirit of truth (1QS 4 : 2-3) there is only one passage which explicitly

---

[64] *Die Söhne des Lichtes*, Wien/München, 1954, p. 179.

[65] 'The Epistle to the Ephesians in the Light of the Qumran texts', above, pp. 121-6.

[66] I make my own the opinion of Benoit with regard to the authorship of Ephesians. In his view, Paul, as a result of his reaction to the Colossian crisis, would have penetrated more deeply into the implications of his ecclesiological synthesis and spoken of it to his disciples, one of whom would have been commissioned to commit it to writing (cf. 'Rapports littéraires entre les épîtres aux Colossiens et aux Ephésiens', *Neutestamentliche Aufsätze* (Festschrift J. Schmid), ed. J. Blinzler *et al.*, Regensburg, 1963, p. 22); 'Paul. Ephésiens (Épître aux)', *DBS*, vol. VII, pp. 204-10). Cf. also my study, 'Who wrote Ephesians?', *The Bible Today*, April 1965, pp. 1201-9.

[67] That is, the immediate source of this doctrine in Eph is the teaching of the Essenes. The closest O.T. parallel to Eph 5 : 9 is not Mic 6 : 8, as Kuhn suggests, but 2 Chron 31 : 20: 'He did what was good *(twb)* and right *(ysr)* and true *('mt)* before Yahweh.' Cf. also Jer 4 : 2; Ps 45(44): 5.

associates the three virtues: The Essene is required 'to depart
from all evil and to cleave to all works of goodness *(m'śy twb)*
and to do truth and righteousness and justice' (1QS 1 : 5). This
is far from an exact verbal parallel to Eph 5 : 9 but the spirit
animating both passages is the same. 'Goodness' is not mentioned
in the catalogues (1QS 5 : 4, 25; 8 : 2) which invariably include
the virtues of truth, humility, righteousness, and loving affection.
But since these virtues are to be exercised 'towards one another'
(1QS 5 : 25; 8 : 2), might not *agathōsunē* be said to sum them
up?

The *Kampfsituation* of the Christian depicted in Eph 6 : 10-17
is fundamentally identical with that of the Essene and his community.[68] The believer must be perpetually on guard, for he is
constantly exposed to the powers of evil and attacked by tempta-
tions to sin. These 'flaming darts' (v. 16) of the Evil One find
a good parallel in 1QH 2 : 26, where the psalmist speaks of himself as encircled by enemies 'the flaming of whose spears was like
a fire consuming trees'. To resist the believer must buckle on the
armour of God. The list is comprehensive: girdle, breastplate,
shoes, shield, helmet, sword.

Similar catalogues are found in the O.T.: Is 11 : 4-5 : stick,
girdle; Is 59 : 17—breastplate, helmet, tunic, cloak; Wis 5 :
17-20—breastplate, helmet, shield, sword. The theme, therefore,
was a common one. What is surprising is that it was not exploited
by the Essenes. Apart from the very material description of the
weapons (shield, sword, spear) to be borne by the sons of light in
their war against the sons of darkness (1QM 5 : 4-14) the idea
of armour does not occur in the Qumran literature either in a
literal or a figurative sense.

The first step in assuming this armour is 'to gird oneself with
truth' (v. 14). The War Scroll speaks of 'girding oneself' as the
fundamental preparation for battle (1QM 15 : 14). That the
girding should be effected by 'truth' manifests a literary depen-

---

[68] Kuhn (above, p. 117) notes that the phrase 'in the strength of his might'
which occurs at the beginning of this section finds a parallel only at Qumran:
'the might of his power' (1QH 4 : 32), 'the strength of his might' (1QH 18 :
8). The same author sketches the background to this passage in *TWNT*,
vol. V, pp. 297-300.

dence on Is 11 : 5b which presents the loins of the messianic king as girt with truth (MT : *'mwnh*; LXX : *alētheia*),[69] but it should be remarked that Is 11 : 1-5 was well known at Qumran and appears as the central portion of the blessing of the Prince of the Congregation (1Q28b 5 : 26). How does the Christian gird himself with 'truth'? Schlier justly remarks that with regard to the spiritual weaponry two points must be noted : (i) they are an objective divine gift, and (ii) they are a modality of man's being *(Seinsweise des Menschens)*.[70] The meaning, then, is that divine truth must become the existential environment in which the Christian lives, moves and has his being. He girds himself with 'truth' in becoming aware of the change that has been effected in him through his contact with Truth. This is not a speculative recognition of his reception of the 'word of truth' (Eph 1 : 13), or of his subsequent ever deeper immersion in it (Eph 4 : 20). It is achieved only by 'living the truth in love' (4 : 15).

Here we must draw attention to an important point (already touched on in note 62). In 1 Thess 5 : 8 the triad faith-hope-love is expressed in function of the theme of spiritual armour, and in other epistles we find references to 'weapons' (2 Cor 6 : 7; 10 : 4) and to 'the armour of light' (Rom 13 : 12). The theme, then, is authentically Pauline. But here in Eph we find it not only greatly amplified but associated with the idea of 'truth', which is given the key role in its explication. This is significant in view of the position we have adopted with regard to the authorship of Eph, because in every case in which the idea of 'truth' is introduced in Eph (with the exception of 1 : 13 which merely reproduces Col 1 : 6) it is as an *addition* to an authentically Pauline theme.

The fourth instance of 'truth' in Eph occurs in a context which, as 1 Cor 5 : 8, manifests the eternal Christian tension between the *de facto* and the *de jure*. The Christians have apparently carried over into their new state traits more appropriate to those who are 'strangers to the life of God' (4 : 18). To remedy this

[69] The LXX version of Ps 91 (90) : 4 is also a good parallel: *hoplō kuklōsei se hē alētheia autou*. The MT, however, is somewhat different: *ṣnh wsḥrh 'mtw*.

[70] *Der Brief an die Epheser*, Düsseldorf, 1957, p. 295.

situation the author of the Epistle evokes for them once again the basic obligations involved in 'learning Christ' (4 : 20). These are three, and each is introduced by an infinitive which has the force of an imperative.[71] The believer must :

1. put off the old man who is falling to corruption through the desires of deceit *(kata tas epithumias tēs apatēs)*
2. be renewed in the spirit of his mind *(tō pneumati tou noos)* and
3. put on the new man created according to God in righteousness and holiness of the truth *(en dikaiosunē kai hosiotēti tēs alētheias)*.

This passage manifests a definite literary dependence on Col 3 : 9-10 : 'Strip off the old man with his practices and put on the new being renewed to true knowledge *(eis epignōsin)* according to the image of him who created him.' In the light of the underlying allusion to Gen 1 : 26ff. the meaning of this latter text is clear. 'Man was created "according to the image of God" (Gen 1 : 26ff.) but fell through seeking knowledge of good and evil in a manner contrary to the will of God. The new man, recreated in Christ (who is himself "the Image" of God, cf. Col 1 : 15; 2 Cor 3 : 18; 4 : 4), recovers this pristine rectitude and this time arrives at true moral knowledge (it is this that is in question in the context, cf. 1 : 9).'[72]

The problem then is : why should the author of Eph have adapted this passage in the way he did? Why expand the notion of 'old man' with explicit reference to 'deceit'? Why isolate renewal of knowledge instead of permitting it to remain as the primary characteristic of the new man? Why explicate the virtues of the new man? And having decided to do so, why emphasize righteousness and holiness and explicitly link them to truth?

It is suggested here that all these questions acquire an answer

[71] Cf. Schlier, *op. cit.*, 217, 220. In some witnesses to the text of v. 23-24 the imperative has actually been substituted for the infinitive. Thus P[46], 69, lat sy.

[72] P. Benoit, *Les épîtres de S. Paul aux Philippiens, à Philemon, aux Colossiens, aux Ephésiens*, Paris, 1953 (2nd ed.), p. 66.

if Eph 4 : 22-24 is understood as a reworking of Col 3 : 9-10 by someone steeped in the ideas of Paul who also had an extensive knowledge of the thought and vocabulary of the Essenes. What has been noted above apropos of Eph 5 : 3-15 shows that this hypothesis is not *a priori* entirely improbable. More specifically Eph 4 : 22-24 would appear to be a conscious Christianization of the 'Treatise on the Two Spirits' of the *Manual of Discipline*.[73] This approach is also recommended by the fact that it throws light on two of the notable exegetical difficulties of the passage, the formula *pneuma tou noos*,[74] and the genitive *tēs alētheias*.[75]

The starting point was certainly the text of Col. Its catalogue (3 : 5-9) of the vices which the converts are urged to put off with the 'old man' would have suggested to one familiar with the doctrine of the Essenes the characteristics peculiar to those under the dominion of the spirit of deceit (1QS 4 : 9-11). The lists do not match each other point for point, but that is not to be expected. The resemblance is certainly close enough to sow the germ of an idea, and to make it unnecessary to repeat the

---

[73] Another example of the Christianization of Essenian ideas is to be found in 2 Cor 6 : 14-7 : 1 (cf. refs. in note 104). If Carmignac's interpretation be correct, the *Odes of Solomon* also provide an interesting parallel. Cf. J. Carmignac, 'Un Qumrânien converti au christianisme : l'auteur des Odes de Salomon', in *Qumran-Probleme* (Vorträge des Leipziger Symposions über Qumran-Probleme vom 9. bis 14. Okt. 1961), ed. H. Bardtke, Berlin, 1963, pp. 75-108.

[74] The embarassment this phrase has caused to commentators and translators is evident in the variety of their interpretations. *Pneuma tou noos* is : the mind as such (Staab, Meinertz), the mind viewed in its profoundest depths (Bengel, Ewald, Abbott), the mind as open to, or as being acted on by, the Spirit (Westcott, Haupt, Huby, Schlier). 'Ils seront renouvelés par l'Esprit agissant sur leur jugement' (Masson). 'Pour vous renouveler par une transformation spirituelle de votre jugement' (Benoit).

[75] The variety of opinions with regard to the meaning of this phrase is only slightly less. The difficulty was felt very early, for a number of witnesses have the dative *alētheia* (D* G it). This correction had its origin in an evident failure to understand the value of the genitive. For Scott 'truth' here is the divine essence of things as opposed to earthly appearances. At the other end of the scale it is understood as a simple adjective opposing genuine justice and holiness to intrinsically worthless piety (Haupt) or to real but imperfect piety (Ewald). A middle road is followed by Swete : 'the righteousness and holiness which spring from and are in harmony with truth' (*The Holy Spirit in the New Testament*, London, 1909, p. 240). He is followed by Huby, Masson and Schlier. The latter, however, goes a little further, seeing 'truth' as the area of being in which the new man has his 'Gerecht- und Fromm-sein' (*op. cit.*, p. 222).

catalogue in Eph, where it is simply evoked by the mention of the first vice listed, 'inextinguishable desire *(rhwb npsh)*', with the indication that its source is Deceit.

The location of the old man among the 'sons of Deceit' led naturally to the identification of the new man with the 'sons of Truth', and to the attribution to him of the virtues peculiar to the latter. But only those virtues are chosen from the catalogue in 1QS 4 : 2-6 which are compatible with the Christian life and which do not find a place in the list of Col 3 : 12. Right at the beginning of the list comes 'walking in the ways of righteousness of truth *(drky sdq 'mt)*' (line 3). The genitive is to be noted. As Wernberg-Møller suggests, it may have been originally a gloss.[76] The three succeeding virtues, humility, patience and compassion, are mentioned in Col. The fourth is 'goodness' which will appear with justice and truth in Eph 5 : 9. Then follows a series of intellectual virtues (lines 3-4) which may reasonably be considered to be englobed in the idea of the renewal of the spirit of the mind. It is not difficult to see why a disciple of Paul should omit the next—'zeal for just ordinances'—as being liable to misconception in Judaeo-Christian circles because *mšpty sdq* was a quasi technical term for the moral teaching of the sect (cf. 1QS 3 : 1; 9 : 17; CD 20 : 30). Then we find, 'a holy intention (with) a steadfast purpose *(wmhšbt qwdšh bysr smwk)*' (line 5). Would the essence of this composite virtue be badly rendered by *hosiotēs*? The succeeding virtue in the *Manual* is 'great affection towards all the sons of truth' and it is omitted because it exhibits a limitation incompatible with Christian love, which is moreover mentioned in Col 3 : 14. The remaining virtues of the sons of truth are not considered; 'avoidance of idolatry' as too obvious, and the others as implying an element of secrecy (with regard to the knowledge of the mysteries) incompatible with the publicity that must be given the Good News.

Thus the virtues attributed to the new man are 'righteousness of truth' and 'holiness'. To emphasize the parallel with Deceit, 'truth' is placed at the end of the phrase and qualified by the definite article, hence 'Truth'. As the vices of the 'old man' flowed

[76] *The Manual of Discipline*, Leiden, 1957, p. 73, n. 6.

from Deceit, so do the virtues of the 'new man' have their source in Truth. Thus broken down, the construction of the phrase gives an impression of extreme artificiality. But is not this a mode of procedure characteristic of the author of Eph, as has been frequently noted apropos of his treatment of Col? Benoit, for example, notes 'the conscientious plagiarism, successful but laborious, which makes Eph an imitation with respect to Col'.[77]

The necessity of expanding the concept of the 'new man' in function of his virtues meant that the formulation of Col, which closely links the putting on of the new man with renewal of knowledge, had to be broken up. But this latter idea could not be omitted, primarily because it was found inextricably associated in Col with the change from the old to the new, but also because it was a cherished concept at Qumran.[78] Hence it is noted separately between the characteristics of the old man and those of the new as if forming the bridge between them. The formula *pneuma tou noos* which has occasioned so much difficulty to commentators because of the complete absence of parallels is unfortunately not found at Qumran, but nonetheless Kuhn has pointed out that this pleonastic accumulation of synonymous terms is a stylistic feature of the Essene writings,[79] where it appears to be merely a literary device to emphasize or intensify an idea. This tends to confirm the opinion of Abbott, etc., who have considered the phrase to denote the rational part of man in its profoundest depths. A renewal so complete would certainly imply the perfection of moral knowledge emphasized in Col, as well as the possession of the intellectual virtues appropriate to the 'sons of truth'.

This grafting of the 'Treatise on the Two Spirits' on to the

[77] 'Rapports littéraires entres les épîtres aux Colossiens et aux Ephésiens', *Neutestamentliche Aufsätze* (Festschrift J. Schmid), ed. J. Binzler *et. al*, Regensburg, 1963, p. 21.

[78] For the Essenes, entry into the state of salvation involved a transformation of the mind. The members of the community were essentially 'those who know *(yd⁽ym)*' (1QH 11: 14), 'men of knowledge' (CD 20: 4), and this understanding was given by God (1QH 11: 10 and passim), through the communication of the spirit he has put in them (1QH 11: 12; 13: 18-19) which strengthens man's own spirit (1QH 7: 6; 9: 12, 32).

[79] 'The Epistle of the Ephesians in the Light of the Qumran Texts', above, p. 117.

specifically Christian theme of the 'old-new man' inevitably implies a radical revaluation of its key terms. In the Treatise 'truth' appears as a moral force. What does it mean in Eph 4 : 24? The key to the answer lies in v. 21 : 'You did not so learn Christ. You heard him and were instructed in him *as he is truth in Jesus*.'[80] 'Jesus' without qualification is rarely met with in the Pauline corpus, but when it does appear it is always to evoke the object of the kerygma—the death and resurrection of Christ, his parousia and his glory.[81] Schlier is almost certainly correct in seeing this phrase as a polemic against a Gnostic tendency to divorce the saving Christ from the Jesus of history.[82] The messianic Lord revealed to the believers in the 'word of truth' (Eph 1 : 13) is true only if he has attained his dominion through the humiliation of the cross and the glory of the resurrection. 'Truth', then, in v. 21 is essentially a qualification of the gospel, characterizing it as the proclamation of the redeeming death and justifying resurrection of Jesus Christ.[83] As endowed with his saving power (Rom 1 : 16) it is a dynamic dimension of Christ. It is this 'truth' (Christ in his word) that is the ultimate source of the being of the new man and all his splendour of virtues. Because it is rooted in a historical Person the Christian concept of 'truth' is immeasurably superior to the Essenian.

[80] For the justification of this translation, cf. I. de la Potterie, 'Jésus et la vérité d'après Eph 4: 21', *Studiorum Paulinorum Congressus Internationalis Catholicus 1961*, Rome, 1963, pp. 245-8.

[81] 1 Thess 1: 10; 4: 14; 1 Cor 12: 7; 2 Cor 4: 5, 10, 11, 14; 11: 4; Gal 6: 17; Rom 3: 26; 8: 11; Phil 2: 10. Cf. de la Potterie, *art cit.*, p. 253. On the central place of the death and resurrection in the kerygma, cf. L. Cerfaux, *Le Christ dans la théologie de S. Paul*, Paris, 1951, pp. 124, 369.

[82] *Op. cit.*, p. 217. Though its formulation is more subtle the same idea is to be found in Col 2: 6: *hōs oun parelabete ton Christon Iēsoun ton Kurion*. . . . Lightfoot indicated the true sense of this expression by inserting a comma after *Christon* (*St Paul's Epistles to the Colossians and to Philemon*, London, 1904, p. 174). In the *Bible de Jérusalem* Benoit translates: 'Le Christ tel que vous l'avez reçu: Jésus le Seigneur. . . .' It is noteworthy that in presenting this idea in a clearer way the author of Eph once again introduces the idea of 'truth'.

[83] De la Potterie confirms this conclusion by two converging arguments: 1) the relationship between truth and the plan of salvation revealed and realized in Jesus—2 Cor 4: 2, 1 Ti: 3: 1; 6: 2) the relationship between the death and resurrection of Christ and the paraenesis whose foundation it is—Rom 6: 4, Gal 6: 14, Heb 12: 1 (*art. cit.*, pp. 252-4).

As the passage just discussed has amply demonstrated, 'truth' is very definitely an analogous concept when applied to the life of the Essene and to that of the Christian. Despite certain characteristics in common the two realities are ontologically different. This difference is further highlighted in the final passage (4 : 15) that remains to be considered. It is found in a context which manifests the exigency of the Christian life to develop and grow. This characteristic is not entirely absent in the life of the Essene, but it there occupies a comparatively minor place. Progress for an Essene is growth in stature within the community. As one who is 'in the lot of truth' (CD 13 : 12) he is already saved, but he can advance in the perfection of his knowledge of the Law and of his response to it, and on this growth his promotion within the community depends (1QS 5 : 21-24; 6 : 16-23; 9 : 15). His progress is essentially a growth in truth.

For the Christian, however, growth is something much more organic. As Eph 4 : 10-16 shows, he is incorporated into the Body of Christ whose conditions of growth he assumes.[84] He grows with it and through it, and in turn helps it grow. How? By 'living the truth in love' (v. 15).[85] This is the most specifically Christian characterization of the life of faith as 'truth'. The Essene also associates love with his living out of truth, but the emphasis is very different. 'I love thee freely and with all my heart, and with all my soul I purify—(text corrupt)—[not] to depart from all that thou has commanded and I will keep near to the Many—(text corrupt)—[not] departing from all of thy precepts' (1QH 15 : 10-12). Love is here subordinate to truth.

---

[84] Cf. G. Montague, *Growth in Christ*, Fribourg, 1961, p. 161.

[85] *Alētheuontes en agapē*. *Alētheuō*, according to Arndt-Gingrich (*op. cit.*, p. 36) means 'to be truthful, to tell the truth'. This meaning does not fit the context, which is a warning not to false teachers but to those in danger of being misled by them. Abbott moreover points out that verbs in *-euō* express the doing of the action signified by the corresponding substantive in *-eia* (*A Critical and Exegetical Commentary on the Epistles to the Ephesians and to the Colossians*, Edinburgh, 1909, p. 123). Confirmation is found in the use of this verb in Prov 21 : 3 and Is 44 : 26. With Abbott and Spicq (*Agapè dans le NT*, vol. II, Paris, 1959, p. 230) we join *en agapē* to *alētheuontes* because this seems the most natural, and because 'growth' is fully defined by the following words which include mention of 'love' (v. 16).

To love God is to obey his Law, and this obedience involves loving the other members of the community (1QS 4 : 5)—and them alone (1QS 1 : 3, 10; 2 : 5-18; but cf. 10 : 18). Obedience is thus the mainspring of growth. In Eph the power that sweeps men up into the Plenitude of Christ is love (4 : 16). This love is expressed not in scrupulous obedience, but in filial imitation, because whereas the Essene 'walks in truth', the Christian 'walks in love' : 'Be then imitators of God as beloved children; and walk in love as Christ also loved you and gave himself up for us, an offering and sacrifice to God as an agreeable odour' (Eph 5 : 1-2). The essence of the Christian's life as a child of God is defined not in terms of truth but in terms of love. If he measures up to the ideal set by the sacrificial love of Christ the exigencies of truth will be more than satisfied. But if this love be lacking, the most exact compliance with the law is of no avail (1 Cor 13 : 3). The sometime Essenian, now a disciple of Paul's, had well assimilated the most profound lesson of his master.

IV. KNOWLEDGE OF TRUTH

The theme of conversion is a common one in the Pauline corpus and is expressed by a variety of terms signifying the adhesion of the believer to the word of God.[86] In the Pastorals an entirely new vocabulary appears : conversion is a coming to 'knowledge of truth'. God wills that all men be saved by 'coming to knowledge of truth *(eis epignōsin alētheias)*' (1 Tim 2 : 4).[87] To this end Paul is appointed an apostle to lead the elect to faith and to knowledge of truth (Tim 1 : 1). Those who accept the preaching are those 'who have come to know the truth *(epegnōkosi tēn alētheian)*' (1 Tim 4 : 3), and opposed to them are those who seek this knowledge from wrong motives and with unworthy dispositions and thus do not achieve it (2 Tim 3 : 7),

[86] These are discussed in my study, *Paul on Preaching*, London, 1964, pp. 217-32.

[87] The expression appears only in the Pastorals, but Dupont's suggestion that it underlies the *epegnōte tēn charin tou theou en alētheia* of Col 1 : 6 is quite plausible (*Gnosis. La connaissance religieuse selon S. Paul*, Paris, 1949, p. 12, n. 1).

and those who actively reject it but to whom in God's mercy it may one day be given (2 Tim 2 : 25).

The detailed exegesis of these passages having been thoroughly worked out by Dibelius[88] and Spicq,[89] we can start from where they leave off. The phrase *epignōsis alētheias* means, in the words of Spicq, 'exact knowledge of the true religion'.[90] Both these authors assert that the background of this formula is to be sought in the O.T. idea of knowledge as a vital orientation of the whole personality, and that it bears no relationship to the Greek concept of knowledge as a speculative regard. This is true but too vague to be helpful. In fact the only instances of the formula as such are to be found in Philo (*Omn. Prob. Lib.*, 74), and Epictetus (*Diss.* II, 20-21), but Bultmann correctly points out that these are parallels in form only, since they concern knowledge of reality in general.[91] Dupont can find only one instance where conversion is expressed as a turning to truth, and that in Philo (*Spec. Leg.*, IV, 178).[92] Hence to find the formula *dʿt ʾmt* not once but three times in the Qumran literature may be very significant.

Towards the beginning of that section of the *Manual of Discipline*, which Guilbert[93] with reason entitles 'Rules for the Recruitment and Formation of New Members', we find this instruction to the 'wise man' : 'Let him exhort to knowledge of truth *(lhwkyḥ dʿt ʾmt)* and the practice of justice those who choose [the] way' (1QS 9 : 18). At first sight the stress seems to lie on the quality of the knowledge, and the genitive appears to have an entirely adjectival function, 'exact knowledge'. The same might be said of *epignōsis alētheias*. But just as in that phrase the adjectival function does not exhaust the value of *alētheias*, so too here, the Essenian use of *ʾmt* as the term par excellence to characterize revelation as such should give us pause, for this 'truth' is an object to be known, as the continuation of the instruc-

[88] '*Epignōsis alētheias*,' in *Festschrift G. Heinrici*, ed. A. Deissmann und H. Windisch, Leipzig, 1914, pp. 178-89.

[89] *S. Paul: Épîtres Pastorales*, Paris, 1947, Excursus XVI, pp. 362-5.

[90] *Op. cit.*, p. 362. Cf. R. Bultmann, *TWNT*, vol. I, p. 706.

[91] *Art. cit.*, p. 706, n. 70.

[92] *Gnosis*, pp. 9-10.

[93] J. Carmignac-P. Guilbert, *Les Textes de Qumrân*, vol. I, Paris, 1961, p. 60.

tion makes clear. 'He shall guide them with knowledge and instruct them in the mysteries of wonder and truth . . . so that they can walk flawlessly with one another in everything which has been revealed to them' (1QS 9 : 18-19). It was obviously just as important to the Qumran community that its new members possessed an accurate comprehension of the truth revealed to it, as it was to Paul that his converts should have a precise grasp of the revelation brought by Christ—the knowledge in both cases being expected to flower into moral endeavour.

A significant point of contact between Paul and the above passage is the term 'way' *(drk)*. In 1QS 9 : 19-21 'way' occurs four times. Twice it lacks the definite article (lines 18, 20b), but in the latter case it is made definite by the pronominal suffix (the reference being to God), and the fact that line 20a is introduced as the explanation of line 18 makes it necessary for the sake of coherence and intelligibility to supply it there also : 'those who choose *the* way'. The validity of this approach is borne out by line 21 : 'These are the rules of the way.'[94] The theme of 'way' is a common one in the O.T. (especially in Prov and Ps) and is found under many forms.[95] The fundamental idea of *drk* in a religio-moral context is 'mode of acting' : 'to walk in the ways of the just' (Ps 11 : 6) is to exhibit the mode of life proper to a pious Israelite. Here, used absolutely, *'the* way' can only mean the manner proper to the sect of envisaging fidelity to the Law, and then by metonymy the sect itself (cf. 1QS 10 : 21).[96] A number of times in Acts 'The Way' is used in the same absolute fashion to designate the movement embodied in the primitive Church—twice in the mouth of Paul (22 : 4; 24 : 14) and always in a context involving him.[97]

---

[94] Cf. V. McCasland, 'The Way', *JBL* 77 (1958), p. 225.

[95] Cf. F. Nötscher, *Gotteswege und Menschenwege in der Bible und Qumran*, Bonn, 1958. French resumé in 'Voies divines et voies humaines selon la Bible et Qumrân', *La Secte de Qumrân et les origines du christianisme* (Rech. Bibl. 4), ed. J. van der Ploeg, Louvain, 1959, pp. 135-48.

[96] Line 19 of the passage under consideration impresses on new members that 'this is the time for levelling the way towards the wilderness'. This is a clear allusion to 1QS 8 : 13-14, where Is 40 : 3 ('In the wilderness prepare the way of . . . [= Yahweh]') is applied to the community precisely as the depository of revelation (8 : 15-16).

[97] 9 : 2; 18 : 25-26; 19 : 9, 23; 22 : 4; 24 : 14, 22.

H

The two remaining instances of *d't 'mt* in the *Scrolls* both occur in the same hymn (1QH 10 : 20, 29). Unfortunately the text is rather badly preserved. 1QH 10 : 20 is so corrupt that all attempts at restoration are of necessity very subjective. Consequently we prefer to leave it out of account. 1QH 10 : 29 is somewhat better conserved but the lacunae make its interpretation difficult. The context appears to concern the order of members within the community. The hierarchy is based on knowledge, for it is according to his perfection in knowledge that one is ranked above the other (10 : 27-28). This is the consistent teaching of the *Manual of Discipline* (1QS 2 : 20; 5 : 23; 6 : 22; 9 : 14-15). Then speaking of himself in the third person the author continues: 'Thou hast enlarged his inheritance through the knowledge of thy truth and according to his knowledge. . . .' (10 : 29). In view of the context 'thy truth' can hardly refer to the divine fidelity, for the object of the knowledge on which perfection depends is God's revelation as manifested in the Law. Admission to the community (1QS 6 : 18) and promotion within its ranks (1QS 5 : 21-24) are conditioned by the calibre of the individual's 'knowledge and actions in Torah'. Confirmation is supplied by 10 : 31 : 'My heart rejoiceth in thy covenant and thy truth delighteth my soul'. This verse with its evocation of two passages of Ps 119(118), vv. 162 and 14, suggests that here as elsewhere 'truth' and 'covenant' are synonyms for the Law.[98] The context here is not one of initiation but it does show the emphasis laid on 'knowledge of truth' as a quality of the genuine member. And in this we have a perfect analogy in 1 Tim 4 : 3 where it is confirmed believers who are described as 'those who know the truth'.

We now turn to the problem of the acquisition of this knowledge. Paul on a number of occasions touches on this problem indirectly, and it is clear that if the appropriation of revelation is to be at all possible, divine assistance is absolutely necessary.[99] The *Hymns* are also quite clear on man's radical incapacity to

---

[98] For 'covenant' in this sense, see 1QS 5 : 19 which identifies 'those who know not his covenant' with 'those who despise his word' (cf. 1QH 15 : 15). Note the same parallelism in 1QH 4 : 34-35 : 'the wicked arose against thy covenant and the wretched against thy word'.

[99] Cf. J. Murphy-O'Connor, *op. cit.*, pp. 236-45.

know God or his works if left merely to his own resources,[100] and passages such as 1QH 11 : 11; 13 : 18-19 offer very good parallels to 1 Cor 2 : 14-15. More within the scope of this paper, however, is the analogy between 2 Tim 2 : 25-26 and 1QS 4 : 23-24 on the precise point of the rejection of 'knowledge of truth'. The former reads : 'He (the Bishop) should correct his opponents with mildness, in case God should give them repentence unto knowledge of truth and they return to soberness from out of the snare of the devil by whom they have been taken captive to his will.' The passage from the *Manual of Discipline* forms part of what has been termed 'The Treatise on the Two Spirits' (3 : 15-4 : 26). The essence of this well-constructed and apparently self-contained account of the basic beliefs of the Essenes may be summed up in three points : (i) God has ordained all that happens in the world; (ii) All human behaviour is determined by the influence of the spirits of truth and deceit; (iii) In the future evil will be destroyed and truth alone will prevail.[101] But until the End arrives, 'until now the spirits of truth and deceit struggle in the heart of man, (some) walking in wisdom and (some) in vileness. According to his share in truth *(ykpy nḥlt 'yš b'mt)* and righteousness, thus a man hates deceit, and according to his assignment in the lot of deceit and ungodliness thus does he loathe truth *(yt'b 'mt)'* (4 : 23-24). Licht points out that 'man' in this treatise stands for mankind generally and that the treatise does not visualize the two spirits as competing for the soul of the individual person.[102] He admits, however, that some isolated passages could be interpreted in this way, and in particular the one under discussion.[103] In the perspective of the treatise, 'truth' is known only in virtue of the influence of the spirit of truth, whose relationship to a particular individual is an effect of divine predestination (3 : 17-18). On the other hand, if truth is rejected,

[100] Cf. 1QH 7: 32; 10: 5ff; 15: 21, and the magnificent summary in Holm-Nielsen, *Hodayot*, p. 275.

[101] Cf. J. Licht, 'An Analysis of the Treatise on the Two Spirits in DSD', *Scripta Hierosolymitana* 4 (1958), p. 89.

[102] *Art. cit.*, p. 91, n. 13.

[103] Davies maintains that all men share in both spirits ('St Paul and the Dead Sea Scrolls: Flesh and Spirit', *The Scrolls and the New Testament*, ed. K. Stendahl, New York, 1957, p. 172).

it is because the individual is under the dominion of the spirit of deceit. Elsewhere it is said that he belongs to 'the lot of Belial' (1QS 2 : 5) or that he is 'under the dominion of the spirits of Belial' (CD 12 : 2)—a term used in 2 Cor to symbolize the forces of evil (6 : 15).[104] This brings us very close to the 'devil' who impedes accession to 'knowledge of truth' in 2 Tim. The closeness of the analogy is reinforced when, a few verses later and speaking of this same group, Paul says : 'As Jannes and Jambres resisted Moses, so do these resist the truth' (3 : 8). For these two were considered by the Essenes to be a special manifestation of the spirit of deceit : 'In ancient times Moses and Aaron arose by the hand of the Prince of Lights (= the spirit of truth, 1QS 3 : 20) and Belial raised Jannes and his brother by his evil device' (CD 5 : 18).

In spite of, or rather because of, the similarity in 'mentality' it is important to note the difference in 'spirit' between Paul and the Essenes on this point of the rejection of truth.[105] The doctrine of predestination in the 'Treatise on the Two Spirits' leaves no room for human responsibility.[106] Man's belonging to the domain of the spirit of deceit (or of truth) depends on a choice that is God's and not in any sense his. For Paul, on the contrary, salvation is always contingent on a personal decision. If God sends a 'working of error' into the hearts of men which induces them to believe in the lie, it is only 'because they have not welcomed the

[104] Braun lists sixteen authors who maintain that Qumran influence appears in this passage ('Qumran und das NT', *TRu* 29 (1963), p. 221), but its value as an argument is rendered doubtful by the fact that it is an interpolation. Cf. J. Gnilka, '2 Cor 6: 14-7: 1 in the light of the texts from Qumran and the Testaments of the Twelve Patriarchs' (Chapter 3 in this volume).

[105] For this distinction cf. J. Guitton, *Le Temps et l'Éternité chez Plotin et S. Augustin*, Paris, 1933, pp. xi-xix.

[106] The view of predestination expressed in the Treatise is due to outside influences, presumably Zoroastrianism (cf. K. G. Kuhn, 'Die Sektenschrift und die Iranische Religion,' *ZTK* 49 (1952), pp. 296-316) and is not reconciled with the O.T. view of man as freely meriting reward or punishment which from time to time shows through in the writings of the sect. The inconsistency to which this can lead is clear in the case of apostasy. According to 1QS 7: 23-24 apostasy is the unforgivable sin, but CD 20: 4-5 presupposes the possibility of re-admission to the community and 1QS 7: 18-19 makes provision for just such an eventuality by determining the penance to be imposed.

love of truth unto their salvation *(anth' hōn tēn agapēn tēs aletheias ouk edexanto eis to sōthēnai autous)'* (2 Thess 2 : 10). As noted above, the majority of commentators considers 'truth' here to be the Gospel, but with Spicq I prefer to understand it in a much wider sense : truth as such, which naturally englobes the Gospel as a particular manifestation.[107] This openness to truth is the first grace accorded by God to all. Only in those who refuse it does the word of God, when proposed, fail to evoke a response. Thus does the genius of Paul outline the 'solution' to the problem of the reconciliation of divine omnipotence and human responsibility, a problem that does not appear to have cost the Essenes a moment's thought.

Thus, if the Pastorals show the influence of Essene terminology Paul was certainly conscious of the limitations of the doctrines it expressed. 'Knowledge of truth' for the sectaries, as for the Apostle, evokes the idea of salvation. But for the former this knowledge was limited to their own little group in a very jealous fashion.[108] It is possible that 1 Tim 2 : 1-4 constitutes a conscious reaction to this conception, so diametrically opposed to the mind of Christ (Mt 5 : 43-45; 18 : 21-35, etc.). 'First of all, I urge that petitions, prayers, . . . be made of behalf of *all men*. . . . This is good and acceptable in the sight of God our Saviour, who wills *all men* to be saved and to come to knowledge of truth.' The final phrase is redundant, but its presence is well explained by the hypothesis of an intention to combat the influence of the sect, while borrowing from it formulae capable of being endowed with a new depth of meaning and used in the service of the Gospel.[109]

V. FOUNDATION OF TRUTH

Another point of contact between the Pastorals and Qumran is to be found in the phrase 'foundation of the truth'. We read in 1 Tim 3 : 14-15 : 'I write these things hoping to come to you very soon, that you may know—in case I delay—how you ought

[107] *Agape dans le NT*, Paris, 1959, vol. II, p. 35.
[108] Cf. 1QS 1 : 3, 9-10; 2 : 5-10; 8 : 6-7; 9 : 16-17.
[109] Cf. Stauffer, *TWNT*, vol. II, p. 362, n. 15.

to act in the house of God, which is the Church of the living
God, pillar and foundation of the truth *(stulos kai hedraiōma
tēs alētheias)*'. The formula *stulos kai hedraiōma tēs alētheias*
is unique in the bible. The translation, however, poses no difficulties, for even though *hedraiōma* is not attested in Greek prior
to 1 Tim, its meaning is not in doubt : foundation, base, support.
Hē alētheia means the Christian revelation, as frequently elsewhere in the Pastorals. On any other assumption the relationship
between v. 15 and v. 16 (the mystery of piety) is inexplicable.
The symbolic force of 'pillar' is identical with that of 'foundation' : solidity, stability, utter dependability (cf. Ps 75(74): 4;
Job 38 : 4-6). What rests on them is absolutely secure. The
reality hidden beneath these symbols, therefore, is the mainstay
of revealed truth.

Here an awkward question immediately arises : do 'pillar'
and 'foundation' symbolize Timothy or the Church? The vast
majority of commentators, both ancient and modern, opt for
the ecclesial interpretation, considering the natural sweep of the
phrase to render any further arguments superfluous. However,
in a communication to the Pauline Congress held in Rome in
1961 Miss Jaubert[110] gave a new lease of life to the interpretation
of the Cappadocians, Gregory of Nyssa,[111] Gregory of
Nazianzus,[112] and Basil of Caesarea,[113] who take the symbols to
apply to Timothy, understanding Paul's construction as elliptical :
'I write these things that you Timothy may know how you ought
to act in the house of God, you who are a pillar and foundation
of the truth.'

In the perspective of the first interpretation the Church is
represented as the guardian of revealed truth, preserving its
purity inviolate in the face of the world's attempts to contaminate
it. In the second opinion this role is played by Timothy within
the Church; on him lies the burden of keeping sound and healthy
the faith of its members. It cannot be denied that the latter

---

[110] 'L'image de la colonne (1 Tim 3 : 15)', in *Studiorum Paulinorum
Congressus Internationalis Catholicus 1961*, Rome, 1963, vol. II, pp. 101-8.
[111] *Vita Moysis*, II, 184; *PG* 44, 385. *Comm. Cant.*, 14; *PG* 44, 1076-7.
[112] *Letter 44*; *PG* 37, 92.
[113] *Letter 243*; *PG* 32, 908.

rather than the former is the perspective of 1 Tim. In this Epistle no mention is made of the action of the Church as such. But Timothy's role in the preservation of the faith is greatly emphasized. He must stop those whose teaching is upsetting the faith of his subjects (1 : 3). He must fight for the faith (1 : 19-20) and strive to minimize the damage done by those who depart from it (4 : 1-6). He must be a model of virtue for all (4 : 12). Finally, he must guard the authentic deposit (6 : 20) and teach it in all its purity (6 : 3, 21). Knowing how well Timothy would carry out these duties, it is easy to visualize Paul addressing him as 'pillar and foundation of the truth'.

This interpretation, as Miss Jaubert points out, finds confirmation in the fact that elsewhere in the Pauline corpus the images of 'pillar' and 'foundation' are applied not to the Church but to those who have been entrusted with authority within it. James, Cephas and John, the leaders of the Church at Jerusalem, are described as 'pillars' in Gal 2 : 9, and Barrett very plausibly suggests that this title was given them because of their positions of fundamental importance in the Temple of the New Age.[114] In Eph 2 : 20 the 'foundation *(themelios)* of the spiritual temple is constituted by the apostle-prophets. In 1 Tim 3 : 15 also the formula may well have been evoked by the mention of the 'house of God'.

Against this mass of convergent evidence the argument that the reference to the Church is the more natural stands alone.[115] Its force cannot be denied, and the number of illustrious commentators, among them St John Chrysostom,[116] who uphold the ecclesial interpretation commands respect. Nonetheless, the arguments in favour of the individual interpretation appear more weighty, particularly since the genesis of the other view can be adequately explained in function of a growing recognition of the Church's position *vis-à-vis* the world.

[114] 'Paul and the "Pillar" Apostles', *Studia Paulina in honorem J. de Zwaan*, ed. J. N. Sevenster and W. C. van Unnik, Haarlem, 1953, p. 12.

[115] Spicq's rejection of the interpretation of Gregory of Nyssa as being out of harmony with the context 'which here has the Church in view' (*S. Paul: Épitres Pastorales*, Paris, 1947, 105) is perhaps beside the point, for the question is: from what angle is the Church viewed?

[116] *In Ep. I ad Tim.*, hom. 11; *PG* 62, 554.

The Qumran documents make a real contribution to the understanding of the background of the formula 'foundation of the truth'. It is a curious coincidence that the image of a foundation is applied therein both to a collectivity and to an individual —the two senses postulated for 1 Tim 3 : 15. We shall examine each of the relevant passages in turn, and it is possible that a decisive argument may emerge to settle the doubt concerning the interpretation of this latter text.

Community: Hans Conzelmann,[117] a protagonist of the ecclesial interpretation of 1 Tim 3 : 15, was, to my knowledge, the first to point out that this passage has a parallel in the *Manual of Discipline* : 'They shall lay a foundation of truth *(mwsd 'mt)* for Israel, for the community of an eternal covenant' (1QS 5 : 5). The term *mwsd* is not very common in the O.T. Vocalized as *môsād* it evokes the solidity and permanence of the foundations of the mountains (Dt 32 : 22; Ps 18(17): 8), of the earth (Is 24 : 18, Prov 8 : 29), and of the heavens themselves (2 Sam 22 : 8). The vocalization *mûsad* is much more significant, for it evokes the foundation of the Temple (2 Chron 8 : 16), and especially the Isaian prophecy concerning the posing of the foundation-stone of the New Jerusalem (28 : 16). This is indeed the perspective of 1QS 5 : 5. The Essenes believed that they were living in the last times. The members of the community withdrew from the 'assembly of deceit' (1QS 5 : 1-2) precisely in order to lay a foundation of truth for Israel. 'Israel' here does not have the limited signification it has in 1QS 5 : 6 and 8 : 5, 9, where it designates the lay members of the community as opposed to its priests (Aaron). It means the new Israel of the future age, which will be the community bound in a covenant that will never need to be renewed. This eschatological community has begun to be realized by the establishment of the community at Qumran. Its foundation has thereby been laid. The context suggests that 'truth' here is not to be understood as an allusion to revelation but as a characterization of the quality of the foundation. The Essenes lay the foundation of the New Israel by the perfection of

---

[117] *Die Pastoralbriefe*, Tübingen, 1955, p. 49.

their obedience to the Law. They are a 'community in the Law' (5 : 2), that is, entirely devoted to its study. Their observance is characterized above all by 'truth' (5 : 3), no one 'walking in the stubbornness of his heart in order to go astray after his heart' (5 : 4). It is precisely as the concrete embodiment of perfect fidelity that the Essenes are a 'foundation of truth' (cf. 8 : 4).[118]

This, of course, implies that the community is the sole upholder of the genuine revelation but only indirectly. Hence, the analogy with 1 Tim 3 : 15 is reduced to a purely verbal parallel. And even as such it is defective, for in 1 Tim 'truth' is qualified by the definite article.

Individual: A change in vocabulary marks the appearance of this second aspect of the theme.[119] We find *yswd* 'foundation' used to characterize both the responsible members of the community,[120] and its fundamental doctrines,[121] but apart from a rather indirect link established by 1QS 7 : 18, this term is never associated with 'truth'. Hence we leave these passages out of consideration, some of which, moreover, are of rather doubtful interpretation. A more fruitful area of research is suggested by a remark in the *Konkordanz zu den Qumrantexten* (p. 90, n. 2) pointing out that in the Qumran documents there is frequently no difference in meaning between *yswd* and *swd*.

This is very clear in 1QH 6 : 26 and 7 : 9. 'Thou layest *swd* upon the rock and cross-beams to the right measure and a plumbline [. . . .] to [. . . .] chosen stone for a strong building which shall not be moved.' (6 : 26). 'Thou makest me as a strong tower, as a high wall, and on the rock thou establishest my building and eternal foundations *('wšy 'wlm)* for my *swd*, and all my walls as a tried wall which is not shaken' (7 : 9). Neither of the biblical meanings of *swd*—(i) confidential talk, a secret; (ii) a group of intimates (1QS 8 : 5)—makes any sense in either of

[118] For Theodore of Mopsuestia the Church was the pillar and foundation of the truth precisely as the assembly of the faithful. *In Ep. B. Pauli Commentarii*, ed. H. B. Swete, Cambridge, 1882, vol. II, p. 131.

[119] *Mwsd* occurs only once more: 'the foundations of the mountains' (1QH 17 : 13).

[120] In the singular: 1QS 8 : 5; in the plural 1QSa (= 28a) 1 : 12.

[121] In the singular: 1QS 7 : 17-18; 8 : 10; in the plural: CD 10 : 6.

these passages. The whole context demands that it be understood as 'foundation', a meaning well attested in later Hebrew.[122]

This does not mean, however, that in every instance *swd 'mt* may be translated as 'foundation of truth'. The meaning 'secret' is also attested for *swd*,[123] and in a number of passages where it is combined with *'mt* this gives an eminently satisfactory sense. Thus 1QH 10 : 4; 11 : 4, 9, 16. Brown in his study on 'mystery' at Qumran has felt that this meaning is not adequate in other cases, and suggests that in 1QH 2 : 10; 5 : 9, 26 *swd 'mt* 'seems to mean a (secret?) source of truth'.[124] This is a precious intuition whose value will soon become apparent, but in each of these instances a good case can be made for meaning 'foundation of truth'.

Before embarking on the examination of each of these passages in turn an important preliminary observation must be made. In his very detailed study on the Teacher of Righteousness Gert Jeremias has shown : (i) that the *Hymns* from Qumran as a whole are not a literary unity, and (ii) that a certain number of hymns are so closely linked in thought and vocabulary that they must be considered as one literary *totum* : these are 2 : 1-19; 2 : 31-39; 3 : 1-18; 4 : 5-5 : 4; 5 : 5-19; 5 : 20-7 : 5; 7 : 6-25; 8 : 4-40. After a minute analysis of each of these hymns he concludes ('mit Sicherheit') that in each the same well-known personality speaks, viz. the Teacher of Righteousness.[125] We accept these conclusions as a *point de départ*.[126] It is extremely significant

---

[122] 'Foundation' is given as the primary sense of *swd* in G. Dalman, *Aramäisches-Neuhebräisches Wörterbuch*, Frankfurt, 1897, Teil, 1, p. 272, and in M. Jastrow, *A Dictionary of the Talmud*, New York/Berlin, 1926, vol. I, p. 961.

[123] It is found in parallelism with *rz* in 1QH 11 : 9. Compare 1QH 4 : 27 and 12 : 12 with 1QH 2 : 13 and 7 : 27.

[124] "The Pre-Christian Semitic Concept of "Mystery" ', *CBQ* 20 (1958), p. 389, n. 84.

[125] *Der Lehrer der Gerechtigheit*, Göttingen, 1963, pp. 171-3.

[126] *Op. cit.*, p. 264. Holm-Nielsen, who also groups these hymns together (adding 9 : 1-36; 14 : 23-28; 16 : 1-20; 17 : 9-25), is unnecessarily reserved with regard to their individual character. He will admit that the 'I' here does not designate the community as it does in another group of hymns, yet does not consider that it is wholly individualized, since it represents the priests and the teachers of the Law or in general those who hold positions of authority : ' "Ich" in den Hodajoth und die Qumrangemeinde', *Qumran-Probleme* (Vorträge des Leipziger Symposions über Qumran-Probleme vom 9. bis 14. Okt. 1961), ed. H. Bardtke, Berlin, 1963, pp. 220, 224.

that all the instances in which *swd 'mt* certainly means 'secret of truth' fall *outside* this group. This, to say the least, makes their value for the interpretation of *swd 'mt* within the group problematical. It is noteworthy, too, that both certain instances of *swd* = foundation occur *within* the group.

> (*a*) 'Thou hast made me a reproach and a derision to the false,
> But a *swd* of truth and knowledge for the righteous of way'
> (2 : 9-10).

The use of 'Way' as a technical term for the sect has already been noted. The absence of the article is not to be pressed, for 'the righteous' can only designate the members of the community (cf. 1QS 4 : 22). 'The false' may be those who deserted the Covenant (Mansoor) or those who never belonged to it (Holm-Nielsen). 'Foundation' is the only meaning of *swd* that makes really good sense here. It is the translation adopted by Holm-Nielsen, Dupont-Sommer and Bardtke, among others. Jeremias (with Mansoor and Maier) prefers 'secret' because of the meaning of *swd 'mt* in 1QH 1 : 27; 10 : 4; 11 : 5, 9, 16.[127] As noted above the force of this argument is greatly diminished by his own observations on the literary unity of the *Hymns*. Moreover, how can the Teacher be said to be *made* a 'secret of truth'? Jeremias replies : 'The Teacher does not merely know this salvific truth, nor is it just embedded in his heart (5 : 9). He incarnates it for his community.'[128] What is of value in this rather strained interpretation is fully preserved if *swd* is translated as 'foundation'.

'Truth' here must mean revelation.[129] An adjectival force of *'mt*, which may be suggested by the context of opposition, is excluded by the association of *'mt* with 'knowledge', and in particular by line 13 which clarifies the meaning of 'foundation of truth and knowledge'. 'Thou hast made me a banner unto the chosen of righteousness and an interpreter of knowledge (*mlys d't*) concerning the mysteries (*rzy*) of wonder to test [the men] of truth'. This text shows that the Teacher has been granted an exceptional grasp of the salvific doctrines proper to the sect,

[127] *Op. cit.*, pp. 198-9.
[128] *Loc. cit.*
[129] Cf. above, pp. 190-1.

not for himself, but in order to mediate this truth to others.[130]
According to lines 17-18, adversaries seek the life of him (the
Teacher) 'within whose heart thou hast set understanding to
open the fountain of knowledge to all who understand'. His
proclamation of revelation is the test (2 : 8; 7 : 12).[131] By rejecting
it men manifest themselves as 'sons of deceit' (line 16). By accept-
ing it they show themselves to be 'men of truth', and their
knowledge has that of the Teacher for foundation. The Teacher's
role, however, extends beyond the communication of knowledge.
He also fulfils a function with regard to its object (7 : 26-27),
truth. In virtue of a special disposition of divine providence he
is its 'foundation', that is to say, its unshakable support (7 : 8-9),
the guardian of its integrity. The Teacher, then, does much more
than embody truth—which any of his genuine disciples could
be said to do (14 : 15).

> *(b)* 'And concerning the secret *(rz)* which thou hast hidden in
> me they go around with slander to the children of destruc-
> tion . . . and because of their guilt thou hast hidden a
> fountain of knowledge and a *swd* of truth' (5 : 25-26).

The content of the 'secret' is in part clarified by line 11 : 'Thou
hast hidden thy Law [within me].'[132]—Compare 'Thy Law
which thou hast impressed upon my heart' (4 : 10). But it
almost certainly englobes also the inspired interpretation of the
Law proper to the sect. In any case we have here an allusion to
the Teacher's special knowledge. Revelation is put in his heart,
not that it may not be seen, but that it may be at the very centre
of his being, the norm and inspiration of every thought and
deed. It is this which enables him to be for the community 'a

---

[130] Holm-Nielsen approves Richardson's opinion (VT [1955], p. 167) that
mlyṣ means 'official spokesman', and by a reference to 1QpHab 8 : 16
underlines the quality of special insight suggested by the text. ' "Interpreter",
therefore, is not to be understood merely as the representative, but in the
sense of the necessary link to make contact between the two parties'
(*Hodayot*, 35, n. 29).

[131] H. Michaud insists strongly that it is by his *teaching* that the Teacher
snares his enemies and heals those who heed him ('À propos d'un passage
des *Hymns*—1QH 2 : 7-14', *RQ* 1 (1958-9), p. 415).

[132] The reconstruction of the end of the phrase as *b[y ']d* is accepted by
Dupont-Sommer, Holm-Nielsen, Jeremias, Maier, Mansoor, Mowinckel
('Some Remarks on *Hodayot* 39 : 5-20,' *JBL* 75 (1956), p. 266).

fountain of knowledge and a *swd* of truth'. We would expect the article were this phrase a reference to revelation, but if it is understood as an allusion by the Teacher to himself the omission can be explained by his humility (4 : 35). Apart from the marked analogy with 2 : 10, two further reasons militate against taking this phrase as a reference to revelation, which must be the case if *swd* is translated as 'secret'. Firstly, the parallel with line 11, where God both hides his *revelation* within the Teacher and conceals *him*. 'Hiding' here is to be interpreted as meaning the exercise of God's protective care (2 : 34-35).[133] Secondly, the difficulty of explaining why 'fountain of knowledge' and 'secret of truth' should *both* be used, since either one is sufficient to denote the totality of revelation (11 : 16). This difficulty disappears if *swd* is understood as 'foundation' and the whole phrase referred to the Teacher. With respect to his followers he is the mediator of revelation and thus a source of knowledge. Compare : 'Thou, O my God, hast put in my mouth as showers of early rain for all [. . . .] and a spring of living waters' (8 : 16). With respect to truth itself he is its mainstay and its guardian.

    (c) 'Thou hast set me in a place of exile . . . and there thou hast established me *lmšpt*, and the *swd* of truth thou hast consolidated *('mṣth)* in my heart and [thence][134] (comes) the covenant to them that seek it' (5 : 8-9).

Were this the only instance of *swd 'mt* one would automatically translate it by 'secret of truth', especially in view of line 11, which alludes to the Law being hidden within the Teacher. Against this, however, is the meaning of the formula in the two passages just discussed, and which bracket this one.[135] Moreover, the verb *'mṣ* 'to strengthen, consolidate, fortify' is much more

---

[133] 'Truth' is said to be hidden in 1QH 9 : 24. The text, however, is corrupt and the allusion appears to be to the eschatological triumph of truth spoken of in 1QS 4 : 19 (cf. 1QH 6 : 12).

[134] Reading *wmzh* instead of *wmyh* with Dupont-Sommer, Holm-Nielsen, Jeremias, Maier, Mansoor, Mowinckel.

[135] Jeremias here, as in 5 : 26, takes *swd 'mt* to mean 'secret of truth' on the grounds that it is 'ein festgeprägter Ausdruck' (*Der Lehrer*, 219, n. 3; 222, n. 8) and refers to his treatment of 2 : 10. We fully agree that the formula has a fixed value in the group of hymns under discussion, but maintain that the evidence indicates its constant meaning to be 'foundation of truth'.

appropriate with 'foundation' than with 'secret'. Mowinckel, who prefers the meaning 'foundation', thus interprets the phrase. '[It] obviously means that God strengthened the very foundation of truth, of the right religion and the right relation to him, in his heart. He became again a true and steadfast believer and "servant" (line 15) of God, surrendering and overcoming "the [evil] desires of his nature".'[136] The accent is on 'foundation' rather than on 'truth'. This foundation is the Teacher's attitude towards the Revealer and his word. On the concrete level where God acts through human instruments, the Teacher's union with God is the support and guarantee of the revelation confided to him (line 11). This accords perfectly with the two phrases which immediately precede and follow. 'Thou hast established me *lmšpt*' has been variously understood.[137] Inspired by Hab 1 : 12 ('Thou hast ordained him for judgment . . . established him for correction') a number of commentators (Dupont-Sommer, Holm-Nielsen, Maier, Mansoor) give *mšpt* the sense of 'judgment' and interpret the phrase as a judgment on the wicked. Jeremias, seeing in the phrase a reminiscence of Is 42 : 4, understands *mšpt* as 'divine justice'.[138] This difference is at most one of emphasis, because as 7 : 12 shows, one interpretation necessarily implies the other. As its sure foundation the Teacher embodies truth. Those who oppose him and refuse to submit to his teaching merit God's wrath, but those who hear his words receive the covenant (4 : 24, 34-35) and are thereby delivered from judgment (1QpHab 8 : 3).

The harmony of thought and vocabulary between these three passages is remarkable and fully bears out Jeremias' conclusions regarding the literary unity of the hymns to which they pertain. It is in virtue of his special relationship to God, which involves the possession of a unique knowledge (cf. Eph 3 : 3), that the Teacher is a 'foundation of truth'. And, humanly speaking,

---

[136] 'Some Remarks on *Hodayot* 39: 5-20', *JBL* 75 (1956), p. 273.

[137] Mowinckel (*art. cit.*, p. 273) suggests that *ysrtny* should be read in place of *ysdtny* giving the sense 'Thou hast instructed me aright', but this appears unnecessary.

[138] *Der Lehrer*, p. 222.

revelation needed just such a reliable support and guarantee, because the atmosphere of these passages is heavy with hostility. Another passage shows clearly that the Teacher was persecuted not so much for what he was but for what he taught : 'They have devised against me to exchange thy Law which thou hast impressed upon my heart for hypocrisy unto thy people, and they withhold the drink of knowledge from them that thirst, and for their thirst they gave them vinegar to drink' (4 : 10-11). The Teacher's every effort is directed to preserving the purity of the doctrine entrusted to him for others. His authentic teaching is the touchstone on which humanity is tested. Those who seek a truth of their own devising (4 : 14-15) are repelled by it. But those who seek God's truth find in him a fountain of pure knowledge, and to drink from this source is to receive the Covenant.

The analogies between this conception and 1 Tim 3 : 15 interpreted as referring to Timothy are remarkably close. In both an individual is the 'foundation of truth' precisely because his role as a mediator of revelation demands that he exercise ceaseless vigilance to prevent its contamination by heterodox teaching. The concrete situation is the same in both, because this danger is not hypothetical but an actual fact.

What contribution does Qumran make to the understanding of 1 Tim 3 : 15? At the very least it adds another argument to the weight of evidence amassed by Miss Jaubert in favour of the individual interpretation. It may be, however, that Paul consciously draws on Qumran terminology to characterize the head of the Church in Ephesus. As Eph shows, Paul was definitely in contact with someone who knew Essenian teaching thoroughly. Timothy belonged to the same circle. What could be more natural therefore, that Paul in writing to him should employ a formula whose overtones were clear to both? It emphasizes what Timothy must be in the face of opposition, but it also offsets this hostility by its implication of divine support and assistance. To underline the difference between the mission of the Teacher and that of Timothy, Paul would have added the definite article before 'truth'. Both their functions concerned 'truth', but that handled by Timothy (2 Tim 2 : 15) is *'the* truth', for revelation is no longer the Law but Christ 'the great mystery of piety'.

CONCLUSION

When we come to sum up the results of this investigation, we must be content to let the various sections speak for themselves. This rather cautious approach is recommended by the varying degrees of authenticity attributed to different Epistles, for it is noteworthy that the divisions imposed on our study by the material investigated coincide with the great divisions of the Pauline corpus. The idea of the Law as the form of knowledge and truth is found only in Rom. Except for one aside in 1 Cor the conception of the Christian life as truth is in evidence only in Eph. The expressions 'knowledge of truth' and 'foundation of the truth' do not occur outside the Pastorals. The theme of truth-revelation runs through all groups of Epistles : once each in Gal and 2 Cor, once each in Col and Eph (in the form 'word of truth'), but frequently in the Pastorals. In other words, the most characteristic aspects of the Pauline concept of truth are almost exclusively associated with definite blocks of Epistles and not scattered throughout the corpus. This poses a dilemma with regard to the passages studied. Did Paul emphasize one or another facet of his idea of truth at different times due to the influence of Qumran? Or were those who penned epistles (under his aegis but with varying degrees of freedom) influenced by different applications of the Essenian concept? The latter hypothesis is certainly to be preferred in the case of Eph, and one may wonder if it is not also the one best adapted to explain the occurrences of truth in the Pastorals. In both cases an idea found in Epistles whose authenticity in the fullest sense is unquestioned is applied in a unique way. Beyond this we cannot go, for the precise point studied in this essay is too narrow a base to give security to any sweeping conclusions.

INDEX OF SUBJECTS

Aaron and Israel, community as temple of, 168-9; *see also* Essenes, concept of two Messiahs
ablutions, ritual, 7; *see also* baptism
Agathosunē, 204-5
Alētheia: *see* truth
Allo, E. B.:
on jurisdiction in Church of Corinth, 70, 81
on subordination of women, 35n, 36n, 43n
'Mt, concept of, 182, 189-90, 214, 216, 222-5, 227
angelous in 1 Cor 11: 10, 31, 33-34; 38-47
angelology:
in Judaism, 4
in OT and Rev, 41
in Paul, 20, 31-47, 150
in Qumran, 17, 41-42, 164, 165
anomia:
use of term by Paul, 57, 65-66, 68n
in Scrolls, 65
Antichrist in Pauline theology, 140, 156-8
apistos, 57, 68n
apocalyptic doctrines, 3-4
apostles:
eschatological judgment by, 81, 82, 84
witnesses to event of Christ, 105-6
arbitrators: *see* justice in Church of Corinth, 70, 81
armour metaphors, 205-6
assembly of the Many, 78-79, 80, 84

baptism:
and dying to sin, 126-9
justification through, 26, 109-10, 166
of penance, 7-8
Bardtke, H.:
on jurisdiction in CD, 73, 75
on the Hodayoth, 87, 96
Beelzebul, 10; *see also* Beliar

Beliar (Belial):
adversary of God, 55, 66, 141n; of the Messiah, 55-56, 61
use of term in OT, 54; by Paul, 10, 53, 54, 55n; in Qumran writings, 54-56, 60; by XII Patriarchs, 55-56
Benoit, P., on authorship of Ephesians, 204
beth din, 77
bishops:
colleges of, 16
in the early church, 16
judicial functions, 77
relations of *episkopos to mebaqqer*, 14-15
Braun, H., on Pauline angelology, 46-47
'brood of vipers', concept of, 8
building metaphors, 170-3, 177-8, 219-21, 223-4
Bultmann, R., on *alētheia*, 180
Burrows, M.:
on jurisdiction in CD, 75
on similarities between Paul and Qumran, 85

Cadbury, H. J., on Pauline angelology, 45-46
calendar, Qumran, 5, 17
Carmignac, J., on wilderness, 60n
Casel, O., on mystery, 132
celibacy, Essene concept of, 9
Cerfaux, L.:
on authorship of epistles, 154
on mystery, 158
Christ: *see* Jesus Christ
Christian life, the:
as 'truth', 202-13
love as mainspring, 212-13
Christians:
as temples of God, 51-53, 62
attacks of the Evil One on, 205
separation from unbelievers, 50-53, 57-61, 62

231

INDEX OF BIBLICAL REFERENCES

OLD TESTAMENT

INDEX OF PSEUDEPIGRAPHIC REFERENCES

TESTAMENTS OF THE XII PATRIARCHS

INDEX OF DEAD SEA SCROLLS
REFERENCES

Indices prepared by Brenda Hall

227
M97

41112

Date

Reserve

SEP 8 '78

NOV 27 '80

FEB 17 '82

DEC 15 '82

MAR 29 '83

Thesis
Spring 84

MAR 1 '85

DEC 18 '85

DEC 11 '86

Demco 38-297   Lincoln Christian College